Sociology of Children and Families

Series editors: **Esther Dermott** and **Debbie Watson**, University of Bristol, UK

The *Sociology of Children and Families* series brings together the latest international research on children, childhood and families and pushes forward theory in the sociology of childhood and family life. Books in the series cover major global issues affecting children and families.

Forthcoming in the series

Adult-Children Raised by LGBTQ Parents Stories of Kinship and Connection
By **Eliza Garwood**

Out now in the series

Critical Perspectives on Research with Children Reflexivity, Methodology, and Researcher Identity
Edited by **Sarah Richards** and **Sarah Coombs**

Race, Class, Parenting and Children's Leisure: Children's Leisurescapes and Parenting Cultures in Middle-class British Indian Families
By **Utsa Mukherjee**

Childcare Provision in Neoliberal Times: The Marketization of Care
By **Aisling Gallagher**

Find out more at
bristoluniversitypress.co.uk/
sociology-of-children-and-families

Sociology of Children and Families series

Series editors: **Esther Dermott** and **Debbie Watson**,
University of Bristol, UK

International advisory board:

Harry Brighouse, University of Wisconsin-Madison, US
Sara Eldén, University of Lund, Sweden
Mary Jane Kehily, The Open University, UK
Zsuzsa Millei, University of Tampere, Finland
Tina Miller, Oxford Brookes University, UK
Meredith Nash, University of Tasmania, Australia
Emiko Ochiai, Kyoto University, Japan
Gillian Ranson, University of Calgary, Canada
Anna Sparrman, Linköping University, Sweden
Ulrike Zartler, University of Vienna, Austria

Find out more at
bristoluniversitypress.co.uk/
sociology-of-children-and-families

THINKING THROUGH FAMILY

Narratives of Care Experienced Lives

Janet Boddy

with Fidelma Hanrahan and Bella Wheeler

First published in Great Britain in 2025 by

Bristol University Press
University of Bristol
1-9 Old Park Hill
Bristol
BS2 8BB
UK
t: +44 (0)117 374 6645
e: bup-info@bristol.ac.uk

Details of international sales and distribution partners are available at bristoluniversitypress.co.uk

© Bristol University Press 2025 excluding Chapters 1, 2 and 7 © Janet Boddy 2025

The digital PDF and EPUB versions of Chapters 1, 2 and 7 are available Open Access and distributed under the terms of the Creative Commons Attribution-NonCommercial-NoDerivatives 4.0 International licence (https://creativecommons.org/licenses/by-nc-nd/4.0/) which permits reproduction and distribution for non-commercial use without further permission provided the original work is attributed.

British Library Cataloguing in Publication Data
A catalogue record for this book is available from the British Library

ISBN 978-1-5292-1471-0 hardcover
ISBN 978-1-5292-1472-7 paperback
ISBN 978-1-5292-1473-4 ePub
ISBN 978-1-5292-1474-1 ePdf

The right of Janet Boddy, Fidelma Hanrahan and Bella Wheeler to be identified as authors of this work has been asserted by them in accordance with the Copyright, Designs and Patents Act 1988.

All rights reserved: no part of this publication may be reproduced, stored in a retrieval system, or transmitted in any form or by any means, electronic, mechanical, photocopying, recording, or otherwise without the prior permission of Bristol University Press.

Every reasonable effort has been made to obtain permission to reproduce copyrighted material. If, however, anyone knows of an oversight, please contact the publisher.

The statements and opinions contained within this publication are solely those of the authors and not of the University of Bristol or Bristol University Press. The University of Bristol and Bristol University Press disclaim responsibility for any injury to persons or property resulting from any material published in this publication.

Bristol University Press works to counter discrimination on grounds of gender, race, disability, age and sexuality.

Cover design: blu inc
Front cover image: alamy/Rawpixel Ltd

Sensitive Content in this Book

Please be aware that this book contains sensitive content, including some detail of harsh, abusive and neglectful experiences in participants' accounts of their lives.

This book is dedicated to the people whose words form its heart.

And to our own families, in all their variety.

That's us:

        Small chickens
        Learning to hatch.
Different eggs
In the same nest.
        (from Lemn Sissay, 'The Nest', 2016, p 80)[1]

Contents

List of Figures and Table		xii
Acknowledgements		xiii
1	Why Think Through 'Family'?	1
2	Learning From Care Experienced Perspectives	18
3	Doing Family: The Significance of the 'Ordinary'	43
4	Re/Configuring Boundaries: Who Counts as 'Family'?	70
5	'How Can We Not Talk about Family When Family's All That We've Got?': Care and Connectedness	95
6	Understandings and Experiences of Parenthood	120
7	Thinking Through Family: Implications for Theory and Practice	152
Notes		167
References		171
Index		189

List of Figures and Table

Figures

1.1	'A New Family Politics'	10
4.1	William's picture of 'Two Moons'	81
4.2	Rebecca's picture of her toothbrush	85
5.1	Anna's photograph of her stepmother's wax print dress	108
6.1	Rosa's picture of her child's art	138

Table

2.1	Participants in the two studies: assigned pseudonyms, age and gender	40

Acknowledgements

Thanks are due to many people. Above all, we are grateful to everyone who took part in the two studies on which this book is based, and especially the 35 people in England whose experiences form the focus of the analysis presented here. Their patience with our questions and generosity with their time made it possible for us to learn, and we hope this book does justice to the trust they have placed in us as witnesses to their experiences.

The research projects on which the book is based both involved large teams of collaborators. *Against All Odds?* was led by Elisabeth Backe-Hansen at OsloMet University (NOVA) and funded by the Research Council of Norway (Norges Forskningsråd; grant number 236718). The study involved colleagues in Norway (Elisiv Bakketeig, Tonje Gundersen and Marianne Dæhlen, also at NOVA and OsloMet), Denmark (Jeanette Østergaard, Mette Lausten at VIVE in Copenhagen, and Signe Ravn, now at the University of Melbourne) and England (myself and Fidelma Hanrahan at University of Sussex and Charlie Owen at Thomas Coram Research Unit, UCL Institute of Education). The *Evaluation of Pause* was a cross-institutional collaboration in England, funded by the UK Department for Education (as part of Wave 2 of the DfE Children's Social Care Innovation Programme) involving myself and Bella Wheeler (formerly University of Sussex), Chris Hale, James Kearney and Claudia Mollidor (Ipsos MORI) and Julie Wilkinson, Susannah Bowyer and Oliver Preston (Research in Practice). It has been a privilege to work with such brilliant and supportive colleagues and we extend our heartfelt thanks to them, as well as to Norges Forskningsråd and the Department for Education for funding the two studies. The views expressed in this book do not necessarily reflect those of the funders of the two studies, nor of the participants or other collaborators in the research.

For the Pause evaluation, particular thanks are also due to the research advisory group – expertly chaired by Karen Broadhurst, and including Jennifer Beecham, Pamela Cox, Angela Frazer-Wicks, Katherine Gieve, Jules Hillier, Lisa Holmes, Sue Mann, Ellen Marks, and Richard White – who made such collegial and insightful contributions to the development and analysis of the evaluation. I am also ever grateful to Josey Wilkin who provided professional support to the Pause study, for her patience, expertise and lynchpin role within our consortium team. The Pause evaluation was made possible by the facilitation of Pause staff and trustees, in particular Ellen Marks, Jules Hillier, Rosanna Thomasoo, Matthew Stancliffe-Bird and Clare Laxton, as well as the practice leads and practitioners in the practices where we conducted research. Their generous support in enabling the evaluation research often added considerably to substantial existing workloads.

This book was written during the extraordinary years of the COVID-19 pandemic, with all that entailed, and I am extremely grateful to Esther Dermott, Emily Ross and Anna Richardson at Bristol University Press for their support. Thanks are also due to a much wider group of friends and colleagues at the University of Sussex and at NOVA, OsloMet, who have encouraged me to write this book – listening, questioning and offering invaluable suggestions. They are too many to mention, but particular thanks must go to Rachel Thomson and Gillian Hampden-Thompson at Sussex, and Monica Five Aarset and Marie-Louise Seeberg at NOVA. I am lucky enough to co-convene a Family Research Network at NOVA with Monica Five Aarset, and the supportive feedback of Monica and the group on the very first draft of the very first chapter made an enormous difference to the rest of my writing. I also owe my thanks to Monica for introducing and explaining the 'New Family Politics' of Kjell Ingolf Ropstad (see Figure 1.1 in Chapter 1).

At an early stage of the research design for *Against All Odds?*, Fidelma and I were privileged to be able to consult with an expert panel of care experienced young adults who work with *Become*, a national non-governmental organization in England that provides support and advocacy for young people who are care experienced. The advisory group for the *Evaluation of Pause* benefited from a membership that included experience of child removal, as well as academic and professional stakeholders, and we were also helped by consultation with Pause about the acceptability and accessibility of our methodological approach. We are grateful to all these experts for their good advice and critical questioning.

Finally, we thank our own families, for their patience and encouragement and emotional and practical support. Particular thanks go to Gabriel, Oszi, Patrick and Kasia for all their help and good advice – from reading drafts and checking references, to trying to restrain my evident tendency towards the cheesy in exploring possible cover images.

A note on authorship and language

The thinking behind this volume has been inextricably shaped by my conversations with colleagues within and beyond the study teams, during the two studies and subsequently. During both studies, I worked closely with Fidelma Hanrahan on *Against All Odds?* and Bella Wheeler on the *Evaluation of Pause*. Together, we conducted fieldwork in England, although Fidelma and Bella carried out most of the interviews. The idea for this volume – bringing the two studies together – is mine, as is the writing contained in these pages. But the substance of the book would not exist without collaboration, over the course of the two studies, with all the colleagues thanked here – and particularly, without both Bella and Fidelma's involvement, questioning and insights. The book also draws together ideas and material linked to my contributions to several existing publications from the research, which are cited throughout the text (Boddy, 2019; Boddy et al, 2019; Bakketeig et al, 2020; Boddy, Bakketeig and Østergaard 2020; Boddy et al, 2020b; Boddy and Wheeler, 2020). Throughout I use 'we' when I refer to ideas we developed through our discussions, and 'I' when discussing an idea or experience for which I personally bear responsibility.

Janet Boddy
Brighton, December 2022

1

Why Think Through 'Family'?

> Create a single story, show a people as one thing, as only one thing, over and over again, and that is what they become. It is impossible to talk about the single story without talking about power. There is a word, an Igbo word, that I think about whenever I think about the power structures of the world, and it is 'nkali'. It's a noun that loosely translates to 'to be greater than another'. Like our economic and political worlds, stories too are defined by the principle of nkali. How they are told, who tells them, when they're told, how many stories are told, are really dependent on power. Power is the ability not just to tell the story of another person, but to make it the definitive story of that person.
>
> Chimamanda Ngozi Adichie, *The Danger of a Single Story*, 2009

Introduction

This is a book about family, based on learning from the narratives of young adults who were in state care in childhood. By thinking through 'family' in care experienced lives, we aim to move beyond the pervasive story of the conventional family, building new insights into complex connected lives, identities and practices.

The book is based on two studies, both of which involved care experienced people living in England who were in early adulthood (all of whom were aged 16–30 years at the time of joining the research). These young adults are diverse, but they have in common that they spent time during childhood living apart from their birth parent/s: 'looked after' under English law, in court-ordered or voluntary arrangements that included residential care, foster care with unrelated families, kinship care with family or friends, and in some cases, legally permanent arrangements including adoption. As discussed in more detail in Chapter 2, these young adults are part of a diverse population, with varied experience in terms of reasons for entering the care system as well as the timing, nature and duration of their placements. But under English law – the Children Act 1989 – a common purpose for placement is clear: to safeguard or promote the child's welfare.[1] As such, placing a child in care is an intervention that inevitably involves thinking about family.

Yet this is not primarily a book about public care: it is a book about family. There are two reasons for this. First, it is imperative that policy, research and practice concerned with public care systems think through the meanings of family for this population: supporting people who have been in care, through childhood and beyond, depends on recognizing the continuing and distinctive complexities of their family relationships. Second, learning from diverse experiences helps to think through the concept of 'family': challenging normative binaries between the 'ordinary' and the 'troubled' (McCarthy et al, 2019) and enriching wider understandings of the concept of 'family'. There is an ethical imperative for this shift, because of the ways in which certain family lives and family stories are socially and culturally marginalized, as 'sad and secret' stories that do not fit dominant narratives (Steedman, 1986, p 124). Writing about working class childhoods, Steedman notes that through history, such stories have often remained untold or unheard, or are homogenized and pathologized through comparison to an imaginary bourgeois 'norm': 'But it is the story itself that does not fit: all its content and its imagery demonstrate its marginality to the central story, of the bourgeois household and the romances of the family and the fairy-tales that lie behind its closed doors' (Steedman, 1986, p 139).

Steedman argues that an analysis like this 'denies its subjects a particular story, a personal history, except when the story illustrates a general thesis' (Steedman, 1986, p 10). Her arguments resonate with the epigraph from the novelist Chimamanda Ngozi Adichie that opened this chapter. Although writing about very different geographical, historical and cultural contexts, these authors make a similar point – about which stories may be told, or heard. Their observations are highly relevant to thinking about meanings of 'family' for people who have been in care. Adichie was discussing the colonial power play involved in the reductive problem-focused construction of a 'single story of Africa'. But her words resonate in considering policy and media constructions of 'family' in contemporary England (the focus of this book), where austerity politics have been implemented through state-crafted stigma and a political economy of disgust (Tyler, 2020). The Igbo concept of *nkali*, 'to be greater than another', as Adichie explains, can be seen to play out in reductive politicized constructions of some families as 'ordinary' and some as 'troubled', problematic, abject and 'other'.

As Jamieson (1998) observed, class, race and gender privilege coincide in the powerful storying of the conventional modern family: 'The most pervasive public stories are typically produced and reproduced by people occupying positions of power and authority, that is, they operate from and on behalf of powerful institutionalized structures. Their stories are never "just stories"' (Jamieson, 1998, p 12).

Stories serve political functions and, in our late neoliberal age, the curation of storytelling – and the privileging of particular kinds of stories and story tellers – determines whose lives are recognized and how (Fernandes, 2017). Research can play a critical role in relation to pervasive public stories, providing evidence that disrupts stigmatizing binaries and hierarchies by allowing 'the fullness and complexity of experience to be expressed' (Fernandes, 2017, p 4). This is our aim, in thinking through meanings of 'family' in care experienced lives. Through the focus and analytic strategy of the book, we respond to this challenge: bringing forward the stories of family that our research participants have shared; treating them analytically with respect for their integrity and particularity, and with sensitivity to their accounts of complex and sometimes very difficult experiences.

The studies

The book draws together narrative material from interviews with young adults in England who took part in two different studies conducted between 2015 and 2020:

- *Against All Odds?* was a Norwegian Research Council funded study which involved interviews with 75 people (aged 16–32 years) in Denmark, England and Norway, who were in care in childhood. At the time of recruitment to the research all the participants were in education or employment, full- or part-time (including voluntary work). For this book, we draw on interviews with the 21 young adults who took part in the research in England.
- The *Evaluation of Pause*, funded by UK government, examined a programme which provides intensive, individually-tailored practitioner support over an 18-month period for women who have had children removed into care and who are judged to be at risk of future removals of children.[2] For this book, we draw on interviews with 14 women who were part of a 'care leaver pilot' (and were aged 18 to 25 years at time of referral to Pause), all of whom had experienced the removal of at least one child into care or adoption.

The studies differed in many ways, discussed in more detail in Chapter 2, but both used qualitative longitudinal methods concerned with understanding lives over time. While conducting interviews, I was struck by both similarities *and* differences in participants' experiences across the two studies, and this prompted the idea of bringing the two samples together in a new analysis. The aim is not comparison, nor is it to identify pathways to risk or protective factors, as this carries the danger of essentializing the experience of participants in *Against All Odds?* as 'doing well', or defining women who took part in the *Evaluation of Pause* in terms of their child/ren's removal. That would not only be an oversimplification, it would be an injustice to all those who took part.

As we have written about elsewhere (for example, Boddy et al, 2020b; Bakketeig et al, 2020; Hanrahan et al, 2020; Gundersen, 2021), life was far from straightforward for the people who took part in *Against All Odds?*. As researchers, we must recognize the stigma and challenges they face, as well as their strengths and opportunities. And the same is true for women who have worked with Pause: it is crucial that we do not reify them as definitionally vulnerable (see Butler, 2016), effacing their agency and resistance by writing about them only in terms of the difficulties that they have navigated. Instead, writing about participants in both studies, we need to recognize and engage respectfully with complex experience. In a previous study (of family lives in India and the UK), we used the metaphor of 'juxtaposition' to create a research narrative that would challenge the false 'universalism' of the single story, in order to 'argue for a more nuanced and contextually situated analysis entailing recognition of... commonalities and differences' (Boddy et al, 2021, p 18). Throughout this book, we apply the same metaphor in thinking across the two studies discussed here. Considering the experiences of these young adults together illuminates the diversity of care experience. Recognizing their lives as varied, specific and socially and biographically located means paying attention to what is 'ordinary' as well as what is 'distinctive' in their stories of family, rather than emphasizing (or reducing them to) their differences or the difficulties they have experienced.

The analysis presented in this book focuses on England, but the insights it generates are relevant for other nation states. Thinking through family entails thinking about welfare policy and practice, because familial and intergenerational resources are increasingly expected to compensate, as 'the protective carapace of the welfare state no longer promises social reproduction or cradle-to-grave social security' (Thomson and Østergaard, 2021, p 1). With these arguments in mind, this book forms part of a growing body of evidence for the importance of family-minded approaches to welfare policy and practice (Featherstone et al, 2014).

Conceptualizing 'family'

Before we start to think through the ways in which family lives and practices may be shaped by child welfare interventions – and specifically, by the placement of a child in care – it is necessary to set out the understanding of 'family' that we employ in this book. This explanation matters because the idea of 'family' in popular and political discourse tends to be highly normative. Jamieson (1998, p 11) refers to the normative construction of the conventional modern family as a 'pervasive story' – 'a repertoire of themes, stereotypes and judgements' which shape both public and private lives, and Morgan (2011) similarly warned of the dangers associated with the 'thing-like' quality of the concept of 'The Family'. He highlighted the imaginary of the 'cornflakes packet' family – the purported 'norm' against which a problematic 'other' can be constructed. To take an illustrative example of this metaphor, a 1960 Kellogg's cornflakes advertisement[3] depicts a mother standing and serving her husband and child. The caption – promising the cereal will 'bring you much more essential goodness than whole grain' – illuminates the morality inherent in this story of this modern, White, middle-class heterosexual-couple family, in which the mother ensures everyone's wellbeing and visible happiness. This representation can be understood as contributing to what Gillis (1996) termed 'the families we live by' – imagined families that do symbolic work: 'Constituted through myth, ritual and image, they must be forever nurturing and protective, and we will go to any lengths to ensure that they are so, even if it means mystifying the realities of family life' (Gillis, 1996, p xv).

Heaphy (2018, p 163) argues that these normative understandings continue to pervade academic scholarship, as 'the sociology of family lives in the shadow of a cultural imaginary of the conventional family', even while the essential diversity and fluidity of family forms and family lives has long been recognized (for example, Morgan, 1996; 2011; 2019; Jamieson, 1998; Finch, 2007; Dermott and Seymour, 2011). In this light, thinking through family in *care experienced* lives has the potential to nuance and extend existing theoretical conceptualizations of family, and so to enable new sociologically informed approaches to family in child welfare policy and professional contexts.

Within contemporary family studies, some scholars have argued for a need to move beyond the language of 'family' to allow expanded and/or alternative conceptual frameworks, for example, focusing on 'personal life', kinship or intimate relationships (for example, Jamieson, 1998; Smart, 2011). But recognition of the normative implications of reifying 'the family' does not negate the value of attention to 'family' (Edwards et al, 2012). Family matters – within relational practices and identities, in everyday lives *and* over the life course. There remains a need to attend to 'what is being evoked in the relational language of family togetherness' (McCarthy, 2012, pp 70–71), while recognizing the diverse and multiple possible meanings of 'family' and the inherent interdependency that characterizes all our lives. These arguments have sharpened relevance for child welfare contexts, because they highlight the need for policy and practice concerned with children's best interests to recognize the relational child. As Featherstone and colleagues (2014) argued:

> We need to change because more and more we have seen a decoupling of the child from their family in a *child-focused* orientation. This

orientation concentrates on the child as an individual with an independent relation to the state, thus ignoring the most fundamental of insights about our relational natures. (Featherstone et al, 2014, p 152)

Talking in terms of *relationality* also allows that families are active and dynamic, and not 'simply given (and hence unchanging) through one's position in a family genealogy' (Smart, 2011, p 17). Roseneil and Ketokivi, (2016, p 149) observe that both the 'individual' and the 'family' must be understood as in a 'state of becoming', constructed through dynamic and relational processes, rather than existing as 'pre-given bounded entities'. Placement of a child in care is an intervention that highlights the active and dynamic nature of family, because it reconfigures family in complex ways. Beyond the circumstances and experiences that led to placement, family is shaped through the legislative provision and entitlements offered by care and aftercare systems; by the timing and nature of placement/s in the child's life; and by frameworks for regulating family involvement (for example, contact arrangements). These systems and frameworks shape children's experiences of family, both during and after their time in care, including their relationships with family members – and those who they understand to be family, including kin and unrelated carers.

'Doing' family: practices and display

In writing about the dangers of the 'cornflakes packet' imaginary, Morgan (2011) suggests that a productive alternative is to treat the word 'family' as an adjective and verb, so it is possible to think about 'doing family'. This makes it possible to recognize 'family' as active, fundamentally social and dynamic. Thinking about the 'doing' of family practices and about family 'display' is thus particularly useful for understanding family meanings and practices when 'the family' does not conform to conventional structural forms (Finch, 2007). As Dermott and Seymour (2011, p 12) observed:

> A focus on practices and display is useful in managing the challenge of deepening our understanding of families and personal relationships while navigating through a wide range of settings and circumstances, as practices and display offer the possibility of moving away from thinking about families in terms of categories which are supposedly, a priori, significant.

Thinking about the diverse ways in which family may be practised by people with care experience is also helpful in thinking through the distinction between family and intimate practices. As I will discuss in Chapter 4, this is especially apparent in placement contexts where practices of upbringing are the responsibility of carers who may or may not feel like family to the child. Some significant intimate practices 'do not include any strong sense of family' (Morgan, 2011, p 37). Equally – and especially evident in the experiences of care experienced women whose children are in care or adopted – practices that are inherently about family (such as a mother's display of her child's picture) can occur in contexts where opportunities for relational intimacy are highly constrained. These considerations are discussed in Chapter 6.

Thinking about family *display* has particular value in attending to the risk of reproducing stigma in giving an account of care experienced lives. Finch and Mason (1993, p 27), writing about families' public identities, highlight the external audience, 'who observe what goes on and make judgements about it'. While all our family lives are observed within our social worlds, this experience of observation and judgement is especially acute for care experienced families, whose biographies are shaped by professional evaluation and intervention, and by the stigma that can often be faced by those with care experience (for example, Rogers, 2016; Roberts, 2021). As Finch (2007, p 66) observed, 'the meaning of one's actions has to be both conveyed to and understood by relevant others if those actions are to be effective as constituting "family" practices'.

Throughout this volume, our account is focused through a narrative analytic lens. As discussed further in Chapter 2, this approach involves recognizing narratives as 'a means of exchange' (Steedman, 1986, p 132). When participants respond to questions about family, or talk about family within the interview conversation, their accounts can be recognized as a form of family display, constructed with and for the interviewer (Phoenix et al, 2021). Listening to participants' explanations of what family means to them demands respectful recognition of complex and diverse experience – from us as researchers and from you as readers. Only by attending to their perspectives – on what is difficult, distinctive and ordinary, and what matters from their point of view – does it become possible to counter the *mis*recognition that positions some accounts of family as 'wholly other or simply invisible' (following Fraser, 2001 p 24).

Thinking beyond childhood

Our focus on the perspectives of *young adults* who have been in care highlights the ways in which family continues to matter in lives over time. As Finch and Mason (1993) documented in their classic study of family responsibilities, the significance of relationships between adult kin includes – but extends far beyond – their importance as sources of practical and financial help: 'Much more is at stake therefore, than simply the material value of the goods and services which are exchanged. People's identities are being constructed, confirmed and reconstructed' (Finch and Mason, 1993, p 171).

Nevertheless, kin do play a crucial role in practical and financial support: this is shaped by the ways in which family lives and practices are subject to wider welfare contexts, and so reveals tensions in between state and family responsibility. Finch and Mason (1993, p 8) highlighted the long history of politicians and policy makers who 'have sought to draw a line between the responsibilities which the state is going to assume for the welfare of its citizens, and those which can be presumed to be taken care of by the family'. As we will document through this volume, the politicized delineation of 'family vs state' responsibility has particularly sharp consequences for care experienced people of all ages. Children are described as 'looked after' by the state as 'corporate parent' within the underpinning legislation of the Children Act 1989 – a role defined in statutory guidance to the Act as 'acting as any good parent would' (Department for Education, 2018, p 8). But what does this mean *beyond* childhood?

Young adults who have been in care often face accelerated and compressed transitions out of state care (Stein, 2006) and so the presumption that family will take care of responsibilities instead of the state is especially problematic. Unlike young people from more privileged backgrounds, they are unlikely to be able to rely on the 'propulsive power' of parental capital, increasingly critical for negotiating early adulthood in societal contexts of widening inequality (Toft and Friedman, 2021; p 105). As well as experiences of stigma, the resources afforded them through relational interdependence are likely to be especially precarious, or simply inaccessible (see also Bakketeig et al, 2020; Boddy et al, 2020b; Glynn and Maycock, 2021; Gundersen, 2021; Roberts, 2021). To understand how best to support young adults who have been in care, it is necessary to think through family – particularly in times when the shrinking of state responsibilities presumes increasing reliance on informal and familial resources.

Austerity and 'the other'

The two studies which form the basis of this book were conducted between 2015 and 2020, in a sociopolitical context of austerity policies in England. Funds available to councils to fund local services have fallen by an average of 24 per cent per person in the last decade, with the largest cuts in the most deprived urban local authorities (Harris et al, 2019). Cuts to universal and targeted welfare provision have disproportionately impacted children, young people and families who are already disadvantaged in other ways, as a narrowing of support coincides with increasing rates of material deprivation, labour market insecurity and income inequality for families (for example, Shildrick et al, 2012; Furlong, 2015; Bywaters et al, 2018;

Bilson and Bywaters, 2020; Sanderson, 2020; Batchelor et al, 2020; Webb et al, 2021; Rehill and Oppenheim, 2021). Rehill and Oppenheim (2021, p 3) document the 'hollowing out' of services designed to support families who are struggling; spending reductions have particularly affected public health and preventative services for children and families. At the same time, as Gupta and Blumhardt (2016, p 170) argue, the role of social work has increasingly been narrowed 'from support to policing', while the 'distortion of relationships caused by a risk-saturated system mitigates against effective work to support families'.

Political justification for changes to the welfare state rely on a particular 'austerity story' about 'the family', as Featherstone et al (2018b, p 149) observe: 'Like all good and memorable stories, it has a plot, heroes and villains and a clear moral, is full of metaphors and very memorable and easily grasped.' Rooted in a political economy of stigma, this 'austerity story' marks some people and families as responsible for their own and society's problems (see Tyler, 2020; Featherstone et al, 2018a, b; Gillies et al, 2017). The story of the troubled, or problematic family (McCarthy et al, 2013) is constructed in contrast to the imaginary of the "ordinary" family "doing their best" (in the words of former UK Prime Minister Theresa May, 2016). This political conceptualization of family can be recognized as a dividing practice (see Foucault, 1983) – a practice of exclusion and objectification that positions some families as essentially 'other'. Thus, stigma becomes part of the machinery of inequality, producing stress and discrimination which has cumulative effects on stigmatized groups over time, such that the stigmatizing construction of the other in itself perpetuates disadvantage (Tyler, 2020).

Thus, the families we live by (see Gillis, 1996) are constituted politically through the legal and cultural legitimation of particular kinds of family (Cooper, 2017), which coincide with the 'cornflakes packet' imaginary. The Kellogg's cornflakes advertisement I described is 60 years old, and of course the representation of family within advertising has changed throughout that period – but arguably, not that much. In late 2020, the UK supermarket Sainsbury's experienced racist trolling on social media after screening a Christmas advertisement, Gravy Song,[4] which featured a Black (heterosexual couple) family. The advert was widely defended (including by other supermarkets), but the fact that it was distinctive enough to trigger a racist response and public defence indicates the persistent dominance of the White normative 'ideal type'. This is evident in another exemplar image[5] (Figure 1.1), taken from a video published in 2019 by the Ministry for Children and Families in Norway. The Minister at that time, Kjell Ingolf Ropstad from the Christian Democratic party, sets out his vision for a 'new family politics' (*En Ny Familiepolitikk*) – presented over a backdrop of vintage footage of White Norwegian families from years gone by, engaged in traditional gendered family practices (such as women making sandwiches for children).

Figure 1.1: 'A New Family Politics'

Source: Norway Ministry for Children and Families, https://www.facebook.com/ barnedep/id eos/608193516366950/

This normative imaginary of the 'good enough' family can also be seen to inform contemporary family policy through the persistent influence of Baumrind's (for example, 1975) concept of 'good enough' parenting. Her typology of parenting 'style' was derived from research with White, middle-class, highly educated, heterosexual couple families in California, and she acknowledged the specificity of this selective sample of 'urbane families ... nontraditional, child centered, and rational' (1975, p 14). More recent research raises questions about the universal applicability of Baumrind's notion of parenting 'styles', for example, documenting the need for greater sensitivity to cultural and contextual variations (Smetana, 2017). Yet, the qualities of parenting that Baumrind identified among these 'urbane' White Californian families continue to shape policy and political understandings, as demonstrated in Dermott and Pomati's (2016) research in England, which suggested that 'the most educationally advantaged fraction of the middle class is setting the tone and standard in terms of key markers of educationally 'appropriate' and 'supportive' parenting' (p 138). In this way, societal inequalities are obscured. The stigmatization of low-income families is reinforced, while those who are among the most well-resourced, educationally and economically, are represented as 'ordinary' through governmental discourses of evidence-based parenting (Jensen, 2010; Dermott and Pomati, 2016; Gillies et al, 2017; Boddy, 2023).

Writing about the US, Cooper (2017) documents a contemporary political discourse of family crisis, which has led to 'the strategic reinvention of a much older, poor-law tradition of private family responsibility', such that 'welfare has been transformed from a redistributive program into an immense federal apparatus for policing the private family responsibilities of the poor' (p 21). Her observations are equally pertinent for other contemporary neoliberal welfare states including England.[6] As Jensen (2010, p 2) writes: 'This sort of talk is not simply an evasion of socioeconomic class; it is also part of a much longer and broader rewriting of the very terms of social differences and inequalities, a rewriting which goes back to distinctions between the deserving and the undeserving poor.' The 'evidence' that is drawn on to inform policy and practice understandings of family is thus likely to reinforce unhelpful binaries, as McCarthy et al (2019, p 2214) observe:

> The real and apparent danger ... is that the dichotomy between mainstream and problem-oriented family studies, besides creating academic siloes, risks constructing unrealistic binaries between 'good' and 'bad' families, the 'ordinary' and the 'problematic', often on the basis of taken-for-granted assumptions about what family lives 'should' look like, what family practices are entailed, and what meanings are invoked in the attribution and legitimation of the powerful language of 'family'.

Thinking beyond the 'troubled' family?

The tendency to academic siloes (see McCarthy et al, 2019) is also a danger in research concerned with care experience, where a substantial literature has documented that young people who have been in care face heightened risk of disadvantage across multiple domains (for example, Stein and Dumaret, 2011; Courtney et al, 2011; Kääriälä et al, 2018; Häggman-Laitila et al, 2018; Jay and McGrath-Lone, 2019; Berlin et al, 2021). While it is crucially important to understand the barriers and challenges that care experienced people face, restricting their stories to assessment of risk, or evaluating their lives in relation to narrowly defined outcomes may inadvertently function to (re)produce stigma and social inequality, if such work contributes to the assumption that care is associated with lifelong problems (see also Bakketeig et al, 2020).

In considering this tendency to think in siloes in the context of 'family' and 'care experience', it is helpful to borrow from a distinction noted by Phoenix (for example, 1987) in her writing about parenting and ethnicity. Phoenix defined a couplet of 'normalized absence and pathologised presence', observing that families from minoritized ethnic groups are customarily absent from research on 'ordinary' family lives and tend to be included only when research is risk- or problem-focused. Arguably, this tendency to normalized absence and pathologized presence can be seen in research with other groups within society – including care experienced people – who face stigma and are commonly defined as vulnerable or at risk. Diverse family lives and practices are either rendered invisible or else pathologized, discursively constructed through problem-focused research and problem-saturated narratives. In this light, the normalized absence/pathologized presence couplet can be understood to contribute sociopolitical *misrecognition* in Fraser's terms: 'When ... institutionalized patterns of cultural value constitute some actors as inferior, excluded, wholly other or simply invisible, hence as less than full partners in social interaction, then we should speak of misrecognition and status subordination' (Fraser, 2001, p 24). Phoenix's (1987) couplet of normalized absence/pathologized presence highlights the need for research that takes a holistic approach that recognizes nuance and subjectivities in care experienced people's lives (see also, for example, Reimer and Schäfer, 2015; Brady and Gilligan, 2018; Rees and Munro, 2019; Join-Lambert et al, 2020). This means engaging with the complex and dynamic diversities of family lives in time and across space, place and generations (Edwards, 2020), working to 'destabilize any tendency to write about "family" in conventional terms, while still centralising the importance of writing about family' (McCarthy et al, 2019, p 2214).

Here, we can draw a parallel with Heaphy's writing about same-sex couple families. He argues that attention to the *ordinary* aspects of unconventional family lives makes it possible to understand their 'double nature', recognizing both the normative and non-normative aspects of family relationships and practices and enabling insights 'into the everyday possibilities and troubles' that families encounter (Heaphy, 2018, p 174). Thinking through 'family' for people who have been in care also necessitates this kind of 'double thinking'. By attending to meanings of family for marginalized and stigmatized groups within society (Edwards et al, 2012; Wilson et al, 2012), it should be possible to challenge policy discourses that rely on 'impoverished stories about family life' (Smart, 2011, p 16), stories constructed in opposition to the imaginary of an 'ordinary' other. This approach also has practical and political consequences. By revealing the lie of the austerity narrative that constructs some people as deserving of their hardship, we enable the development of humane, family-minded policy and practice in child and youth welfare (Featherstone et al, 2018b). Moreover, as Heaphy observes, 'double thinking' can build a better understanding of 'family' as a contemporary social institution, disrupting unhelpful academic siloes between mainstream family studies and child and youth welfare research (Heaphy, 2018).

Thinking through 'family' in care experienced lives

For people with care experience, placement in care is an intervention which fundamentally reconfigures family for children and adults alike.

The nature of that intervention inevitably depends on the wider welfare system in which it is situated: 'social, political, economic and systemic contexts matter for why and how decisions are made' (Burns et al, 2017, p 2). Cross-national research highlights the ways in which child welfare policy and systems are shaped by wider welfare contexts, as well as how different approaches shape experiences of family – for example, in relation to use of adoption or in the extent to which family involvement is related to use of voluntary and court-ordered arrangements (see Boddy et al, 2013; Skivenes and Thoburn, 2016; Boddy, 2017; Burns et al, 2017). Drawing on Gilbert's (for example, 2012) typology of welfare systems, Burns and colleagues' cross-national analysis describes England as a risk-oriented 'child protection' system – with high thresholds for intervention – in contrast 'family-service' oriented systems (for example, in Nordic countries), which place greater emphasis on early intervention to promote healthy childhoods as well as mitigating risks.

The underpinning legislation for children in care in England – the Children Act 1989 – could be seen to have a strongly child-centred family service orientation. The Act was designed to protect the best interests of the child within a legislative framework that encompasses several different aspects of family lives, uniting previously disparate 'legislation relating to child protection, the support of families in difficulties, and decisions about the care of children whose parents were divorced or separated' (Hetherington and Nurse, 2006, p 55). A key principle of the Act is that local authorities should work in partnership with families and that children are best brought up within their families, so local authorities should provide support and services to enable that to happen. In addition, the Act sets out a definition of parental responsibility, referring to 'all the rights, duties, powers, responsibilities and authority which by law a parent of a child has in relation to the child and his property' (Children Act 1989 Section 3 (1)). Parental responsibility can be awarded to others through legally permanent arrangements (including Special Guardianship Orders and Placement Orders for adoption) and can be shared with the local authority.

Family is further emphasized in statutory guidance on planning for permanence, defined in terms of ensuring that: 'Children have a secure, stable and loving family to support them through childhood and beyond and to give them a sense of security, continuity, commitment, identity and belonging' (Department for Education Children Act Guidance 2015, pp 22–23). This conceptualization of permanence spans all forms of intervention under the Act, ranging from family support to placement of a child in care. It can be also seen to accord with the UN Convention on the Rights of the Child and the European Convention on Human Rights, both of which set out the child's right to a family life.

Despite the emphasis on family and partnership with parents within the Children Act 1989, the influence of neoliberal ideology – embedded in the history of child and family policy in England (Cunningham, 2006) – means that policy and provision are dominated by a targeted or 'residual' approach. Family is seen as a private domain and difficulty in linking the 'parallel tracks of child protection and family support' persists (Hetherington and Nurse, 2006, p 82), with early intervention and family support conceptualized as corrective interventions rather than as a matter of child or family rights, or an expression of state responsibilities to families (see Boddy et al, 2013; 2014; 2023; Gillies et al, 2017). As Gupta and Blumhardt (2016) observed, this tendency is heightened in times of political austerity. It obscures recognition of the impacts of poverty on child and family lives, within and across generations, and fails to recognize the strengths of families and communities, so that ultimately, 'the orthodoxies are masking complexity and making children less safe' (Featherstone et al, 2014, p 152).

If policy and practice are to provide adequate support for children and families who encounter care systems, we need to respect the complex diversity of care experienced people (discussed further in Chapter 2) and their correspondingly diverse experiences of 'family'. We must recognize the contingency and the ambivalent complexity of lived experience, recognizing how care experience shapes 'unconventional' and diverse family forms and relating practices (for example, Gabb, 2011a; b; Heaphy, 2018), illuminating fluidity and ambiguous boundaries, while recognizing the enduring importance of family in people's lives over space and time.

The structure of this book

The first two chapters set the context for the volume as a whole, including this introductory chapter (Chapter 1), and a contextual framing of the focus on care experienced people and the two studies on which the book is based (Chapter 2). The second chapter begins with an overview of key policy and legislative contexts for young people in and after care, reflecting on how key family-related features of children's lives and care experiences (including the presence of siblings, recurrent removal of children into care from the same parent/s and so on) are recognized within policy and published data. The chapter then goes on to discuss ethical and methodological debates in researching vulnerability. It sets out the argument for taking a narrative approach to thinking through family in care experienced lives, including the need for methodological and analytic approaches that avoid the enforced narrative of the 'terrible tale' (Steedman, 2000), challenging the tendency for categorizations of 'vulnerability' to disempower, silencing narratives of resistance (Butler, 2016). This discussion links to an overview of the two studies, addressing methods, study contexts, and sample recruitment and characteristics, and the details of the analytic approach to linking the two datasets.

Drawing on Morgan's (2011) conceptualization of family as entailing a sense of the active, and seeking to highlight the (continuing) significance of birth families in care experienced lives, Chapter 3 addresses the significance of the 'ordinary'. Undeniably, care experienced people have often faced significant challenges within their family lives. But if we focus only on documenting those adversities we risk engaging in a dividing practice (see Foucault, 1983) as discussed before, whereby care experienced people – and care experienced families – are reduced to the problems they have faced. Accordingly, this chapter draws attention to 'ordinary' memories within extraordinary childhoods, encompassing narratives of regular, ritual and habitual family practices and the importance of these within participants' accounts.

Chapter 4 considers how family practices shape family boundaries, considering who 'counts' as family and examining family connections over time and through experiences of placement in childhood. Participants in the two studies had very varied experiences of placement – ranging from a single foster or kinship placement from early childhood to adulthood, to experiences of 20 or more placements, and of residential care and mother-and-baby placements (especially in the Pause sample). This chapter addresses participants' narratives of the practices that enable a placement to feel 'like family' – or not – and explore the different possibilities for doing 'family' that participants highlight in their narratives of placement.

Chapter 5 builds on the material discussed previously to consider care and connectedness, and the challenges, responsibilities and resources that are part of those linked lives. In line with previous research concerned with young adults who had been in care (for example, Wade, 2008; Havlicek, 2021), participants in both studies had contact with their birth families and gave accounts of practices of care within and across generations. This chapter draws on these accounts to think about the sharpened significance of family connections for care experienced young adults living in a historical moment of heightened precarity and political austerity.

Chapter 6 turns to understandings and experiences of parenthood. It begins by focusing on the experiences of participants who are parents (all but one of whom were mothers), including the implications of child removal for understandings of parenthood and family. The chapter will consider how participants practise family at-a-distance, and how they manage and maintain identities as parents separated from their children, taking account of different permanence, placement and contact arrangements. Finally, this chapter engages with participants' narratives of future imagined families, and the ways in which those are positioned in relation to their past and present experiences, including relationships with partners and children not-yet-born, as well as the potential return of children who are currently in placement.

Chapter 7 concludes the book by drawing together learning from the preceding chapters to consider the value of a sociological lens, and of attention to family practices, for thinking through the conceptualization of family for people who have been in care. We argue that learning about 'unconventional' family lives from the perspective of people who are care experienced enriches the theorization of 'family' more generally – in terms of understanding family practices, fluidity and continuities, for example. This in turn helps with identifying the implications for the politics, policy and practice of child and family welfare, highlighting the importance of thinking through 'family' when working with children in care and with families who encounter public care systems, through childhood and beyond.

Summing up

This chapter began by quoting Adichie's warning of the danger of the single story. The aim of this book is to enable new, more nuanced narrative understandings of what 'family' means for care experienced people: 'To expand and legitimise opportunities for different types of dialogue, storytellers and audiences' (Featherstone et al, 2018b, p 2). We live in a historic period of precarity for young adults, who are increasingly reliant on familial support. This has sharp implications for those who have been in care, who may have complex intergenerational responsibilities yet fewer intergenerational resources than their peers, and so there is an urgent need to attend to their experiences of family in early adulthood. Achieving the aspirations of statutory guidance for the Children Act 1989 – ensuring a secure, stable and loving family, and enabling a corresponding sense of security, continuity, commitment, identity and belonging through childhood and beyond – depends on listening and learning from people whose families have been shaped by encounters with care systems. It requires that we think through what family means and how family matters in complex and diverse lives, over time.

By learning from care experienced people's perspectives and experiences, this book moves beyond the existing 'single story' of care experienced family lives. A narrative approach makes it possible to curate diverse stories of family – recognizing the ordinary and extraordinary, and challenging stigmatizing constructions. The aim is to illuminate features of complex family lives that might otherwise be missed, or misrepresented; attending to relationality, care and connectedness; recognizing the significance of the mundane; and considering how family lives over time – including experiences as a child, sibling and parent – can be distinctively shaped, supported and challenged by being in care. Thinking through 'family', as expressed in our participants' narratives, should help policy makers and practitioners think how best to support people who encounter care systems in their family lives, while building new understandings that connect the conceptualization of 'family' in mainstream family studies and in child and youth welfare research.

2

Learning From Care Experienced Perspectives

> Is the possession of a terrible tale, a story of suffering, desired, perhaps envied, as a component of the other self? ... To do with a bourgeois self that was told in terms of a suffering and enduring other, using the themes and items of other, dispossessed and difficult lives.
>
> Carolyn Steedman, *Feminism and Autobiography: Texts, Theories, Methods*, 2000, p 36

Hearing a different story?

In Chapter 1, I drew on Adichie's (2009) discussion of the Igbo word 'nkali' to argue for the need to move beyond a troubled 'single story' of family for people who have been in care, recognizing dynamic complexity and diversity – and strengths as well as challenges – in order to avoid reinforcing stigmatizing binaries. This was an explicit focus of the *Against All Odds?* study, as our research team has written elsewhere: 'If care experienced people are predominantly viewed (and studied) through a problem-focused lens, policy and professional approaches may become dominated by an inadvertently stigmatizing hegemonic discourse, focused on measurable risks and outcomes' (Bakketeig et al, 2020, p 1). As we discuss in that paper, there is substantial international evidence that care experienced people face heightened risk of disadvantage across domains including education, employment, housing, financial security and health (for example, Stein and Dumaret, 2011; Courtney et al, 2011; Kääriälä et al, 2018; Häggman-Laitila et al, 2018; Berlin et al, 2021). Research on risk of disadvantage is hugely important in highlighting support needs for young people in and after care (and so informing the development of policy and professional frameworks), but we would add a note of caution. If research focuses *only* on risk, it may have the unintended consequence of exacerbating stigma: complex and diverse lives may be reduced to hegemonic narratives of the vulnerable or damaged subject. A growing body of work has documented the heterogeneity of care experienced lives, for example, modelling the relative contribution of experiences pre-care and while in placement (for example, Fowler et al, 2017; Rebbe et al, 2017) and illuminating the ways in which care systems may be protective for young people (for example, Arnau-Sabatés and Gilligan, 2015; Sebba et al, 2015; Holmes et al, 2018; Hanrahan et al, 2020). These studies demonstrate the value of building understanding of dynamic complexity and diversity – as we also aim to do in this book. In this chapter, I begin by considering the context of care experience in England and then go on to reflect on the implications for methodology: first considering the politics – and ethics – of researching care experienced lives and subsequently discussing the implications for the two studies that form the basis of the book.

Care experienced lives in context

To understand what 'family' means in care experienced lives, we must begin by recognizing that people who have been in care in childhood are not a homogeneous group. The diversity of the population also intersects with the complexity of the multifaceted systems that care experienced people encounter. Child welfare policy and service contexts intersect with individual lives and biographies and with wider social, economic and cultural contexts, and this in turn shapes experiences of family through childhood and beyond.

Childhood and placement experiences

The original and underpinning legislative framework for children in care in England is the Children Act 1989. This legislation introduced requirements for work in partnership with parents, including conceptualizing placement in care as a support for upbringing (see Skivenes and Thoburn, 2016; Lynch, 2017). It also establishes expectations for the state's role in the care and upbringing of children, referring to children and young people as 'looked after' when accommodated in care through voluntary or court-mandated measures. As discussed briefly in Chapter 1, this also means that the state has statutory duties for looked-after children and care leavers under principles of 'corporate parenting' (DfE, 2018).

Most children in care in England live in family-based placements. To take the example of recent data published by the Department for Education: among 80,080 children who were 'looked after' under the Children Act 1989 on 31 March 2020,[1] 58 per cent were living with unrelated foster carers, and another 14 per cent were in 'family and friends' placements. Reflecting a longstanding policy emphasis on achieving permanence through adoption 3,440 children were adopted in England in 2020, joining a legally permanent alternative family. In the same year 3,700 children moved to a legally permanent arrangement through a Special Guardianship Order (SGO),[2] most commonly with biological kin (88 per cent of SGOs were made to family or friends).

Most children in care in England continue to have contact with some family members after placement (see Iyer et al, 2020 for a review). The majority also have established relationships with their families of origin at the point that they come into care. Among children starting to be looked after in 2020, almost two-thirds were aged five years or older, and 81 per cent were over one year old. Recent years have also seen an increasing proportion of care entrants aged 16 years and over. Moreover, placement in care does not mean the child is given a permanent alternative family, nor is that the intent of care entry for every child. Among the 29,590 children who ceased to be looked after in the year to 31 March 2020, almost one-quarter (22 per cent) left to live with parents or other relatives (with or without parental responsibility, not including Special Guardianship Orders). A significant minority of children who return home from care subsequently enter the system again; Farmer (2018) reported DfE data which record that 30 per cent of children who returned home from care in England in 2006–2007 re-entered care within five years (see also Farmer and Wijedasa, 2012; Farmer, 2014). A fifth of 16–17 year olds who ceased to be looked after in 2020 had two or more periods in care – presumably returning to their family of origin before re-entering the system. The fluidity of family for children in care is further complicated because it is relatively common for placements to change: in the year to 31 March 2020, DfE data record 56,330 placement changes.[3] A third (34 per cent) were linked to the child's care plan (for example, a move from emergency to long-term placement), but changes can occur for a variety of other reasons including carer requests (16 per cent of changes) or, less often, child requests (4 per cent). Almost 40 per cent of children ceasing to be looked after in the year to 31 March 2021 had three or more placements, and nearly a thousand had ten or more placements during their time in care.

The data summarized here indicate the complexity and diversity of experiences of family in the 'care population'. Understandings of family are inevitably influenced by factors such as the child's age, family structure, placement and permanency arrangements and whether reunification is being planned or considered. A teenager who is accommodated in short-term residential care under voluntary arrangements will have very different relationships with their birth family compared to an infant removed at birth and subsequently placed for adoption, and family boundaries are also likely to feel very different for children in kinship arrangements compared with unrelated foster care. Experiences and understandings are also likely to vary over time. Moreover, children in care may be in family placements that do not *feel* like family – or be intended to provide long-term care and upbringing (Thoburn and Courtney, 2011). Equally, children may not have legally permanent arrangements (such as adoption or special guardianship), but still live permanently with a foster family and feel a strong sense of familial belonging (Schofield et al, 2012). Children and young people may also experience boundary shifts in their understandings of family as a result of placement, or over time while living in a placement (Schofield and Beek, 2009; Ellingsen et al, 2011; Wilson et al, 2012; Biehal, 2014).

As we will discuss further in the chapters that follow, children's families of origin also feature significantly in their lives while in care. Most children have some kind of contact with one or more family members. But even if there is no direct contact, families remain important for children's understandings of their identities and because they care for – and often worry about – relatives including parents and siblings (for example, Monk and McVarish, 2018; Iyer et al, 2020). Many looked after children also return to their families of origin as young adults: 11 per cent of 18 year olds and 43 per cent of 17 year olds who leave care are living with parents or relatives. Wade (2008) found that 80 per cent of young adult care leavers in England were in contact with birth-family members.

Early adulthoods

Across the two studies discussed in this book, participants were aged 16–30[4] years at the beginning of the research. The high (and increasing) proportion of people in the general population who live with parents when in their early twenties is therefore an important part of the context for thinking through our participants' experiences of family – and for considering the relative role of family and state in aftercare support for young adults who have been in care. Stein and Ward (2021, p 219), introducing a special issue of *Child & Family Social Work* that historicizes understandings of transition from care to adulthood, note 'an unresolved tension between two conflicting policy objectives: the need to reduce dependency on the state and the need to ensure that care leavers receive the support that all young people need as they emerge into adulthood'. They observe that, in England, fear of prolonged welfare dependency has its roots in 19th-century Poor Laws. They comment that this fear continues to underpin contemporary concerns about public expenditure, which 'remain very real factors in the development of practice and policy concerning care leavers' (Stein and Ward, 2021, p 219), contributing to the 'compressed and accelerated transitions' that exacerbate the disadvantages faced by young people as they age out of formal care systems (see also Stein and Munro, 2008; Palmer et al, 2022). This accelerated independence contrasts with the increasingly normative practice of living in the family home through early adulthood.

The UK Office for National Statistics (ONS) estimates that in 2020, the first age at which more than 50 per cent of the population left the parental home was 24 years; this pattern is also gendered: 32 per cent of young men aged 20–34 years and 21 per cent of young women in this age group were living with their parents. Our review of Eurostat data for the *Against All Odds?* study (Boddy et al, 2019) indicated that the practice of extended transition is particularly common in the UK: almost four times as many young adults in their twenties were living in their parental home in the UK than in Denmark, and more than twice as many as in Norway. These patterns also reflect the importance of familial support for young adults facing insecure labour markets, as increased rates of living with parents correspond to an increasingly difficult economic climate (for example, Bucx et al, 2012). Again, the least advantaged young adults encounter the sharpest consequences of these shifts, as Berrington et al (2009, p 35) observe: 'At the oldest ages examined here – those in their early thirties – it is the most economically disadvantaged, for example those with no educational qualifications and the unemployed, who are most likely to remain living within the parental home, suggesting that this is the result of external constraints.' Berrington et al's (2009) analysis suggests that extended support is likely to be particularly important for people navigating multiple disadvantages, and we might expect young adults with care experience to be in this category. But recent policy changes mean that transitions for the most vulnerable young people in care are becoming *more* accelerated and compressed. At the time of writing, a new piece of secondary legislation in England – the Care Planning, Placement and Case Review (England) (Amendment) Regulations 2021[5] – has limited the requirements for regulated settings to those aged 15 and under. This change means that semi-independent, independent and supported accommodation settings are no longer required to provide day-to-day care for young people aged 16–17 years. At its heart, this regulatory change is about the extent to which the state is prepared to function as 'family' for these young people. Writing in August 2021, Carolyne Willow, the Director of Article 39 (a children's rights charity in England) issued a statement about the changes which highlighted the contrast with normative family practices:

> Families up and down the country have this past week been holding their teenagers close as they received their A Level and GCSE results and made big decisions for the next part of their lives. Yet in this new legislation we have the Education Secretary saying it is perfectly acceptable for children in the care of the state who are still in compulsory education to be living in places where they receive no day-to-day care from adults. That means children sorting out their own school uniforms, making and going to health appointments on their own, and not having family holidays or having someone in a parental

role who's going to know when they're upset or need cheering up, and can just be there for them. (Willow, 2021, np)

Willow's list describes familiar practices of family care: sorting clothes; organizing medical appointments; planning holidays; cheering up. These are all things that I have done this week, as a mother of two young adults. They are practices of *looking after*, expressions of *care*. What does it mean when the state is legally mandated to 'look after' a young person, as their 'corporate parent' – but regulates to remove responsibility for family practices of care? Attention to the quotidian practices of family lives for people with care experience helps us to understand the implications of such policy moves.

Becoming a parent

The UK as a whole has relatively high rates of early parenthood compared with other European countries. Early parenthood has been a matter of policy concern in England for many years and was the focus of targeted investment through New Labour's ten-year Teenage Pregnancy Strategy (TPS), launched in 1999. Early conception and parenthood are associated with factors including socio-economic deprivation, lower levels of educational attainment and receiving sex education from sources other than school (Wellings et al, 2016). Awareness of these factors shaped the formation of the TPS, as a multicomponent programme which targeted higher levels of investment in areas of greater deprivation and sought to deliver improvements in sex education and sexual health services, alongside support for young parents to access education and employment, and a national media campaign.[6]

Research has consistently documented the increased likelihood of early pregnancy and parenthood for young people in or leaving care (for example, Biehal and Wade, 1996; Barn and Mantovani, 2007; Vinnerljung and Sallnäs, 2008; Chase et al, 2009; Roberts et al, 2018; Roberts, 2021) and perhaps this is not surprising, given that people who have been in care also experience a clustering of risk factors associated with teenage pregnancy. They disproportionately come from backgrounds of relative poverty (see Bywaters et al, 2018; Elliott, 2020) and they are also very likely to face disrupted education both before and during their time in care (for example, Jackson and Cameron, 2012; O'Higgins et al, 2017; Brady and Gilligan, 2018). The challenges that care experienced people face if they become parents are likely to be exacerbated because welfare systems such as Universal Credit disproportionately disadvantage young parents – those under 25 receive lower rates of benefit than older parents – and such inequalities are likely to have greatest impact on parents who cannot rely on intergenerational support from family. A significant international literature has documented the importance of supportive family networks, and grandparent involvement in particular, for scaffolding young families' journeys through parenthood (for example, Neale and Clayton, 2014; Emmel and Hughes, 2014; Sjöberg and Bertilsdotter-Rosqvist, 2017). Once again, this evidence highlights the critical tension between state and family responsibility. For young care experienced parents, who may not be able to rely on informal intergenerational support, what does it mean when the 'corporate parent' becomes the 'corporate grandparent'?

Bekaert and Bradly (2019) noted that the Teenage Pregnancy Strategy corresponded to heightened public scrutiny and increased stigma towards young parents, and a body of research (for example, Barn and Mantovani, 2007; Chase et al, 2009; Roberts, 2021) demonstrates how this tendency is exacerbated when young parents have been in care. Roberts (2021) reviewed a range of previous research which indicates 'the potential for early pregnancy and parenthood to be viewed as a positive aspiration and choice by young people in and leaving care' (p 73); her research also documents participants describing pregnancy as a time of optimism, pride and hope for the future. Yet for mothers and fathers in her study, these feelings were counterbalanced by concerns about stigma and the (lack of) support that they received:

> Assessment and intervention for care experienced parents is portrayed as routine; resented by some, normalised and tolerated by others. Moreover, young people perceive professionals' knowledge and access to historical information as consolidating risk and compounding stigma. ... Crucially, the reflections of parents in this study provide no indication that corporate parenting responsibilities prompt additional supports or safeguards. (Roberts, 2021, pp 91–92)

Roberts' (2021) analysis powerfully documents the critical consequences of lack of support, including the heightened risk for care experienced parents of losing a child to care or adoption. If we consider this risk in light of the state's putative responsibilities as corporate (grand)parent, it is worth noting a distinction drawn by Sjöberg and Bertilsdotter-Rosqvist (2017) in their study of grandparental support for young parents. They drew a stark contrast between support that they characterized as *'be-there-no-matter-what'* and the more ambivalent or adversarial experiences described by some participants, which they felt inhibited the development of their identity as mothers:

> In our understanding, the 'riskiness' lies not only in 'Who is the mother?' but also in the power and control that grandmothers have over young (insufficient) mothers and how their choice to provide (or not to provide) support and their way of supporting their daughters

or grandchildren can very much set the conditions for the young mother's maternal identity work. (Sjöberg and Bertilsdotter-Rosqvist, 2017, p 325)

This *'inhibition'* repertoire of grandparent support resonates with Roberts' (2021) analysis of care experienced parents' descriptions of corporate grandparenting, highlighting critical questions about how the lack of (familial or corporate) grandparental support for young parents who have been in care can heighten the challenges they face and inhibit their journeys into parenthood.

As noted in Chapter 1, one of the studies that forms the basis of this book, the *Evaluation of Pause*, involved interviews with care experienced mothers who had experienced the removal of one or more children into care. Within the last ten years, a growing body of evidence documents the risk that women who have had a child removed, many of whom have been in care themselves, will go on to experience the loss of future-born children into care or adoption. Broadhurst and colleagues' landmark analyses of CAFCASS data on 65,000 family court proceedings (for example, Broadhurst et al, 2015; 2017) revealed how commonly recurrent child removal takes place, reporting that one in four women returned to the family court with subsequent children. This research also documented the multiple disadvantages faced by these women. Most had histories of significant complex trauma including domestic violence; approximately 40 per cent had been in care in childhood (and late care entry and multiple placement moves were reported by half) and at least two-thirds had experienced abuse and/or neglect in childhood. Women in recurrent proceedings were also likely to have been younger when they had their first child (45 per cent were under 20 years). Broadhurst and colleagues' studies also revealed the collateral consequences of child removal (Broadhurst et al, 2015, 2017; Morriss, 2018; Broadhurst and Mason, 2020), highlighting the need for policy and services to respond to the support needs of mothers as well as the risks for their children. Broadhurst and Mason (2020) document the ways in which the trauma of child removal in the absence of support exacerbates risk in other aspects of women's lives, both in terms of the immediate psychosocial crisis that follows the loss of a child, and in enduring and cumulative effects. These include impacts on welfare entitlements – for example, when housing benefits are reduced through the so-called 'bedroom tax' when a child's room becomes a 'spare room'.[7] This research also shows how a sense of being pre-judged can contribute to women's isolation and make it more difficult for them to access support. Schofield and colleagues' (2011) research with parents of children in foster care similarly documented their fear (and experiences) of 'being seen as, or even having become, a 'different' as well as unworthy person' (p 83).

Summing up

This section has discussed aspects of care experience which are relevant to thinking through family for the studies discussed in the book. First, we noted the diversity of the care population – and experiences of placement, contact and permanence – as critical for understanding what family might mean to children who are 'looked after' by the state. Second, we noted the contrast between increasing intergenerational support for young adults in the general population and limits on support for young adults who are care experienced. Finally, we considered young parenthood, again highlighting questions about how the state functions as corporate parent – or grandparent. I will return to these considerations in discussing analysis in the chapters that follow. But the literature we have discussed here also has implications for the discussion of methodology in the remainder of this chapter, in raising a fundamental conceptual challenge: how to strike a balance between recognizing the distinctive challenges and disadvantages that care experienced people may face, without reinforcing stigmatizing binaries through the depiction of the problematic, risky or vulnerable 'other'.

Politics and ethics: researching 'family' in care experienced lives

In the epigraph that opened this chapter, Steedman (2000) was writing about 'enforced narratives' – the stories that can be told about the lives of the marginalized and stigmatized. A historian, she was writing about Victorian philanthropy, but her point is highly relevant to researching care experience *and* to research in a context of political austerity, in thinking about the stories we tell and the need to reflect on our relation to 'the dominant culture':

> First of all, delineation of emotional and psychological selfhood has been made by and through the testimony of people in a central relationship to the dominant culture, that is to say by and through people who are not working class. ... Superficially, it might be said that historians, failing to find evidence of most people's emotional or psycho-sexual existence, have simply assumed that there can't have been much there to find. Such an assumption ignores ... the way in which the lived experience of the majority of people in a class society has been pathologized and marginalized. (Steedman, 1986, p 12)

The researcher's relationship with the dominant culture cannot be assumed, of course, and is shaped by the intersections of class, ethnicity, gender, dis/ability and place (Crew, 2020). In the book quoted, *Landscape for a Good Woman*, Steedman's challenge to the dominance of privileged minority perspectives in historical research is situated in an autobiographical analysis of her own working-class family background. And as Hey (2013, p 108) writes: 'Privilege is not quite the right word to characterise what is "attached" to the role of professor when it is not embodied by hegemonic, heterosexual White men. Something more elusive goes on when the title is conferred on "other" bodies.' Yet, reflection on power and privilege is necessary, both ethically and politically. As researchers we are often funded, employed, and even promoted on the basis of our studies of 'other, dispossessed and difficult lives' (to paraphrase Steedman) and so we must consider our position in relation to those with whom we conduct our research. Not least, problem-focused narratives can obscure nuance and diversity, and function as 'dividing practices' of exclusion and objectification in Foucault's (1983) terms, whereby the scientific classification of the 'other' highlights difference rather than mutual recognition, contributing to the stigmatization of an already stigmatized group. To paraphrase Gunaratnam's (2003, p 4) arguments for a post-structuralist approach to researching 'race' and ethnicity, 'to fail to recognize the contingency and the ambivalent complexity of lived experience maintains an essentialist view'.

When researchers undertake to study the challenging lives of other people – and to interpret and convey their accounts as we do in this book – heightened responsibilities arise. Those include respectful recognition of diverse experiences, remaining cognizant of differences in relationships to dominant cultures. Recognition of power, in the functioning of those dominant cultures, also demands that we pay attention to the political uses of storytelling (Fernandes, 2017) and the potential for research narratives to engender sociopolitical stigma: 'a way of seeing, classifying and understanding a vast array of discriminatory social attitudes and practices' (Tyler and Slater, 2018, p 729). These considerations are especially sharp when we are conducting research with people who have been defined as 'vulnerable'. As Butler writes:

> Once groups are marked as 'vulnerable' within human rights discourse or legal regimes, those groups become reified as definitionally 'vulnerable', fixed in a political position of powerlessness and lack of agency. All the power belongs to the state and international institutions that are now supposed to offer them protection and advocacy. Such moves tend to underestimate, or actively efface, modes of political agency and resistance that emerge within so-called vulnerable populations. (Butler, 2016, pp 24–25)

One of the ways in which the politics of vulnerability shapes researchers' work is through the implications for funding possibilities and priorities. For example, within a residual welfare framework, the commissioning of evaluations depends on the definitions of vulnerability that determine access to support, by defining who is targeted within programmes of intervention (see Gillies et al, 2017; Crossley, 2018; Boddy, 2023). Especially in times of austerity and a shrinking welfare state, who is vulnerable enough to warrant being supported, or to warrant being researched?

As noted earlier, the *Evaluation of Pause* was focused on the work of a non-governmental organization which provides intensive individually tailored practitioner support over an 18-month period, for women identified as being at risk of repeat removal of children into care or adoption. Other such support programmes exist (see for example Cox et al, 2020), but the work we evaluated – and the evaluation itself – were funded by UK government, receiving investment from the Department for Education's Children's Social Care Innovation Programme. The DfE's £200 million Innovation Programme was launched in 2014 'to test and share effective ways of supporting vulnerable children and young people who need help from children's social care services' through support of 98 specific projects which targeted a range of policy priorities (Department for Education, 2020, np).

Funded by the Research Council of Norway as a formative cross-national study, the *Against All Odds?* project began from a different place. Involving participants with care experience, the research was not an evaluation, nor did it attempt to compare the 'effectiveness' of different national systems. Rather, as we have written elsewhere (Boddy et al, 2020a; Bakketeig et al, 2020), the research aimed to move beyond risk-focused accounts: countering stigma and building positive understandings, without ignoring distinctive sources of disadvantage *or* reducing people's complex lives to their care histories. The cross-national approach was not evaluative, but aimed to illuminate the ways in which individual biographies are situated in multiple layers of context (see Brannen and Nilsen 2011), including variations in care systems and wider welfare provision.

Despite the differences in their commissioning and aims, tensions of relative power remain for both studies. Neither was constructed as a wholly collaborative participatory endeavour – although both involved some advisory input from people whose life experience gives them expertise in the matters that concerned the research (see Acknowledgements) and both used 'open' methods (description follows) that aimed to enable informants to tell us about their lives from their point of view. Nonetheless, the focus of both studies (and of this book) means that as researchers we have heightened responsibilities for managing the risks of reproducing 'othering', as Fine (1994) writes:

> But when we look, get involved, demur, analyze, interpret, probe, speak, remain silent, walk away, organize for outrage, or sanitize our stories, and when we construct our texts in or on their words, we

decide how to nuance our relations with/for/despite those who have been deemed Others. When we write essays about subjugated Others as if *they* were a homogeneous mass (of vice or virtue), free-floating and severed from contexts of oppression, and as if we were neutral transmitters of voices and stories, we tilt toward a narrative strategy that reproduces Othering on, despite or even 'for'. When we construct texts collaboratively, self-consciously examining our relations with/for/despite those who have been contained as Others, we move against, we enable resistance to, Othering. (Fine, 1994, p 74)

Grietens (2018) has spoken about these considerations in relation to his research with adults who had been abused as children in foster care:

as a researcher you may be more than just a mere passer-by. ... You may become an I-witness, a co-creator of a hidden and untold story, a container of your participants' experiences and meanings. Participants leave their stories in your hands when you leave them (the end of an interview always feels a bit strange, even scaring to me, the interview is finished and now?!) and you are authorized (mandated) to report on their stories and make them heard. What a power comes with this role! (Grietens, 2018, p 10)

Grietens' metaphor of the 'I-Witness' is helpful in thinking about how to manage the relative power and privilege of the researcher in writing a book such as this, where the work relies on sharing the experiences of people who have faced – and continue to navigate – distinctive challenges in their lives. This entails more than just being conscious of our positionality and difference from the people we research – in my case, as a White middle-class mother of two young adults, from a supportive academic family. Grietens emphasizes that researchers share with participants in 'being a member of the human community' (Grietens, 2018, p 10) and reminds us that researchers can use their relative power and privilege to enable their experiences to be heard. Butler's (2016) writing on resistance and vulnerability illuminates this shared connection. She explains that when we define people only in terms of their vulnerability, we not only fail to recognize their resistance and agency, we also fail to recognize how the connection between Self and Other is rooted in vulnerability as an essential condition of humanity. In recognizing our vulnerability, we can find 'a way of being related to what is not me' (Butler, 2016, p 25): we are *all* vulnerable, because we live interconnected lives and we are all dependent on others.

In order to 'self-consciously examine our relations' (Fine, 1994, p 75) with the people we research, we must acknowledge what Foucault (1983) terms the danger of ethico-political choice: 'My point is not that everything is bad, but that everything is dangerous, which is not exactly the same as bad. ... I think that the ethico-political choice we have to make every day is to determine which is the main danger' (Foucault, 1983, p 343). The poet and critic Audre Lorde's (1984) writing on 'The Transformation of Silence into Language and Action' is valuable in thinking through the responsibilities that this danger entails. She writes:

> And where the words of women are crying to be heard, we must each of us recognize our responsibility to seek those words out, to read them and share them and examine them in their pertinence to our lives. That we not hide behind the mockeries of separations that have been imposed on us and which so often we accept as our own. (p 23)

Rather than hiding behind 'the mockeries of separations', we can recognize that our relative power and privilege as researchers brings a critical choice. We carry the potential for our research to *contribute* to vulnerability, to efface agency or exacerbate stigma. But research can also be transformative, in choosing to speak to everyday and wider politics (Phoenix et al, 2021). Writing about the role of research in challenging dominant societal narratives, Fine observes: 'I want to invite readers to think aloud about how, why, and with whom we design research that can enter and investigate the claims of dominant narratives, lift up counter stories, and dive into the knotty relation between the two as well as generate images of radical possibilities' (Fine, 2016, p 51).

In thinking about how knowledge – including research knowledge – is politically produced, we also need to think about how these categorizations function within our policy frameworks. Our research has been carried out in the context of the austerity policies discussed in Chapter 1, policies which have been shown disproportionately to disadvantage children and families. Fine's exhortation means we need to think about the production of knowledge in the context of political austerity and an increasingly residual welfare state. What kinds of understandings of 'family' for care experienced people are possible in this context? Do we need research to generate a 'terrible tale', to borrow Steedman's (2000) phrase, in order that the affluent will justify support for people who are constructed in public discourse as 'the objects or abjects of stigma' (Tyler, 2013, p 26)? And if researchers only focus attention on defining the vulnerable other, do we risk contributing to the development of a narrative that restricts welfare support to those judged sufficiently deserving or in need? These are dangerous questions and they underpin our approach to the two studies, and to thinking through family within this book.

The two research projects both aimed to employ a methodological approach that would look beyond risk-focused structural and categorizing accounts, enabling participants to talk about what matters in their lives on their own terms. For the purposes of this book I have linked data from the two projects in order to analyse narratives that reflect the dynamism, complex relationality and structural constraints of family. Neither were planned as narrative studies, but both were designed using open methods that would allow participants the space to talk about what they considered to be important at the time of the interview.

The aim is not comparison between the two studies, as this risks essentializing the experience of participants in *Against All Odds?* as 'doing well', or defining the experience of women who took part in the *Evaluation of Pause* in terms of child removal. That would not only be an oversimplification, it would be an injustice to all those who took part. We must recognize the stigma and challenges faced by participants in both studies, as well as their strengths, agency and resistance.

A narrative perspective on care experienced family lives

> To write a novel, it seemed to me, a writer should be living in a world that makes sense, a world that a writer can believe in, draw a bead on, and then write about accurately. A world that will, for a time anyway, stay fixed in one place. Along with this there has to be a belief in the essential correctness of that world. A belief that the known world has reasons for existing, and is worth writing about, is not likely to go up in smoke in the process. This wasn't the case with the world I knew and was living in. My world was one that seemed to change gears and directions, along with its rules, every day.
>
> Raymond Carver, *Fires*, 1997, p 35

The philosopher Galen Strawson (2004, p 428) cautions against the normativity of what he terms the 'ethical Narrativity thesis' – the normative assumption that 'experiencing or conceiving one's life as a narrative is a good thing'. The search for narrative coherence is also *politically* problematic, because it foregrounds some people's voices while rendering others silent:

> This claim of invisible and silenced people gaining a voice through stories is itself a rhetorical construction that amplifies some voices at the expense of others. Those who are able to make their personal experiences legible to the mainstream through drawing on dominant narratives and devices are given a platform while other voices are silenced. (Fernandes, 2017, p 5)

In the extract quoted here, from his book *Fires,* the writer Raymond Carver was commenting on why he wrote short stories rather than novels. His observation that his life could not be conveyed neatly in a singular narrative that will 'stay fixed in one place' is apposite for thinking about the distinctive complexities of, and disruptions to, family experienced by many people who have been in care. Their worlds – and their family lives – may also have changed gears, rules and directions over time, including through placement moves and in their lives after leaving care.

Our aim is to learn from our participants' experiences, while resisting essentializing assumptions of simple narrative coherence. This means attending to the telling of diverse 'family stories' and the insights they afford into 'the more complex and hidden aspects of family lives' (Phoenix et al, 2021, p 10). It means attending to that which is absent, hesitant, or incoherent, as well as to things that do not 'fit' neatly with the dominant narrative in the interview (Squire, 2013). This approach draws on the distinction between *stories* and *story telling* (see Gubrium and Holstein, 1998), recognizing narratives as situated in space, place and time, and storytelling as a practical activity, co-constructed in conversation between researcher and researched. It allows us 'to see more clearly the ways in which both coherence and difference, even authenticity, are socially assembled' (Gubrium and Holstein, 1998, p 166).

Engagement with situated, dynamic complexity underpins the opportunity to transform understandings of family, moving beyond the dangers of the single story to lift up narratives that counter dominant problem-focused hegemonies, without negating the distinctive experiences and challenges associated with having been in care. This kind of insight depends on creating methodological space: giving participants the freedom to talk about both normative and exceptional aspects of their lives and experiences, and maintaining that space for expression in the reporting of their words in this book.

Riessman (2000) reminds us that narratives (and responses to stigma) are often complex and contradictory, as well as being shaped by structural inequalities. This is sharply apparent in both the studies discussed in this book. Seemingly contradictory accounts within and across interviews over time – of meanings of 'family', or in accounts of important relationships – reveal the ways in which our respondents make sense of difficult and disrupted experiences, and how that sense-making may shift over time. Apparent inconsistencies in participants' accounts reflect lived experiences that cannot be told through narratives of neat coherence, spanning an affective continuum between 'the run of the mill affectivity of everyday social life and moments of extraordinary emotional drama' (Wetherell, 2015, p 161).

The studies

Reflecting these arguments, ethics considerations were integral to both studies, from planning and formulation of research design through data collection, analysis, and writing and other dissemination from the research (including in this book). Throughout, we have sought to hesitate and reflect on our power and positionality as researchers in our methodological and analytic decision-making, within a critically engaged ethical approach (Staunæs and Kofoed, 2015), and that includes acknowledging our power as researchers in eliciting and presenting accounts of complex and often very difficult biographical experiences. In both studies, interviews were conducted with an emphasis on ensuring that people who took part could talk freely about considerations that were important to them, and with care to avoid any pressure to participate or to discuss issues that they may have found upsetting or been reluctant to discuss. In the chapters that follow, participants have been assigned pseudonyms[8] and potentially identifiable details of their lives have been withheld or amended in order to protect confidentiality. Very occasionally, I refer to participants without using their pseudonyms, to mitigate the risk that people could become recognizable as a result of linkage of information across different elements of very detailed and holistic accounts.

Against All Odds?

This study was funded by the Research Council of Norway[9] and OsloMet University, and led by Elisabeth Backe-Hansen of the NOVA Social Research Institute at OsloMet. Conducted in Norway, Denmark and England, the research was focused on building new understandings of positive pathways through care and into adulthood by addressing two main research questions:

- What are the meanings of 'doing well' for care experienced young adults?
- What contributes to 'doing well' in their view – what do they see as important?

The study combined secondary analysis of administrative data with in-depth qualitative longitudinal research and a cross-national documentary review that encompassed policy frameworks, legislation and published administrative data relevant to understanding the situation of care experienced by young people as they make transitions out of child welfare services (Boddy et al, 2019). The total sample for the qualitative longitudinal research was 75 young people: 21 from England (aged 16–30 years at first interview), 30 from Denmark (aged 16–32) and 24 from Norway (16–32). All had been in care and were either in education (Norway: 15; Denmark: 25; England: 12);

employment (Norway: 9; Denmark: 5; England: 8) or training (none in Norway or Denmark, one in a workplace apprenticeship in England) at the time they were recruited to the study.

In this book, we focus on qualitative data from interviews in England, which were conducted with ethics approval from the University of Sussex (ER/JMB55/2). All participants were interviewed by Fidelma Hanrahan or Janet Boddy. The 21 young adults who took part in England were recruited through a variety of sources including nongovernmental organizations that support and advocate for children in care and care leavers, local authority leaving care services and 'Children in Care Councils', and through publicity on social media (Twitter and a Facebook group for care leavers). Similar recruitment strategies were employed in Denmark and Norway, an approach that was intended to enhance diversity (including geographical spread) within the sample. We did not seek to construct a sample that would be representative of the heterogeneous population of young adults who have experienced care, but it must be recognized that participants were willing to identify as care experienced and as 'doing well'. This construction can be understood as an 'emblematic', rather than representative (see Thomson, 2009): by building an understanding of what matters in participants' lives, we aimed to think through the complexities of 'doing well', problematizing the conceptualization of 'outcomes' for care leavers.

In line with this discussion, the methodological approach for *Against All Odds?* was designed to avoid the 'enforced narrative' of a life constructed in relation to problematizing questions (Steedman, 2000). Methods were designed to enable participants to narrate their own lives and each participant was interviewed on three occasions using a multimethod approach designed to build a 'mosaic' of understanding (inspired by Clark and Moss, 2011). All received a thank-you gift voucher following each interview. This qualitative longitudinal approach allowed exploration of 'complex timescapes or flows of time' (Neale et al, 2012, p 5), addressing biographical time, as participants looked back and forwards through their lives, as well as the quotidian temporalities of everyday lives:

- The first interviews took place in 2015 and gathered information about participants' current living situation and involved completion of a life chart addressing four domains (living situation, family, education and employment and free time).
- Participants were then given a digital camera and asked to take photos for a week that would show what mattered to them in their everyday life; they were also asked if they would be willing to choose a piece of music to share at the next interview, selecting something with positive associations that would help show what is important to them in their lives (following from Wilson, 2013).

- Conducted at least a week later, the second interview was focused on discussion of participants' photographs and music choices, before ending with questions about expectations for the future.
- Twelve months later, participants were invited for a third interview, which was focused on their account of the last year and incorporated a future life chart (drawing on Thomson and Holland, 2002; Worth, 2011), addressing the same domains as the life chart in Interview 1.

The use of music and photography fulfils several purposes in the design, including encouraging participation, enabling richness of data and disrupting conventional modes of interviewing and power relationships (see for example Wilson, 2016; 2018; Ravn, 2019; Mannay and Staples, 2019; Join-Lambert et al, 2020). The use of photography and music functions to disrupt 'deficit and damage-based seeing' (Luttrell, 2020, p 15), lifting up participants' visions of what they see as important in their lives, giving them time to reflect and make decisions about what to represent in between interviews. Discussion of the photos means that participants' visual representations provide a scaffold for eliciting their perspectives – helping us to learn, and see, differently. Our use of music as an interview elicitation method was directly inspired by Wilson's (2013) research, which highlighted music's potential to create a sensory space, facilitating reflections that might not be brought forward in more 'conventional' dialogue. In addition, by sharing the pictures and music in the communication of learning from the project our aim is to help to encourage policy and practice response by 'opening imaginative spaces in which we can see … why it matters' (Luttrell, 2020, p 14).

Giving participants a week or more to take photographs and to plan and reflect on their music choices also afforded control over what they wanted to share. Responses to these requests varied, but were overwhelmingly positive. In England, one person chose not to take photos, but instead shared a list of 'important things' in their life. Among the remaining participants, the number of photographs taken for a single interview ranged from two to 39. Two participants initially said it was difficult to identify a music choice, but both, as they reflected during the interview, spoke about a particular song that was significant for them. All the other participants decided to share at least one song or piece of music, but some chose several pieces and, in one case, a playlist of ten songs. DeNora (2000) describes music as a time travelling technology and in the course of our study we heard music that was tied to highly significant biographical events (such as special times with friends, or a song played at a parent's funeral). But musical choices also reflected what was current, part of everyday life and listening, as well as music that had particular functions at particular times (for relaxing, or lifting the spirits) that might only be listened to at particular moments. These different practices reflect what DeNora (2000) describes as the power of music as a technology for the constitution of self and self-identity, but also as a practice for care of self, 'to shift mood or energy level, as perceived situations dictate' (p 53). And, as will become evident in the following chapters, and in line with DeNora's (2000) research, participants in our study very often used music to explain and emphasize their *relational* selves, choosing songs that connected them with particular people, including at particular times in their lives.

Evaluation of Pause

The study of Pause started from a different place to *Against All Odds?*, as an evaluation, commissioned by UK government (Department for Education, DfE) as part of a programme of studies evaluating the contribution of service models funded under Round 2 of the Children's Social Care Innovation Programme (discussed before). Pause was one of the first recurrence-focused services to be established in England; initially developed in the London Borough of Hackney in 2013, it has grown into a national organization, supported through substantial investment from government. In 2015, Pause was awarded £4.2 million in Round 1 of the DfE Innovation Programme to expand its intervention support package to seven areas nationally, and in 2017 Pause was allocated a further £6.8 million in Round 2 of the Innovation Programme, to scale up and roll out the model to nine other areas and develop and implement a 'care leaver pilot' targeting care experienced women (aged 16–25) who have had one or more children removed.

The Pause theory of change is predicated on trauma-informed intensive relationship-based practice, driven by women's own perceived needs and priorities. Within each local Pause practice (managed by a Practice Lead), Pause practitioners have small caseloads (up to eight women) and work flexibly and responsively to facilitate change. Their work is supported by a dedicated budget allocation for each woman, designed to 'ensure that practitioners are able to, where necessary, pay for things that might otherwise not be available through normal services' (Pause, 2017, p 32). The relationship with the practitioner is at the centre of the intervention, generating space for change through 'an intensive and tenacious bespoke support package', aimed at three key areas of work. The first is stabilizing lives, for example, through: domestic abuse support; income review and support to take up benefits and address debt; support to access safe and secure housing; support to reduce alcohol or drug misuse; support to reduce offending; and support to engage in learning or work. Second, Pause work is focused on developing a sense of self, for example, involving participation in one-to-one and group activities designed to build strengths, develop new skills and explore new experiences, as well as support to address bereavement and loss and to establish positive relationships. Within the Pause framework (2017, p 18) this relationship-based practice is framed as therapeutic, aiming to enable women with significant histories of complex trauma 'to develop an alternative, richer narrative about the woman which does not define her by the (often) "problem saturated" stories of herself as a mother or her own experiences of childhood'. Third, participation in the programme entails accessing effective contraception and regular sexual-health check-ups. This last criterion relates to a distinctive feature of the Pause model at the time of our evaluation: access to the programme of support was subject to women's agreement to use a method of long-acting reversible contraception (LARC) unless this was contra-indicated for medical reasons. Pause programme requirements for the use of contraception during the intervention have changed since our research was conducted and women may now choose to use other forms of contraception rather than a long-acting reversible method (see Chapter 6 and www.pause.org.uk).

Our focus in designing the evaluation was necessarily shaped by the nature of the Pause programme, as well as the wider context for its commissioning within the DfE Innovation Programme. In common with *Against All Odds?*, our approach was also underpinned by consideration of the ethical responsibilities involved, particularly in conducting research with a population of women who have experienced child removal, who may have had challenging prior experiences of professional involvement (for example, Broadhurst and Mason, 2020; Cox et al, 2020).

The evaluation as a whole was a large multimethod study; the overall design and methodology have been presented in detail elsewhere (Boddy et al, 2020b; see also Boddy and Wheeler, 2020) and are not repeated here. But the evaluation was designed to integrate attention to process and outcome, in accordance with recent UK Medical Research Council (MRC)/ National Institute for Health Research guidance on evaluating complex interventions (Skivington et al, 2021). The multimethod approach included qualitative longitudinal research (QLR) with 49 women who currently or previously worked with Pause; group and one-to-one interviews with Pause professionals (including members of the national team, managers and practitioners); interviews with local authority stakeholders in Pause and comparison areas; secondary analysis of Pause administrative data on women who work with the service; and secondary analysis of published local authority SSDA903 data on rates of infant care entry in Pause and matched comparison areas. Ethics approval for the research was provided by the University of Sussex (Social Sciences and Arts Cross-School Research Ethics Committee ER/JMB55/8).

Participants in qualitative longitudinal interviews were working with Pause at the time the evaluation began, in 2018. All participants in this QLR component were interviewed by Bella Wheeler or Janet Boddy. Women were sampled from a mix of older and more recently established

Pause practices, to represent different local authority and delivery characteristics, including the 'care leaver pilot', which targeted women aged 16 to 25 who had been in care during childhood and had one or more children living in care or permanency arrangements (including Special Guardianship or adoption). All participants were recruited to the evaluation as close as possible to the point of starting work with Pause. Within the QLR sample overall, the average age of participants was 28 years (range 19 to 39 years old); on average, they had 2.4 children (range one to five). None had children living with them at the time of recruitment to the study.[10] Women in the 'care leaver pilot' – who form the focus of our analysis in this book – were younger (average 23 years old) and had fewer children (1.5 on average).

Each woman was interviewed on up to four occasions over a 20-month period, usually twice face to face and twice by telephone.[11] With the women's permission, interviews were digitally recorded and transcribed. Not all women were reachable at all time points and we exercised caution in pursuing women for interview, given their vulnerability and an ethical concern not to disrupt Pause work or put pressure on people who were in a dependent position as recipients of the service being evaluated. Hence, longitudinal data were subject to sample attrition (82 per cent of the sample participated at Time 2, 57 per cent at Time 3, and 37 per cent at Time 4), although at least one post-intervention interview was conducted with 32 women (65 per cent of the sample of 49). All women received a gift voucher in thanks for participation in each interview.

All interviews were open ended, following a topic guide. As with the *Against All Odds?* study, the use of open methods aimed to provide opportunities for participants to 'disavow dominant perspectives' (Riessman, 2000, p 114), with questioning designed to elicit women-centred accounts of their experiences and so to enable a biographically informed and contextualized understanding of the implications of involvement with Pause in their lives over time. In common with (and adapted from) the methods for *Against All Odds?*, we used a life chart as a prompt early in the first interview. By inviting participants to record significant people and biographical experiences across four domains (family; living situation; friends and other important people; and education, work or training), we aimed to centre what women saw as important for us to understand about their lives. Beyond that, the primary focus of all the interviews was on women's experiences of the Pause intervention, including (as appropriate at each time point) processes of engagement with (or referral into) the program, experience of key features of the programme including contraception, and the extent to which the programme meets their perceived needs. The topics covered in the interview included information about current circumstances (including housing, relationships, employment and contact with children) along with any other issues that women wished to discuss. As with *Against All Odds?* interviews, while family was not an explicit focus of interviews in the *Evaluation of Pause*, the open-ended approach to interviewing, combined with attention to biography in women's accounts of their lives, created space for women to talk about meanings of family, and perhaps it is not surprising that this was a significant feature of most interviews with women across the study as a whole.

Bringing the studies together

As discussed in Chapter 1, the aim of this book is to build new understandings by bringing together perspectives from participants in the two research studies. For the remainder of this book, our discussion will focus on just two subgroups of the two larger studies:

- The 14 women in the *Evaluation of Pause* who were part of the Pause 'care leaver' pilot; and
- the 21 people in England who took part in *Against All Odds?*

These 35 young adults have commonalities as well as differences in their experience. As well as having been in care at some point during their childhood, they are similar in age: the 21 participants in *Against All Odds?* were aged 16–30 years at the time of first interview, while the 14 women in 'care leavers' subgroup of the *Evaluation of Pause* were 19–28 years old at the start of the study. Across the two studies, some had relatively stable placement experiences while others – especially, but not only, in the Pause sample – had experienced significant disruption, multiple placements, and abuse from carers while in care. All participants in the Pause evaluation (by virtue of the nature of the service) were female and all were mothers (only one of whom had custody of children by the end of the study), whereas two-thirds of those in the English sample for *Against All Odds?* (14 of 21 participants) were female and just four participants were parents (three mothers and one father, of whom two women had children living in their care).

Table 2.1 shows the age and pseudonym of each participant. Given the risk of identifiability (or recognizability, for people who know them) within these two qualitative samples, to protect confidentiality, other sample characteristics (such as number and age of children, care experience, employment or living situation, sexuality, ethnicity, religion or immigration status) are only discussed where relevant to the analytic discussions in the chapters that follow.

We do not claim that these 35 individuals are statistically representative of young adults with care experience, but their narratives allow us to think through the meanings of 'family' for people who have been in care. Gobo (2004) argues for thinking about *social* (rather than statistical)

Table 2.1: Participants in the two studies: assigned pseudonyms, age and gender

Study	Pseudonym	Age	Gender
Against All Odds?	Charlotte	16	Female
	Rebecca	18	Female
	Sophie	19	Female
	Richard	19	Male
	Toby	19	Male
	Natalie	21	Female
	Maria	22	Female
	Max	22	Male
	Frank	22	Male
	Daniel	22	Male
	Karen	23	Female
	Jack	23	Male
	Rosa	24	Female
	Megan	24	Female
	Nicola	25	Female
	Jo	27	Female
	Claire	27	Female
	Anna	29	Female
	James	29	Male
	Ella	30	Female
	William	30	Male
Evaluation of Pause	Bethany	19	Female
	Skye	20	Female
	Louise	22	Female
	Christie	22	Female
	Joelle	22	Female
	Zoe	22	Female
	Jasmine	22	Female
	Leila	22	Female
	Jade	23	Female
	Alicia	24	Female
	Maya	24	Female
	Michelle	26	Female
	Hannah	26	Female
	Ashley	28	Female

representativeness – we are not concerned with counting the number of people who share an experience or characteristic, or with generalizing from a single experience, but rather with what it is possible to understand when we think with their data.

Similarly, Østergaard and Thomson (2020, p 433) discuss the value of attending to 'the dynamism and particularity of a single case' by applying a narrative logic (following Abbott, 1992). They observe: 'Understood as a narrative, the longitudinal case can be exemplary, enabling a mode of generalisation and theory development that is at once specific, explanatory and critical' (Østergaard and Thomson, 2020, p 433). In the analysis that follows through this book, our aim is not to compare the two samples, nor to evaluate the impact of different experiences of 'family' on 'outcomes' for people in the studies. Rather, as noted in Chapter 1, we set out to consider their accounts together. We use the metaphor of 'juxtaposition' to highlight the value of considering diverse experiences alongside each other within a narrative analytic approach, in order to avoid false universalism and develop a nuanced and contextually situated analysis that attends to commonalities *and* differences over time and to the complexity of family lives and social worlds (see Boddy et al, 2021 for further discussion of this approach). This approach is necessary given our aspiration to avoid essentializing complex and dynamic lives over time on the basis of care experience, and so to address the political problem of assuming a common identity associated with 'care experience'.

In *Gender Trouble,* Butler (1990/2006, p 4) observes that 'gender intersects with racial, class, ethnic, sexual and regional modalities of discursively constituted identities. As a result, it becomes impossible to separate out "gender" from the political and cultural intersections in which it is invariably produced and maintained'. The same is true for 'care experienced' identities (and experiences and understandings of 'family'), which are also produced and maintained within complex political and cultural intersections. With this in mind, our analytic approach follows Jackson and Mazzei's (2012, p vii) exhortation to qualitative researchers:

> to use theory to think with their data (or use data to think with theory) ... qualitative data interpretation and analysis does not happen via mechanistic coding, reducing data to themes, and writing up transparent narratives that do little to critique the complexities of social life; such simplistic approaches preclude dense and multi-layered treatment of data.

For the chapters that follow, interviews were analysed using a case-based longitudinal approach to examine key narratives and areas of interest for the conceptualization of 'family'. For both datasets, the same analytic approach has been used:

- for the purposes of the original studies:
  - within each case, an analytic summary was prepared for each time point;
  - these were then combined into a whole case analysis which took account of change over time;
- subsequently, analytic summaries and transcripts were reviewed for the new analysis of family, in relation to the key foci that form the chapters of this book, and any other considerations identified as important to thinking through family;
- for each case, summaries of key narratives relating to different aspects of family were highlighted and compiled for the purposes of cross-case analysis, to examine commonalities and differences across the sample as a whole.

Given an approach based on thinking with theory and data together (after Jackson and Mazzei, 2012), the chapters that follow do not derive from a thematic analysis of the dataset and do not represent key themes in the data. Each chapter draws in detail on emblematic examples, focusing on data that allow us to think through the conceptualization of 'family' – in relation to birth family, experiences in placement and family lives beyond childhood. The interviews are the core of the book and the inclusion of extended extracts in the chapters that follow is intended to signal our commitment to maintaining the integrity of participants' narratives. As Thomson and colleagues (2011, p 270) have written: 'This focus is partly as a consequence of the centrality of talk to our method, but also because we are interested in the work that stories do in making experiences intelligible and available for representation and response.' In this approach, we are mindful of Lorde's (1984, p 7) exhortation to recognize the responsibilities that come with power and privilege, 'to seek those words out, to read them and share them and examine them'. This book has been written in order to share what we have learned from the people who helped with our two studies and so the chapters that follow foreground their perspectives on experiences of family in their lives.

A note on the transcriptions in this book

The chapters that follow use the following transcription conventions:
- A short pause is indicated by (.) and a long pause by (…).
- Ellipses in square brackets […] indicate that material has been cut from the transcript, to ensure confidentiality or to edit for length within a long narrative.
- Words in square brackets – for example, [child], [age], [sibling] – have been used to replace potentially identifying detail, such as someone's name, or to clarify the referent when it is not obvious from the transcript.
- All names given are pseudonyms and some details have been redacted or amended (for example, the age or gender of participants' children and siblings) to protect confidentiality.

3

Doing Family: The Significance of the 'Ordinary'

> A whole set of what appears to be trivial or even meaningless activities is given meaning through its being grouped together under one single label, that of family. The focus on doing, on activities, moves us away from ideas of the family as relatively static structures or sets of positions or statuses.
>
> David Morgan, *Rethinking Family Practices*, 2011, p 6

Introduction

Undeniably, people who have been in care have often faced significant challenges within their family lives and that is certainly true for the participants in the two studies on which this book is based. But equally striking in both studies were apparently mundane accounts of quotidian or habitual family practices. In this chapter, we focus on participants' narratives of everyday family practices, to reflect on the significance of the ordinary for understanding 'family'. This is important for several reasons. Focusing only on adversity or care-specific experiences risks reinforcing the 'single story' discussed in Chapter 1. When we focus only on difficulties, we risk creating what Steedman (2000, p 36) describes as the bourgeois construction of the 'suffering and enduring other, using the themes and items of other, dispossessed and difficult lives'. If we reduce the complex lives and relationships of care experienced people and families to the difficulties they have faced, we replicate the binary construction of the normative imaginary of the 'ordinary' family and the problematic 'other' – the 'the objects or abjects of stigma', to paraphrase Tyler (2013, p 26). To move beyond such binaries, we need to think through the complex relationality of 'family' for people who have been in care. That means we need to pay attention to *ordinary* aspects of care experienced family lives, as well as what is distinctive, in ways that allow us to question what 'ordinary' means.

The argument for attention to quotidian family lives can also be made in relation to the social pedagogic concept of *lifeworld orientation* (see Grunwald and Thiersch, 2009), whereby the lifeworld (or everyday-world) experiences of an individual are the key reference point for praxis: 'The lifeworld and the everyday manifest themselves as primary and fundamental dimensions of human life situations in all their meaning and dignity' (Grunwald and Thiersch, 2009, p 133). The concept of the 'lifeworld' as set out by Grunwald and Thiersch draws on the work of Alfred Schutz (1932/1967), who was concerned with 'the world of daily life' – and so with understanding the ordinary ongoing processes of interpretation and sense-making in everyday lives. Schutz (1932/1967) emphasized that these processes are biographically shaped and socially oriented and hence he argued that lifeworlds are fundamentally *intersubjective* – both individual and socialized – shaped by societal structures and demands, as well as by life histories and relationships over time. As Trujillo (2018) explains: '"World-experience" is not "private experience". It is "shared experience". The world of daily life is "the 'world for all of us'", not withstanding it is also "primarily 'my' world"' (Trujillo, 2018, p 6, citing Schutz 1970, p 54). If researchers, policy makers or practitioners aspire to respect the 'meaning and dignity' (see Grunwald and Thiersch, 2009) of the lifeworlds of people with care experience (or anyone else, for that matter), then that requires respect for intersubjectivity. A lifeworld orientation therefore depends on recognizing the relationality of everyday life – and this means thinking about family.

What do we mean by 'ordinary'?

In the epigraph that opened this chapter, Morgan (2011) introduced his theorization of family practices by arguing for a sense of the active, such that individuals can be understood to be *doing* family. This active conceptualization avoids the pitfalls of reifying 'family' as a static 'thing', enabling a better recognition of fluidity and permeable boundaries in how family is experienced and practised over time. Particularly relevant for our discussion in this chapter is Morgan's emphasis on the significance of the mundane. The meaning of activities that might otherwise seem to be trivial depends on their being understood as *family* practices. Expanding on this notion of the trivial, Morgan (2011) further distinguishes between two meanings of everyday life:

- First, the everyday refers to activities which are 'unremarkable, hardly worth talking about' (p 6) – regular and taken for granted practices of family living. He notes that these could be common quotidian practices

among a large part of the population (giving the example of taking children to school) or specific to a particular family group (such as a particular 'family joke').
- Second, he refers to events which may not happen every day, but which are experienced by a significant proportion of the population. This category could include 'longer term regularities which have a more seasonal character' (p 78), such as birthdays or religious festivals, as well as exceptional or memorable family events, such as a wedding or the birth of a child. Morgan emphasizes that such events are not always positive or conflict-free, but they illuminate the ways in which the practical and imagined aspects of family life coincide.

Both understandings of everyday practices are crucial to moving beyond what Morgan terms a 'social problems' approach to the study of families, and so are highly relevant to thinking through family in care experienced lives.

The placement of a child in care is of course an intervention that disrupts everyday family practices in both of the senses that Morgan (2011) describes. First, the child moves from one set of regular and taken-for-granted family practices to another household; whatever the form of placement (whether family-based or institutional care), the practices of everyday life will differ and cannot be taken for granted by the child. Second, placement of a child in care is a highly distinctive reconfiguration of family structure and family life. In contrast to Morgan's description of 'everyday' practices of partnering and parenthood that are experienced by a significant proportion of the population, only a small proportion of children will experience placement. According to the most recent government data at the time of writing, 67 per 10,000 children were in care on the census date of 31 March 2021.[1] While rates of children becoming looked after have increased over recent years and are described by government as being at an all-time high,[2] the great majority of the 12 million children and young people (aged 0–17 years) who live in England[3] have not experienced this kind of reconfiguration of family. I will turn to this reconfiguring of family through placement, and the implications of placement for family practices, in Chapter 4.

Focusing on the ordinary and the everyday in participants' narratives of birth families helps to build a nuanced understanding of family lives and practices – mitigating the risk of the single story. As I have written elsewhere (Boddy, 2019, p 2249), 'troubling meanings of "family" for people who have been in care means recognizing what is ordinary as well as what is distinctive'. In this chapter, we discuss young people's experiences within their families of origin, to engage with the significance of 'ordinary' memories within extraordinary childhoods, encompassing narratives of regular, ritual and habitual family practices and the importance of these within participants' accounts. Andrews (2014) writes that: 'Our imaginations, which reflect our own situatedness, play a significant role in which pieces of past experience we bring together, how we assemble them to make sense of our present condition, and what we reach towards in the future' (Andrews, 2014, p 108). In this chapter, we consider how participants in our studies have assembled pieces of past experiences, bringing them together in response to our invitation (in our role as researchers) to tell us what is important to them – to convey their understandings of themselves, their lives and their families. We document participants' narratives through two linked sections, first addressing regular and habitual practices, before turning to ritual practices and special occasions. Through this analysis we will reflect on the ways in which ordinary and distinctive aspects of experience intersect, challenging the policy and political tendency to construct care experienced lives (and families) as inherently 'other'.

The significance of the mundane
(Un)remarkable practices?
People who took part in the *Against All Odds?* study were asked (at the end of the first interview) to bring a piece of music to their second interview, with the broad instruction that it should be something with positive associations that would help show what is important to them in their lives. Our use of this method was inspired by Wilson's (2013; 2016) research with young people, including those with care experience, employing a participatory sensory methodology that included asking people to share music. DeNora (2000, p 66) describes music as a time travelling technology, observing that: 'Music moves through time, it is a temporal medium. This is the first reason why it is a powerful *aide-mémoire*. ... Music reheard and recalled provides a device for unfolding, for replaying, the temporal structure of that moment, its dynamism as emerging experience.' Wilson's (2013; 2016) work shows how this could function to create a reflective space for participants in discussing complex lives, including in relation to difficult family situations:

> Many respondents also identified music tracks and associated videos accessed through youtube™ that they employed to reflect on difficult personal experiences and complex related feelings. Drab, for example, recorded himself watching a music video in which a young boy is shown looking in on his father's new family and later vandalising the bedroom of one of his 'new' children. (Wilson, 2016, p 291)

In the *Against All Odds?* study, memories of family life during childhood were often discussed in relation to participants' choice of music. DeNora (2000, p 33) writes that musical affect arises from human-music interaction, 'constituted reflexively, in and through the practice of articulating or connecting music with other things'. In the examples that follow – from Rebecca and Daniel – the emotional meaning of the music was rooted in the connection that participants made with family relationships and practices. We had asked participants to choose music with *positive* associations partly because of the focus of the study (on what 'doing well' meant for our participants); recognizing that music can be very emotionally evocative, we were also concerned not to prompt distressing memories. In fact, we found that this directive proved helpful in illuminating the 'ordinary' as well as the distinctive aspects of care experienced family lives. Music is increasingly integrated into everyday lives (for example, Krause et al, 2015) and so it is perhaps not surprising that participants' musical memories often related to quotidian family lives and practices. Rebecca described a shared love of music with her mother that continued to the present day. She discussed several musical choices during her interview, including one that she recalled her mother often singing to her as a child:

> 'And like another one, you know, that childhood song like *You Are My Sunshine*, yeah, I grew up with my mum singing that. So that one I've always thought, you know, it was that sort of family love. And like that's always represented like my mother's love, like for me and my brothers and that song's always been about *(inaudible)* stuff to me. And like, the relationship between parents and children which I think is a huge important thing, like there has to be positive otherwise that can easily affect a child which is why I quite like that song. I think that one's (.) even though it's so sort of childish I still love to sing (.) 'cause it's just got all those connotations.'

In this account, Rebecca's mother singing is clearly framed as a habitual family practice. Morgan (2011, p 111) observes that 'emotions are an essential component of everyday family living and routines', and this is evident in Rebecca's narrative. Performing and listening to music are clearly framed as habitual and regular practices – she "grew up with" her mother singing the song – but she also identifies it as an inherently affective practice, representing "that sort of family love". Rebecca gave other examples of music in affective memories which reinforce Morgan's (2011, p 120) observation that 'the emotions we are concerned with are not simply the more dramatic outbursts of anger or affection' but may refer to more 'ordinary' emotional experiences. She described watching the TV show *X Factor* with her mother and brothers on a Saturday night – and spoke about "those fun times" when "me and my brothers would make up routines to the songs and dance about". Her memory acts as an important reminder that fun times with family can be part of a childhood which included significant trauma and hardship. Recognizing one does not negate the other. Rebecca's memories of these times with her family were also important to understand in terms of her understanding of herself, as she explained in drawing a connection between her past and present-day identity.

Daniel's music choice[4] – which was his first musical memory – was also linked to an apparently mundane family practice, but as he explained it was highly significant to his identity as a singer: "So the song is the first song I remember hearing besides the Lion King. [...] [*song plays*] I was about five-ish, because I was still with my birth mum. And it made me cry, but I didn't really understand why. [...] But that song is one of the (.) it is the reason that I started to do music (.) or started to sing." He continued with a vivid narrative of the moment of hearing the song:

> 'My birth mum used to always listen to music anyway, and really, really loud. She loved every type of music pretty much. And I think I was laying in her bed in the morning while she was tidying up and she put this song on. (.) And it was the first time that I'd ever probably sat down and listened to music. And I think within maybe the first 45 seconds I cried, I think. Because I distinctly remember it wasn't that far into the song. And then my mum was like, are you OK? And I was like, yeah; I'm fine. I just didn't know why I was crying. I think she knew why I was crying because it was an emotional song, but I don't think I understood why I was crying.'

Daniel's story illuminates the relational intersubjectivity of his lifeworld (see Schutz, 1932). His understanding of himself as a singer is situated in relation to this moment with his mother, where an ordinary family practice – his mother playing music while tidying up – becomes significant in his narrative because of the connection he makes with his understanding of himself, then and now.

The connection between the significant and the mundane is further exemplified in Nicola's explanation of one of her photo choices for the second interview in the *Against All Odds?* study: a picture she took of an old photograph of a family wedding. This prompted a lengthy account of complex intergenerational relationships in her family, which included a vivid small story[5] of her fond memories of time spent with great-grandparents. The importance of the everyday is visible in her detailed description of spending time in their home, remembered from her perspective as a child:

> 'And I've got fond memories of these two. [...] And they were lovely [...] and they had a really nice way about them. But I think they really helped my mum as well when she was young. That was her go-to place when she was growing up and stuff. I've got fond memories of being in their house. And my nan used to have this fire that had red

and (.) I think it was an electric fire and it had red and orange stones. And I used to take the stones off and clean them; I remember that. [...] And she used to let me play with her tea set. They used to be like these (.) they must have been quite expensive, but she used to let me play with them. So yes, I've got quite fond memories actually of being there.'

Nicola's small story of playing at her great-grandparents' house was juxtaposed in her interview with a much longer account of significantly challenging family relationships, complicated by relatives' mental health and alcohol problems as well as domestic violence. The contrast with her narrative of ordinary domestic play – with the stones on the fire and the expensive tea set – underlines the distinctive kindness and supportiveness of her great-grandparents at that time. Reflecting on the photograph, she observed: "A lot of madness has gone on between that family, but it just feels like that day they were all together and (.) I think me and my mum look at it quite a lot; I think it's quite a significant picture to us." Nicola expanded on this framing of the closeness of her and her mother in the context of complicated intergenerational relationships with her music choice.[6] Playing the song to the interviewer on YouTube, she explained:

'The whole album is probably really significant to our family. [...] That whole album has gone through the generations. But there's always a song I remember. I love all of theirs and they've probably all got good memories to each one. But I don't know why this specific memory stands out, but I was (.) [...] before anything, my mum didn't really date, didn't have any boyfriends, it was just us. And she's always been quite into music. We're quite a musical family, we love music. But I remember her holding me – so I must have been quite young because she was picking me up and dancing around the front room with me to this song. She always used to do it to all the songs really. But I don't know, I think because I used to say to her (.) I didn't really understand (.) it used to get her quite upset because it's about a daddy, and I think obviously (.) she didn't really have a great relationship with her dad and stuff. So even though I was young I picked up on that, so it meant (.) I didn't understand why but I knew there was some emotional attachment with her and the song. And she's quite spiritual so she always used to say to me, I'm singing it about God or whatever, because she could never think about her own dad. So, it's just a fond memory because (.) that specific memory of her picking me up and dancing around the front room with me. But the whole album really. And there's plenty more songs, we've got loads of songs together, but I think this song's quite positive [inaudible].'

Nicola's narrative emphasizes intergenerational connections in her "musical family" and she emphasizes this in her coda, "we've got lots of songs together". But her specific choice – of a song that used to get her mother "quite upset" – also draws the researcher's attention to the intergenerational echoes of difficult family relationships. Recalling a time when "it was just us" (Nicola and her mother), she observes that, even as a young child, she was conscious that her mother could "never think about" her own father.

Daniel, Nicola and Rebecca described memories of apparently mundane family practices, likely to be common to many people in the population: a family watching Saturday night TV; a child playing with a tea set; one mother tidying up; another dancing with her child. These memories are not specific to care experience and can be recognized as 'unremarkable' in terms of Morgan's (2011) conceptualization of everyday family practices. But they *are* remark-able – these memories underpin the stories chosen to tell us as researchers, for the purpose of explaining what matters to our participants in their lives. The emotional significance of these memories is inextricably shaped by the distinctive complexity of family and intergenerational relationships for people with care experience; happy memories, fun times and highly valued emotional connections are part of complex and challenging family lives and relationships. By sharing these memories, our participants help us understand that complexity: 'Some meanings of "family" in everyday lives may thus express forms of connection and relationality for which there is little alternative discursive space available' (McCarthy, 2012, p 86).

Women in the *Evaluation of Pause* did not discuss their everyday childhood experiences as much as participants in *Against All Odds?*. This undoubtedly reflects the different foci and methods of the two studies – while both used life charts with a similar framing prompt ('to understand what's important to you in your life up until now'), the Pause evaluation was (appropriately so, given its aims and funding) more focused on current and recent times in participants' lives. In general, women in the Pause study spoke more about everyday family practices in relation to their own children (discussed in Chapter 6), as well as in relation to the period during which they had been working with Pause. Their accounts of earlier childhood tended to be more focused on placement experiences, discussed further in Chapter 4. Nevertheless, in common with participants in the *Against All Odds?* study, many of the women in the Pause evaluation spoke about the emotional significance of intergenerational connections, with narratives woven through memories of everyday childhoods. For example, Leila's account of sports activities organized by her Pause practice prompted a childhood memory from school:

'I was quite good because I was (.) when I was young there was actually (.) This is quite a funny story, one day I was actually doing 200 metres or 300 metres run and I was nearly there and a girl collapsed on the floor and you know when it's either (.) you feel like you're selfish because you want to win because at that time I was very competitive and I wanted to win, so she collapsed and had asthma and then I went to go and help her and someone else won. I must have come second or something. *(Interviewer: But you did the right thing.)* Yeah, because she collapsed, and I didn't want her to (.) everyone else ignored her they run past her. [...] And I thought I had the heart because I took after my mum with that.'

Previously, Leila had been explaining that she was looking forward to some planned Pause group activities because she had been good at sports as a child. She introduced the memory as "quite a funny story" – a framing that she used quite frequently during the interview, which arguably functions to draw the listener into paying particular attention to what she wants to say. In fact, it is a story that evidences both her athletic skill and her strength of character: she could have won the race but was the only child to stop and help the girl who collapsed. Her final sentence introduces new meaning to this small story, in connecting this character trait – having the 'heart' to prioritize welfare over winning – to her mother. As Muxel (1993, p 193) wrote, 'it is with and through memories that the identity of a social subject pieces itself together'.

The role of the everyday in understanding complex family connections

The connection between family and relational identities was a strong theme in both studies, often highlighted through accounts of everyday family practices. In *Against All Odds?*, Natalie presented what might appear superficially to be contradictory framings of her mother, highlighting the importance of considering time and generation in understanding her experiences and how they connect to her understanding of herself. Natalie was at university when we first interviewed her; she entered care when she was in secondary school and she spoke in her first two interviews about the anger she felt toward her mother: "I was angry at my mum over it happening because, like I said, she was in care herself so she kind of let history repeat itself, so I was really angry with her, so my, like, relationship with her wasn't really that good." Natalie's mother died while she was still at school and her emotional work in coming to terms with that loss, and with her feelings of anger, was evident in her interviews. But when asked who she saw as a role model, Natalie cited her mother: "For some weird reason [...] because my mum was a strong person, and, like (.) She went into care, and she didn't have, like, family there but she was a strong person for putting up with stuff she did for such a long time." She drew a caveat toward the end of this account, commenting that her mother was a role model until she had started a relationship with Natalie's stepfather, which meant that "I lost my mum". But elsewhere in her interview she highlighted her mother's strength in fighting successfully for Natalie to be allowed to go to a mainstream secondary school on the basis of her academic ability, rather than continuing in the special school she had been moved to previously because of her dyslexia.

Perhaps unsurprisingly, Natalie spoke most about her mother in her first interview, while completing her life chart. But in her second interview, she mentioned her mother again, when asked if she had any worries for the future:

'Just me changing really into a person I don't want to be. […] Like it's going back to my mum again. My mum didn't want social workers to be involved with her kids, but because she changed without herself noticing, that's what happened. And she was a lovely woman before she changed. […] It's just something I think it could happen to me without me noticing really. And that's what scares me. […] it's not like I'm really worried about it. It's just a little thing (.) in the back of my head. A big part of me goes, well you've seen it and you know you don't want that to happen, so it won't happen. And it's going back to me getting out of that circle. So a part of me is like, well you're going out of that circle so that won't happen. But it's still a little thing in the back of my head that does (.) remind me about the little fear.'

Natalie still struggled with her feelings of anger and loss and, even as she respected her mother's strength, she lived with the "little fear" of becoming like her. But this fear was not wholly negative in Natalie's telling; she observed that it acts as a reminder to herself, making it less likely that she could repeat her mother's difficulties without noticing. She spoke just once about her mother in her final interview, conducted as she was about to start a master's degree. Asked what had been most important in making a difference to her life, her comments show the significance of quotidian family practices in understanding her sense of self and her complex relationship with her mother: "And it was like, when my mum or my dad would take me up to go to bed, when my mum would tuck me up, my mum would be like, you'll be the daughter getting the big house, you'll go to uni and all that. So they kind of like drilled that into my head. And I just remember when I was younger I always wanted to go to uni as well." Natalie set out this memory in explaining her distinctive position within the family, drawing a contrast between her ability and ambitions and her mother and sister who both became parents at a young age. In the memory of her mother's words when she was being "tucked up" in bed, and when she tells the story of her mother's fight for her to access mainstream secondary education, Natalie presents a sense of self which is partly defined by those positive memories of her mother's quotidian family practices, as well as her broader narrative of struggle, loss and regret. Her narrative is complex, not contradictory or lacking in coherence, and shows what can be illuminated by attention to the mundane and why it is unhelpful to binarize family (or family members) as 'good' or 'bad'.

Ruby, in the Pause study, also highlighted the apparent contradictions and complexities of family in her childhood. She noted that things became difficult after her father died when she was a young child:

> 'My Mum started being, like, abusive towards me, verbally and then physically then, it was just like (.) I had a good childhood apart from my Mum, because when I went to my Nan and Grandad's house, I'd be happy and stuff, then when I'd go back to my Mum, I'd feel horrible. But school, I was popular, I was a happy child. I was not naughty, I was cheeky, you know, secondary school, I was a terror, a terrible teenager. I went into care because of what my Mum did, because I lost a travelcard, so stupid.'

Two key points stand out in the framing of her childhood in this short narrative. First, in Ruby's closing comment, we see how the most significant life events are rooted in quotidian family life. Losing a travelcard – something fairly ordinary, that many people have experienced – prompted what could be seen as an extraordinary sequence of events, both in terms of the wider population and, even in Ruby's life up to that point, as the escalation of her mother's physical violence (not detailed here to protect confidentiality) led to Ruby finally entering care after many years of social services involvement.

The other point that particularly stands out in Ruby's narrative framing is that she firmly defined her childhood as good – "apart from my Mum". This distinction is underlined in her narrative by the brief pause after she tails off in the description of her mother's abuse – (.) – and then shifts into the list that follows: she was happy with her grandparents and happy at school. In this telling, while her mother's abusive behaviour is foregrounded in her narrative – important for understanding past and present struggles in Ruby's life – it can simultaneously be marginalized. It does not define Ruby *or* her childhood. The ongoing significance of her positive family memories was highlighted later in Ruby's first interview through a 'resemblance story' (Mason, 2018), as she reflected that she had agreed to start working with Pause because the practitioner looked like her Nan, whom she described as her "favourite person":

Interviewer:	And were there any things you think that made you particularly think, 'Yes, I do want to work with [Pause practitioner], I do want to give this a try'?
Ruby:	To be honest, because she looked like my Nan. I know it sounds stupid but she looks a lot like my Nan and my Nan's passed away. [...] Yes, she just looks really, really similar to my Nan. I was like, you know, maybe it's like a sign from God, is she going to help me? I'm not a God person but I thought, like maybe it is somebody who can help me, it's a sign from somebody up there or something that can help me. Yes, and they've given me, like a little sign but they don't want to make it too obvious instead of doing it in a different way.
Interviewer:	And you were close to your Nan?
Ruby:	Yes, she was my favourite person. [...] But she was naughty, she gave me my first cigarette. Yes, she was bad but she had [serious mental illness] and stuff so she wasn't thinking straight, but yes I was really, really close to her.

Mason (2018, p 88) writes of the ways in which resemblances can seem 'inherently magical', 'ineffable forces outside of our knowledge and understanding, yet potentially speaking of highly important things'. This is apparent in Ruby's account – the physical resemblance is "a sign from God" even though she is "not a God person". Her words bring to mind Andrews' (2014) reflection on the ways in which narrative imagination connects everyday lives to possible futures: 'Through our narrative imagination, we are not alone, even if there is no one with us. It connects us always to others who are not there, including our past and future selves' (Andrews 2014, p 114). In Ruby's account, her childhood memories of her grandmother made it possible for her to imagine that the Pause practitioner was someone who could help, in spite of a general wariness she described about "sharing her business" with people. One might conclude that this physical resemblance between the practitioner and Ruby's grandmother was simply lucky chance. But she was not the only participant to highlight resemblance in discussing her relationship with her Pause practitioner. In Hannah's first interview, she observed: "I'm always saying to my mum, I swear she could be related to us, yeah, it's made like, we just get each other, we're both Rhesus negative as well, we're both empaths, yeah, we're both into the same kind of stuff." Like Ruby, Hannah's comments are not just about liking, or getting on well, with someone. Both women speak of affinity through familial resemblance; for Hannah, there is a connection through blood type as well as personality. The importance of this perceived affinity is particularly striking given women's circumstances at the time they started working with Pause, struggling with very significant unmet needs but also carrying memories of previous adverse experiences of professional involvement (see Boddy et al, 2020b; Boddy and Wheeler, 2020). Ruby and Hannah's descriptions of their Pause practitioners highlight the potential challenges involved in managing relationship-based work where perceived affinities may make a professional feel like family.[7] Yet their accounts also indicate that building a more nuanced understanding of family relationships in care experienced lives could have valuable practice implications, in line with Featherstone et al's (2014) arguments for the development of humane social work with children and families, in a context where 'welfare practices close down opportunities for vulnerable families to demonstrate their ethic of care, and, by failing to demonstrate care, families are found wanting' (Featherstone et al, 2014, p 144). The value of an alternative, more family-minded approach has been demonstrated through research such as the evaluation of 'Lifelong Links' (see Holmes et al, 2020), developed by the NGO Family Rights Group. As the Family Rights Group website explains:[8] 'An independent Lifelong Links coordinator works with a child in care to find out who is important to them, who they would like to be back in touch with and who they would like to know.'

Holmes and colleagues' (2020) evaluation concluded that the Lifelong Links approach contributed to children and young people's sense of stability and emotional wellbeing, noting the importance of restoring continuity of relationships for children and young people's identity formation. But Ruby's account of meeting her Pause practitioner highlights an additional point. Understanding diverse relationships across the family network is not only helpful for identifying support *within* that network. Developing a nuanced understanding of the relationships and family practices that young people value could help with determining the best approach to support – especially when those young people have had extensive and often negative prior experiences of professional involvement. Resemblance is not only, or necessarily, a matter of physical likeness, but can also 'range and vary across character, spirit, ways of being' (Mason, 2018, p 85). Understanding the relational intersubjectivities of someone's lifeworld can help practitioners to engage with families' complexities and so can illuminate approaches to practice by creating space within which to imagine possibilities for professional relationships and practices.

What is (extra)ordinary?

> What is mundane and ordinary to one person might be quite extra-ordinary to another.
> Susie Scott, *Making Sense of Everyday Life*, 2009, p 2

In considering Morgan's (2011) conceptualization of the everyday as it applies to family lives and practices for people who have been in care, we need to recognize how what is 'ordinary' and can be taken-for-granted depends on the resources and support available to families. As Featherstone and colleagues (2014) observed in discussing child maltreatment, family poverty can be understood as a form of societal neglect, and 'poverty and its associated social inequalities generate experiences that render family life at times risky and harmful for children' (p 143). In Chapter 1, I drew on a range of research to highlight the ways in which rising levels of material deprivation and income inequality for families in England have coincided with significant reductions in universally accessible provision for children and families, such that material deprivation corresponds with increased risk of child protection involvement for families.

For many people in our research, the taken-for-granted nature of family homes and quotidian family practices were often shaped by poverty and compounded by the family difficulties that had led them to be placed in care. Their accounts evoke Scott's (2009) observation, that what is ordinary for some is extra-ordinary for others. This is illustrated by Zoe, who took part in the Pause evaluation. In her first interview, she shared photographs on her phone of the flat where she had recently moved with her partner and spoke of her excitement at having a living room for the first time in her life:

> 'I have one bedroom, we have one living room, which is really cool because I've never had a living room – but I have when I used to live with my foster parents, but now I have a living room, I have one bedroom, a massive kitchen and it is massive and a massive balcony. I enjoy it.'

In the *Against All Odds?* study, Richard's narrative drew attention to the taken-for-granted deprivation of his early childhood. His opening frame – "this is for the tape" – emphasizes the relevance for our research, while his account emphasized his older brothers' hard work in 'trying to make it look normal':

> 'Oh, this is for the tape, [my mother and her partner] painted the window black in the master bedroom so they could sleep in the day and spend the nights getting drunk and high with friends or whatever. Yeah, literally one day it was painted black. It was a dark house to live in (.) it was a dark childhood, figuratively and literally. [My older siblings] were getting ready for school and trying to make it look normal. It was kind of our little secret that no one could know about. [Sibling] would try and provide for us with whatever was in the cupboards. [...] I remember once looking in the oven, seeing the fish fingers cooking in the oven, and thinking to myself, are they going to be white or green like they

were last time? Because they were out of date and that was the only thing we had in. So messed up for a little child to think it is normal.'

As he questions the assumption of his younger self that it is 'normal' to eat mouldy food, Richard reminds us that taken-for-granted quotidian family practices are not necessarily benign. In relation to the *Against All Odds?* study, we have written about the importance of attending to the everyday for understanding what it means 'to live a life that you feel is good for you', in the words of one of the Norwegian participants (see Bakketeig et al, 2020, p 5). Within that analysis, participants' accounts of the significance of apparently unremarkable quotidian practices – like keeping a house clean, or buying fresh food – could be understood to have particular significance in relation to their childhood experiences. In Richard's vivid memory of rancid fish fingers, and Zoe's appreciation of the living room in her flat, we see why memories that are 'ordinary' to some people may feel 'extra-ordinary' to others, and vice versa.

For many participants in our research, the distinction between the ordinary and extra-ordinary aspects of family life was not clear cut. Again, a lifeworld orientation can help to understand how adverse experiences may be part of the regular and taken for granted practices of family living, entwined with mundane routines like having dinner or going to school. This connection was powerfully illuminated by Ella (in the *Against All Odds?* study), who described life with her mother's violent partner and told a detailed story about a day when he threatened her with a knife. Edited for confidentiality, we pick up her narrative at the point when she is hiding in her bedroom:

'And then one day he was eating his dinner or something and then he put this knife to my throat (.) She [Ella's mother] goes, "Leave her alone", and then sending me up to my room. [...] And they were talking about me [...] I remember him saying, "You'd better call her an ambulance because she's going to need one". And he went up the stairs three at a time and I remember thinking, "oh my God he's going to see me". And I even contemplated jumping out of the window. And I had this stupid little lock on the door, and I locked the door, and he was kicking it. Anyway, eventually he went. And then [younger sibling] was like, "Ella, are you OK?". I was like, "Is he still there? Is he still there?" And [sibling] was like, "No, no, he's gone". I said, "Are you sure? You're not just saying that. He's not told you to say it, has he?". "No, no, no". I unlocked the door and that and then I was like (.) Anyway, so he'd gone. [...]

The irony was [sibling] had a swimming lesson up the road, because we used to live near [leisure centre] walking distance up the road. So my mum paid for [sibling] to have swimming lessons but I was the one that had to take [them]. And this is what my mum was like, even though I didn't want to take [them]. And it was dark – it must have been winter time (.) […] I went to go out and my mum went, "Can you take [sibling]? I'm not going out there. He could be out there waiting for me".'

Ella's use of reported dialogue from multiple characters gives immediacy to her narrative and maximizes the affective intensity of her account, as 'through strategies of quotation, the storyteller literally engages in space-time travel' (Koven, 2012, p 8). She makes vivid the family dynamic: the characters involved, the relational contingencies of what happened and the way in which she is positioned within the family. Her narrative switch – "the irony was" – emphasizes how the violence and threat that she describes were woven into her everyday family life, as quotidian family practices – a mealtime, a child's swimming lesson – bookend her account.

Elsewhere in her first interview, Ella recalled spending time with the family of a childhood friend and being starkly aware of the contrast between *their* taken-for-granted family practices and her own experience:

'They'd invite me round after school for tea and we'd have dinner and stuff. It was always a treat because they'd always have pudding and my mum never had pudding and things like that. And they'd have games (.) It wouldn't be like sit in front of the telly, but they'd have all different board games. And I didn't play at hardly any of these and it was such great fun to me. It was always such a joy to go round her house. And I remember back then I was riddled with nits, and they never (.) they had their own kids and they never made me feel bad or (.) they must have seen it, looking back, but they never said we don't want you hanging around with her or anything like that. They were so kind.'

Ella's description highlights what was made visible to her by the contrast with her friend's family, especially, as she says, "looking back". Her account resonates with Grunwald and Thiersch's (2009, pp 137–138) observations about the importance of seeing alternatives to the 'taken-for-grantedness' of the lifeworld:

A final factor determining the nature of the lifeworld is the conflict between the given on the one hand, and the possible and the abandoned on the other. … it can always be asked whether things have to be as they are, whether they could not be different. … In order to open oneself to new options, the taken-for-granted must first be problematised, broken open and 'destroyed'. (Grunwald and Thiersch, 2009)

For several participants in our research, such contrasts were only made visible after they were placed in care. For example, Richard's description of the moment of arriving at his first foster carer's house posed a vivid contrast to the 'figurative and literal darkness' that he said characterized childhood in his mother's house: "And we arrived at [foster carer's] house. The front door opened and it was this nice clean, light house. And there was this woman with three children. [...] She was like, let's watch a film, and sits down and puts on [cartoon]." But for others – as with Ella's experiences with her friend's family, Nicola's fond memories of playing at her great grandparents' house and Ruby's recollections of happy times at school and with her grandparents – the taken-for-grantedness of adverse family practices was countered by the experience of possible alternatives that were part of their everyday childhoods, and their lifeworlds, prior to entering care. The extraordinariness of these ordinary experiences, for participants' lives and their understandings of themselves, is revealed in the importance they attached to their telling within the context of our interviews.

Rituals and celebrations

Morgan's (2011) definition of everyday family practices refers to *a sense of the regular*, which includes practices which may not happen every day, but which are experienced by a significant proportion of the population. He further distinguishes what he terms 'life course rituals' (Morgan, 2011, p 120) – key life events such as weddings and funerals, or rites of passage such as university graduation, as well as less formal events such as birthdays or other family get-togethers. The former he notes are:

> frequently more emotionally charged partly because they are concerned with serious matters, partly because so much (materially and emotionally) is invested in them and partly because the element of display is frequently more obvious. Such events have their own intensity deriving in part from the sense of risk or danger that lies beneath the surface. (Morgan, 2011, p 119)

In the context of our discussion of care experienced people's family lives, we can also understand this conceptualization of 'ordinary' as relating to events and practices which are not specific to care experience. As discussed in Chapters 1 and 2, this is important in our endeavour to challenge the 'single story' of care experience. What matters in people's lives is not defined by their care experience, but as discussed later, ordinary events and practices may be distinctively shaped by people and experiences associated with having been in care.

Informal celebrations

Perhaps unsurprisingly, given the circumstances that led to placement, participants in the two studies rarely discussed events such as birthday celebrations in childhoods prior to entering care. As Ella (*Against All Odds?*) commented, "I've never had parents that have bought me this, that and the other for Christmas and birthdays and (...)". For some people, this pattern shifted on entering care. Rosa (*Against All Odds?*), explained that her move into a residential home coincided closely with her tenth birthday and she recalled how pleased she was about the gifts she received:

'The children's home from the age of nine. It was actually I think a month and eleven days before my tenth birthday. I was a big fan of Barbie, so you can imagine, I got the Barbie case and tons of Barbies. I was well chuffed.'

Like Richard (quoted earlier), Rosa drew a contrast between this early experience in her placement and her life prior to entering care, which she summarized simply as "Neglect, abuse, trauma, isolation (.) that's why I am the way I am now". In Chapter 4, when we discuss the re/configuration of family, we will consider the ways in which such ritual family practices – such as the careful choice of a child's present – can foster a sense of recognition and belonging within the placement.

In the *Against All Odds?* study, Claire's second music choice illuminates the significance of family in another ritual domain of childhood and youth – sporting events. Strandbu et al (2019) discuss young people's perspectives on ideal parental roles in sporting activities, noting that parents' presence was often highly valued: for emotional support, but also – to quote Ingar, one of the young people in their study – to 'have a parent who thinks it's cool what you do' (Strandbu et al, 2019, p 73). For Claire, parental involvement in her sport (gymnastics) was never a possibility, but she explained her music choice with the story of a competition that took place near where her grandparents lived. She stayed with them while she was preparing for the competition and they came to see her compete. Claire surprised them by performing to "my granddad's favourite song", Beethoven's 'Moonlight Sonata':[9]

'And [...] he came to see me compete to it. And I won the competition. [...] Yeah, he was really upset (...) Well I don't think he was upset, I think he was happy and proud. And I think he just wasn't expecting me to have chosen his favourite song. I don't know what he was expecting, but (...).'

Claire's account shows the importance of extended kin in her understanding of family, something discussed further in Chapter 4. She had very little contact with her grandparents during childhood and they were not generally involved in quotidian family practices of care. The time she spent with them around the competition clearly had special significance – expressed through her choosing to perform to his favourite music and also in her choosing to share this memory in our research. Her narrative resonates with Strandbu et al's (2019, p 68) descriptions of the positive affordances of parental involvement, in helping to 'develop and sustain emotionally close bonds'.

Weddings and funerals

Participants' accounts of their young adult lives documented the ongoing significance (and challenges) of key family rituals – both less formal occasions such as birthdays, and more formal lifecourse events such as christenings, communions, weddings and funerals.[10] As Morgan (2011) has noted, formal lifecourse events such as weddings and funerals can surface critical tensions about managing relatedness, because they are practices centred on family gatherings and family display. Writing about heterosexual weddings, Maillochon and Castrén (2011, p 32) observe:

> Individual choices are embedded in social constraints. … The kin group membership is thus open to negotiation. What follows in the context of weddings is that kin from both the bride's and groom's sides are expected to be present, but also that the couple needs to decide on the categories of relatives and the actual people they invite to their wedding.

These tensions were apparent in both studies, in participants' narratives about formal lifecourse rituals and rites of passage such as weddings, funerals and university graduation. In the examples that follow, we consider these tensions – about who to include and how to manage inclusion – as well as the implications for care experienced people who may be managing these key lifecourse events *without* the participation of supportive kin.

Ella (*Against All Odds?*) was happily married and expecting her first child when we first interviewed her. As indicated by the experiences discussed earlier in this chapter, she had a very difficult relationship with both of her biological parents and this was a source of tension for her and her partner in planning their wedding:

> 'And when I got married (.) that was a real (.) bittersweet event because [partner] comes from a traditional family, he wanted a traditional wedding, etcetera, etcetera.
>
> I wanted to go away and do it because I knew all the issues it was going to bring up. And I really agonized for months over what to

do because I was so worried about all the drama that might happen. My mum might kick off, my dad was (...) When I told my dad I was getting married (.) And it's funny because my dad (.) we don't not get on; I've never fallen out with my dad as such, but he's just useless. He's just not very helpful. And he just doesn't bother. And I remember saying to him (...) the first thing he said (.) I said, [partner's] asked me to marry him. And he didn't say, that's great, or congratulations. He just said, well don't expect me to pay for anything; I haven't got a pot to piss in. And it was like, well thanks dad; I knew that already. But congratulations (...) And then he went on to say he wasn't going to go and his girlfriend could go – behind my back he said this. And I can't stand his girlfriend (...) So it all went on. I can't even begin (.) the dynamics. My [siblings] have been in prison, predictable. My mum's got mental health issues. And my [sibling] – as much as [they're] harmless, [they're] late for absolutely everything. I could imagine [them] turning up late for the ceremony. And putting them all together. My mum and dad hate each other (...) it was just (...) I was like, I can't deal with this. So I wrote to them all and said they weren't invited.'

This part of Ella's wedding narrative shows the overwhelming complexity of managing kin. Her comment, "I can't even begin (.) the dynamics" is surrounded by detail of family members' difficulties, lack of care and unreliability. But throughout her interviews, Ella also described strong, supportive friendships and she continued the story of the wedding by explaining that her friends advised her how to handle the situation:

'They're like, you need to do what's best for you at the end of the day, that kind of thing. And [friend's name] I remember her saying – when I said I was going to write letters saying all my reasons and that. [...] She said, "If you're going to write a letter, keep it short and sweet. Just to the point so it doesn't open up a can of worms". Best advice she gave me. And I just wrote (...) everyone had the letter. Something like, this isn't personal (.) it's just causing me a lot of stress (.) and I felt the best way that I can enjoy the day, and I hope you can understand. Or something like that. And the only person obviously that did go was my [younger sibling]; [they] gave me away.'

Ella talked further about the challenges for her younger sibling, who tries to be "everyone's friend", in managing the other family members' curiosity and expectations. But she also spoke of the risk that they might inadvertently give away details of the wedding to her mother; she was "so scared that somebody was going to turn up and cause problems" that she made a "little plan" with friends:

'it was all agreed there were a few people that were going to keep an eye out and just deal with it for me, get her out sort of thing (.) or whoever. Do you know what I mean? And I was just on tenterhooks. I remember the day before crying my eyes out. Just the stress (...) I cannot even begin to tell you the stress. Organizing the wedding and all that is stressful anyway, but with all this emotional stuff as well (...) Unfortunately my husband just didn't understand, didn't get it; he just didn't understand what the big deal was. He thought it was a bit harsh writing everyone but (.) how could he possibly understand.'

Ella's wedding narrative ended with a positive turn, as she introduced a new character: a friend who "was absolutely amazing [...] I cannot begin to explain how fantastic she was". She continued by listing the wedding and bridal traditions that this friend had ensured, including "the glass engraved that said Bride Ella, [...] my sixpence in my shoe and something blue". The significance of this role was marked by her friend's presence in the wedding photo on display in Ella's living room. She explained:

'I said to the photographer, the most important shot is the confetti shot. And we actually had it staged so that they (...) lots of people had confetti and I bought loads of confetti; and I made the photographer, he did it (.) we did two takes because I wanted to make sure I had a good shot. But I think he got it first time anyway. *(Interviewer: Fantastic)* She was absolutely amazing.'

Her repeated description of her 'absolutely amazing' friend bookmarks this part of the narrative, which also reveals the extent to which the practices of a traditional wedding *did* matter to Ella as well as to her partner. Carter and Duncan (2017) argue that tradition is idealized in contemporary British weddings, because it is legitimating: 'the process of creating something special inevitably draws on tradition' (p 18). But their research also highlights the ways in which tradition can be 're-served' through 'a process of bricolage and social negotiation' (p 7). This metaphor of bricolage is very apt for understanding Ella's experience. Unlike the participants in Carter and Duncan's (2017) research, hers was not an ideological rejection or repurposing of tradition, a rejection of consumerism or concern to give the day a 'distinctive' edge. For Ella, the need for bricolage was not a choice; the challenge was how to achieve her and her partner's aspirations for the wedding, given the complexities of her family relationships. Through difficult decisions and the support of close friends, she and her partner were able to create the wedding that she described, retaining important traditional features – such as the confetti photo and being walked down the aisle – but simultaneously protecting Ella from the risks she foresaw in her family's involvement.

Ella described her wedding as "bittersweet", but we can also recognize it as a happy moment in her remaking of family with her partner, a moment that marks 'the recognition of the couple by salient others' (Bernardi and Oppo, 2011, p 96). However, the considerations she navigated, balancing complicated relationships alongside the expectations of tradition, were also apparent in accounts of another key lifecourse ritual: funerals. In a sample of young adults, across the two studies, it was striking how commonly they had experienced – and also been involved in organizing and paying for – funerals of close family members. Here, we consider two examples: James from *Against All Odds?* and Joelle from the *Evaluation of Pause*.

James spoke in his interviews about his mother's funeral. He lived with her for the first ten years of his life and spent the remainder of his childhood moving through multiple placements in foster and residential care. He explained his placement instability in terms of his feelings about leaving his mother, saying that he was never able to connect with his carers: "Because I wanted my mum and because I knew I couldn't have my mum. And I was angry at my mum, I didn't feel safe around my mum (…) And I was just lost really, confused, and I just lashed out at the world." James had siblings, but he was never placed with them – they initially remained with his mother and subsequently the youngest child moved in with his father while the older sibling spent time in foster care before moving back to his mother's home. His mother died when James was in his twenties and in his first interview he expressed pride in how he had managed during this very difficult time:

> 'And I guess looking back on how I managed that situation and dealt with that, I'm quite proud of that. I was there when they turned the machines off and (…) yeah, got to hold her hand and stuff and say a few things (…) and organized the funeral, me and my [younger sibling] organized the funeral, paid for it (…) That was quite a good thing (…).'

Asked how he managed in this situation, his response echoes Ella's account of her wedding – he turned to friends: "I picked up the phone, I asked for help, I talked to people. […] [Two closest friends] particularly, but other people as well. I was very lucky to have a lot of support around me." James returned to the story of his mother's funeral in his second interview. He chose two songs to share, both of which he had played at his mother's funeral. The second song – The Saw Doctors' 'World of Good'[11] – had been introduced to him by his mother during a brief period in his teens when he had returned to live at home. He explained that he chose to play it at the funeral because

> 'it was almost like me saying goodbye. […] And almost like letting her go on really. And some of the words in it (…) "the children in your likeness of the same inspired blood" (.) I think that's a really nice

line. And, "a friend that you can trust" [...] And he says in the song, "if I thought you should take me with you, I know that you would", sort of thing. I kind of like that. It's like, look, where I'm going, you can't come but I know that you'd like it. If I was supposed to, I would. And so, although I'm leaving you, I know that if the right thing to do was to take you then I would definitely take you with me. And I like that. It's like, you've not been forgotten about.'

His description of significant lyrics expresses James's care and thoughtfulness in coming to terms with his mother's death and a "very, very difficult relationship [...] Nothing has beaten that one yet, do you know what I mean? Nothing's been more profound and had the biggest impact on me". Again, he expressed pride in giving her a "good funeral", but he also noted (in an account edited here for length and confidentiality) the challenges of achieving this given long-standing difficult family dynamics:

'My [older sibling] was there, my [lists relatives]. I'm just so different to them and their outlook on life. They just don't get me you know. [...] Well (.) as a child it was like (.) I just remember (.) it was like shame would be imposed on you for feeling, having feelings. Which is quite cold really, emotionless (.) and they don't even know it. They don't have a clue how much they were and they're not really now. But in their heads they never were emotionless. It does my head in a bit really and (...) there's something wrong with me, I've got an issue, a chip on my shoulder or I think the world owes me something. They're the kind of comments they make, and it's like you fucking have got no idea, no idea.'

Having noted these challenges, he continued the narrative, saying:

'But it was a good funeral. [...] Me and my [siblings] did it. *(Interviewer: So your [younger sibling] was there as well?)* Yeah, my [younger sibling], yeah (.) and my [relatives] came to support me and my [siblings], but (.) I think [relative] did support my [older sibling] and stuff. But like (.) you know, I just (.) I don't know (.) none of them were there when my mum was alive. They just all judged her. *(Interviewer: Did you feel pleased about what you managed to do?)* Definitely, it was a good funeral. Looking back, it was a good funeral, yeah. It was a good funeral, yeah. [...] And me and my [younger sibling] paid for it, do you know what I mean? Fucking hell – to pay for my mum's funeral's big, you know. *(Interviewer: It's a lot of money.)* Yeah, and it was before I had my house. *(Interviewer: So when you were saving really hard [for a deposit]?)* Yeah, it did knock me back a bit.'

Funerals, like weddings, are inescapably shaped by tradition, with family relationships and family display embedded in 'normative expectations regarding appropriate content and conduct' (Woodthorpe, 2017, p 596). And as Woodthorpe notes, these expectations and the resulting decisions are also financial decisions. Against a context in which James says that none of his relatives were there for his mother when she was alive, it is perhaps unsurprising that he and his younger sibling had to pay for the funeral, unsupported by other family members even though it did 'knock him back'. Claire (*Against All Odds?*) had also paid for a close relative's funeral and for her this was additionally complicated because she had to negotiate another relative's preferences while still being expected to pay: "We had arguments over the damned coffin, me and my [relative] *[laughs]*, because I was the one paying and [they] was being really difficult. Like in the end I just let [them] have it." In talking about his mother's funeral, James explained that several of his friends had attended to support him, including his best friend, who appeared in several of his photographs, including one taken when they were at the supermarket together. Discussing this photo, he explained (edited from a longer account):

'He's my best friend. He's my best friend. Yeah. He's someone that I (…) He's the only person that I've ever loved without reservation or questioned it. I've never felt scared to have feelings for him. Everyone else who I have feelings for, family included, I always feel like it's not straightforward or it could be a bit dangerous to have that much value placed on them. It can feel unsafe at certain times. But it's never felt unsafe to care about [friend] so much. […] He teaches me a lot. He's very wise. When I'm talking with him, he'll come out with a sentence and I just think. (…) Like he said to me once, when I was really struggling, he said that our thinking is not our destination; it's just part of the journey. And that instantly allowed me to detach from my thinking and not place so much importance on it. And I realized that it was all right, it was going to be OK. And he sang Amazing Grace at my mum's funeral. And he's a really good singer. Yeah.'

James's description draws a stark contrast between the safety he finds with his friend and his feelings about his relatives, including his mother. His reference to the friend singing at the funeral also evokes Carter and Duncan's (2017) concept of bricolage, which they used to describe the remaking of tradition in weddings. The support of his friend made it possible for James to reconfigure family *and* tradition, giving his mother a funeral that he could be proud of, while safely navigating the emotional costs of involving his biological kin. The experiences of James and Ella show the importance of friendships for care experienced young adults who are navigating key lifecourse events, especially when they cannot rely on the support of family. Others in the sample relied on professional support in the absence of supportive friends or family. Joelle, in the Pause evaluation, made no mention in her interviews of family, apart from her child, and she spoke only of one former school friend, who lived some distance away. She said they spoke by phone, but elsewhere in the same interview, she commented that: "I feel alone. I feel like I don't have any friends. My mindset is just that at the moment." At the time of our first interview, Joelle's child (who was born severely disabled and placed in foster care soon after birth) had recently died and it was evident that the only support she had with her bereavement and the subsequent funeral was from Pause. She clearly had a very close relationship with her Pause practitioner and the Practice Lead in the Pause practice. Like some others in the Pause sample, she was nervous about meeting for the first interview; at her request the Practice Lead came to the café where the interview took place and sat at a distance to be available if Joelle wanted her. The first fieldnote records:

> Again, the importance of the close relationship with the Pause workers came through particularly strongly – highlighted by seeing her with the Practice Lead, and the way they hugged when she became upset [talking about her child] during the interview. In talking with the Practice Lead beforehand, we were talking quite a bit – more abstractly – about what 'corporate parenting' really means, and I was reminded of this listening to Joelle, who seemed very young in many ways, especially in the context of having to deal with something as hard and complicated as losing her child and everything that follows that.

In her second interview,[12] which took place in her flat, Joelle shared her Pause 'memory book' – an album of photos and mementos spanning the period of intensive one-to-one support from the Pause practitioner – and showed photos of her child's funeral and the memorial stone on their grave site. The fieldnote records:

> She said she doesn't go to visit the memorial stone any more as she has [the child's] ashes with her, and I realised after she said this that there was a small metal urn on the floor by the sofa.

In her first interview, Joelle spoke very little about her child, beyond stating (in the context of the life chart) that "[they] passed away". She became upset at this point and we paused the interview – and she had the aforementioned hug from the Practice Lead – before we moved on to discuss other things. Joelle's reluctance to talk about her child in the first interview contrasts with the time she spent in the second interview talking about their funeral through her Pause memory book – explaining photos and reading out notes and encouraging statements. Of course, this might simply reflect the passage of time – several months had passed – and her greater confidence with the interviewer on their second meeting. But equally, we might conclude that Joelle's experience has become more tellable because the practices documented in her memory book incorporate recognized traditions relating to grief and loss. As Butler notes: 'The "I" has no story of its own that is not also the story of a relation – or set of relations – to a set of norms' (Butler, 2005, p 8). The care and support of the Pause professionals clearly made it possible for Joelle to navigate the loss of her child and her use of the memory book in the interview indicates that she was able to create her own bricolage (after Carter and Duncan, 2017), incorporating traditional funeral practices such as the memorial stone, even as she lives through the loss of a child in extraordinary circumstances. As for Ella and James, the repurposing of tradition is not a choice for Joelle. To paraphrase one of the key messages of the recent Independent Review of Children's Social Care, apart from the professional support of Pause, Joelle had no 'loving networks of people around her' (MacAlister, 2022, p 144) to support her through this devastating life event.

Conclusion

Relying on a 'single story' of family for care experienced people could mean that we fail to attend to key moments in their family lives, with corresponding implications for their support and family relationships both in and beyond care.

Yuval-Davis (2010, p 266) writes that identities can be conceived as narratives, 'stories that people tell themselves and others about who they are, and who they are not, as well as who and how they would like to/ should be'. The narratives discussed here reflect what participants see as important for the researcher to understand – both in relation to their lives and identities *and* in terms of the wider questions being researched. The narratives they have shared also reveal the impossibility of any single story of family for young people who come into care. Their accounts emphasize the ordinary *and* distinctive aspects of family practices – in quotidian lives and in relation to ritual celebrations and key lifecourse events. The ordinary and extraordinary coincide within everyday lives and relationships, situated in space and time.

The experiences discussed in this chapter highlight a need for policy makers and practitioners to connect thinking about 'family' in childhood and adulthood. Childhood and adult kin relationships for care experienced people span diverse connections that could be supportive, dangerous, or ambiguous, but are often complicated and always emotionally significant. As Wade (2008) documented in his research fourteen years ago, reaching adulthood does not resolve the complexity of family relationships for people who have been in care. Elsewhere, and with other colleagues, I have argued for a need to think beyond 'contact' for young people in care (see Boddy et al, 2014; Iyer et al, 2020); attention to exceptional moments in family lives highlights the need for a long-term view of family connections. Young people in care need support through childhood and beyond, to understand and manage relationships that endure long after their time in placement.

4

Re/Configuring Boundaries: Who Counts as 'Family'?

> 'Ordinary' people are rather good at something that scientists who operate within a single paradigm are famously bad at: namely, traversing and experiencing everyday life connections between, for example, what we might think of as the genetic, the biological, the social, the cultural, the spiritual and so on, and understanding that there are no walls between these. People are routinely used to living such traversings in personal life ... 'the genetic' is never just or only 'the genetic' – it is also always social, and always magical, and always ineffable for example, and these things segue and blur into and out of one another. People know that this is what life is.
> Jennifer Mason, *Affinities: Potent Connections in Personal Life*, 2018, p 111

Introduction

In the first chapters of this book, I argued for the need to recognize the dynamic contingencies and ambivalent complexities of 'family' for people with care experience. Continuing that discussion, this chapter considers how the boundaries of family are configured and reconfigured over space and time, drawing on narratives of kinship and family connection that span families of origin and experiences of placement in care. Thinking across these accounts, we see how meanings of 'family' may be simultaneously constant and fluid. Mason's (2018) account of affinities sets out the idea of *ineffable* kinship, which she defines as 'a something that is in connection, with a charge that feels fixed, immutable and elemental' (p 59). Some of the narratives detailed in this chapter resonate with that definition and show how understandings of family connections can endure despite conflict and complex disruptions. At the same time, as Mason writes in the epigraph to this chapter, the examples presented here show how understandings of kinship – of 'who counts' as family – may also 'segue and blur in and out of one another' (Mason, 2018, p 111), shifting over time.

Attention to the complexities of 'who counts' as family has both practical and theoretical value. Above all, a nuanced conceptualization of the diversity of family connectedness is necessary for policy and practice efforts to support people in navigating the complexities of their family relationships, both in and after care (see Holmes et al, 2020). The next chapter, on Care and Connectedness, will examine the interdependent nature of family connections, illuminating the scaffolding and support that families can provide, as well as the complex and often challenging family responsibilities that care experienced young adults must manage. To understand those connections, and their implications for everyday lives over time, we first need to consider how family may be re/configured as a result of placement or legal entitlements, or over time while living in a placement or after leaving care. In Chapter 3, I drew on Morgan's (2011) theory of family practices to argue for attention to everyday and ostensibly mundane practices; these arguments are also relevant here, because the configuration and reconfiguration of family is *active:* 'Thus family practices are not simply practices that are done by family members in relation to other family members but they are also constitutive of that family 'membership' at the same time' (Morgan, 2011 p 32). The examples shared in this chapter show how the boundaries of family are configured through practices of everyday life, by practices of *doing* family – and, as we shall see, by practices that demarcate relationships as *not-family.*

Thinking through the lens of care experience also helps to disrupt the 'cornflakes packet' imaginary of normative conceptualizations of 'family' (see Chapter 1). This project aligns with the work of queer theorists who have sought to expand and disrupt the definition of family: allowing 'infinite possibilities for family structures' (Acosta, 2018, p 409) and challenging the 'cultural imaginary of the conventional family' by recognizing how traditional family practices may be incorporated into 'non-traditional' family forms (Heaphy, 2018, p 163). These insights have informed my thinking in this chapter, as I continue the discussion of the extra/ordinary in family lives. The examples presented here show how care experience shapes complex and 'unconventional' family forms and practices, illuminating the meanings that are made of kinship and connectedness. Thus, the understandings of family shared by participants whose narratives are included here help us along our continuing journey beyond the conventional ideal-type family and the dangers of the 'single story'.

Defining 'family'

Hantrais et al (2020) observe that 'family' was first formally defined for national census purposes, noting too that the United Nations (UN) international definition 'distinguishes family nuclei within households. ... based on the conjugal (marital) family concept' (Hantrais et al, 2020, p 277). They observe that this UN definition has gradually been expanded; as recently as 2020, the concept of 'reconstituted families' was introduced, recognizing that family forms may change following events such as separation or divorce. The 2020 UN guidance also addresses multigenerational households, but as Hantrais et al (2020, p 281) point out, generational connections are not confined to households: 'complex families and households are highly heterogeneous' (p 281).

Herlofson and Hagestad (2011) note that the lack of attention to extended kin networks beyond the household is an artefact of demographic data collection: 'due to time constraints and the need to limit the length of questionnaires, hardly any survey has included questions about all living generations, ascending and descending' (p 343). Similarly, Furstenberg (2020, p 367) comments that the institutionalization of the household survey as a key method in family research 'could have unwittingly contributed to the narrow focus on family of residence, that is, household composition'.

These arguments about complexity and kinship are highly relevant to thinking through 'family' for the participants in our research. The normative notion of the 'family nucleus' – and the corresponding assumption that 'family' is coterminous with 'household' – is distinctively problematic for people with care experience. Not least, placement comprises an intervention into family structure, household living arrangements and inter- and intragenerational connections. Furstenberg et al (2020, p 1405) suggest that the normative cultural ideal of the nuclear family has receded over recent years, with 'growing tolerance for an increasing variety of family forms'. While they acknowledge that 'ideological battles continue to this day over the legitimacy (often framed as efficacy) of various family forms' (Furstenberg et al, 2020, p 1405), it must be recognized that the tolerance they describe is more apparent for some families than others – as was evident in response to the depiction of a Black family in the supermarket gravy advertisement discussed in Chapter 1. Drew's (2016) analysis of the representation of same-sex families in television advertising found that it functioned to 'idealise and promote same-sex family structures that are normative and conservative in terms of gender and social class and render outside of the frame of the ideal childhood subjectivities that are non-gender conforming and working-class' (Drew, 2016, p 333). This example shows how non-standard family forms can be legitimized in public discourse if they comply in other respects with the normative imaginary of the 'cornflakes packet' family (see Morgan, 2011). The tolerance that Furstenberg et al (2020) describe is *not* extended across the politicized binary constructed between so-called 'ordinary' and 'troubled' families – a distinction that is starkly apparent in the 'poverty porn' genre of reality television and the concept of the 'benefit brood':

'Benefit brood' is a cultural figuration of disgust aimed at families that are deemed to have become 'excessively' large as a result of over-generous welfare entitlements; 'benefit brood' parents are regarded as almost pathologically fertile in their desire to secure greater amounts of welfare payments by having more and more children. 'Benefit brood' narratives form a staple of disgust across news media, lifestyle and 'real life' magazines, and pseudo-documentary (reality) television such as the genre of 'poverty porn'. (Jensen and Tyler, 2015, p 478–9)

Such constructions are highly classed: not all large and complex families are framed as 'feckless' or subject to the same scrutiny and stigmatization.[1] As Crossley (2018) observes, the notion of 'troubled' families is used to problematize those who experience multiple intersecting structural disadvantages including poverty and poor-quality housing, with large and complex family structures singled out for particular concern. To challenge such stereotypes, we aim in this chapter to develop a more nuanced understanding of the complexities of family structure – and what *counts* as family – for people with care experience.

Family structures

Within our two samples, family structures were of course varied, ranging from small close-knit intergenerational units to large, disparate and complicated networks of intra- and intergenerational connections that extended across households. Two contrasting examples from the Pause evaluation – the narratives of Ashley and Jasmine – illustrate this diversity of experience.

Ashley entered care in infancy before being adopted in early childhood and retained strong connections with both her biological and adoptive family. At the time of our first interview – living temporarily in her biological mother's home and with her children in the custody of her adoptive parents – she reflected on the complexity of 'family' in her life:[2] "Ummm, I don't know. Ummm [laughs]. You can't choose your family, but you can choose your friends. No. What is it? You can't choose your family but you can choose your friends, that is the one. But can I write all my family down? *(Interviewer: Yes)* Bloody hell, yes." Ashley's opening "ummms" and laughter reveal her hesitancy as she asks "Can I write all my family down?". Her response, "Bloody hell, yes", foregrounds the scale of the task, as she goes on to explain. I reproduce the detail of Ashley's account in full here (bar editing for confidentiality) to reflect the care she took in documenting the people who represent family for her:

Ashley:	Err so I have got, I have got half-brothers as well and I have got half-sisters. So there is [lists names of siblings]

	they are on my birth dad's side. [...] And then I have got [lists names of other siblings] and obviously me. *(Interviewer: Right)* And then I have got [name] *[laughs]* who is my half-sister and I have got [lists names of other siblings] and then I have got [another sibling]. So they are all from my mum. [counts how many children her birth mother has]. Then obviously my dad he has them [siblings] and us so [counts birth father's children]. Then I have got (.) oh it is so complicated.
Interviewer:	And so do you see them then? Are there any you are particularly close to?
Ashley:	No [two siblings] is the ones that lives in [this city] so I get to see them. And they have got, [lists their children]. And then I have got, who else have I got? Then on my adoption side obviously I have got my mum, dad, umm [lists other siblings]. And they are my adoption family. *(Interviewer: Right)* Obviously we didn't get along that much after I found out at [age] I was actually adopted so I was like a little terror, as you are when you are young, but after I found out I was –
Interviewer:	That must have been quite a shock at that age.
Ashley:	Yes, because I thought they were actually my birth family but then I found out I was actually adopted. And then obviously we do have family get-togethers as well because they [siblings in adoptive family] has got kids themselves as well. [...] But we have family get-togethers on Christmases and birthdays, get-togethers. So like Christmas, birthdays we get together and have a nice family meal, Christmas, birthdays. Sorry, they all mean everything to me, but it is lot to (.) *[laughs]*
Interviewer:	Yes, complicated.
Ashley:	Yes. And then [my half-brother], was to come up and see me [...] but lives in, oh where does he live? It is near [place] but I can't remember where he lives now. [...] No. But his sister is called [name] who is like a sister to me. But we all get along, but [...] them ones we don't hardly see yet until they are old enough to get in touch from my birth mum. But I think that is it for the family. Umm I haven't missed anything off have I? Obviously my partner which is [name]. And I have got their family by my side as well. [Adds detail of his relatives]. And that is I think that is it for the family.

Ashley's careful narrative shows that, despite her initial hesitation, it was important to her that the interviewer understood both the complexity ("oh it is so complicated") and the significance of these relationships ("they all mean everything to me, but it is a lot"). She tails off here and is interrupted by the interviewer's attempt to acknowledge her family's complexity, so we can't know what she means by "a lot". A lot to explain? A lot to deal with? Perhaps both: she opens the narrative with the adage "you can't choose your family" and her account also shows that it is complex to navigate the possibilities of different relationships.

Ashley's account also highlights the dynamic nature of family boundaries and family connections, as she documents how connections shift over time. Notably, she describes how she and her adoptive parents are moving past the rupture in their relationship that was caused by the revelation that she had been adopted: "Obviously we didn't get along that much after I found out." Ashley's narrative shows how intergenerational connections scaffold this reparatory work in her adoptive family. She talks about "get-togethers" – ritual family practices such as celebrating Christmases and birthdays which bring together three generations: her adoptive parents, Ashley and her adoptive siblings, and their children. Her experience resonates with Costa's (2013) observations about family rituals in post-divorce contexts: adults' concern not to deprive children of significant family rituals such as birthdays means that children drive the reinvention of those rituals, 'even in the "most difficult" moments' (Costa, 2013, p 277).

Mason (2018, p 59) comments that kinship affinities may be both '*parochial* and *quotidian*' and '*boundless* and *ethereal*'. This is also apparent in Ashley's interviews as she documents the different ways in which family matters in her everyday life. She lists siblings on her mother's side that "we don't hardly see yet until they are old enough to get in touch". Her narrative recognizes these children as family, but her caveat specifies that they cannot *yet* be known to her. Given her phrasing (and the fact that she was adopted in early childhood) it seems plausible that contact was not currently possible because they are also in care or adopted. She makes their ineffable connection visible in her detailed documentation of kin, but unlike others in the family, they are not a tangible part of her everyday life. By comparison, her account shows that both her immediate and extended kin – her adoptive parents and biological mother, as well as others in her extended family – are embedded in Ashley's regular family practices. Her adoptive parents – who live in a different city with her children – provide financial support for her to travel to maintain regular contact with them and at the time of the first interview Ashley and her partner were living with her biological mother while waiting to be allocated housing. By the time of her second interview, Ashley was living in a flat with her partner; her account of her weekend plans echoes her earlier description of important connections with her siblings: "I'm seeing my niece and nephews from my stepsister's side […] on Saturday. And then I'm seeing my mum on Saturday night. And then it's my niece's first birthday on Sunday, so I'm going to them as well. And they all live near each other, so they're all [in name of area]." And again, in her third and final interview, asked what had been happening since we last spoke, she explained: "Not much really, I've been going to see my sisters, I've been going to see my birth mum and then going to people's birthdays."

Ashley's description of family illuminates the 'double thinking' that Heaphy (2018) discusses in his research with formalized same-sex couples and families, noting the ways in which they can be 'simultaneously viewed as traditionally conventional *and* post-traditional and non-conventional' (Heaphy, 2018, p 163). Heaphy draws on Finch's (2007) concept of family display and particularly the need for nonconventional families to legitimate their status through family *display*. This is apparent in Ashley's account. She makes clear that her family is extraordinary in some respects – distinctively large and complicated and extending far beyond any single household. Yet the practices that Ashley describes in order to display what family means in her life, such as birthday and Christmas celebrations, are ordinary: longer-term regularities that are common to large portions of the population (see Morgan, 2011 and Chapter 3). Her narrative shows us the ways in which ordinary and traditional practices are incorporated within her extra-ordinary family: she describes practices of complex extended kinship within and across generations, highlighting in particular the significance of sibling relationships and geographic proximity. Her experience chimes with the messages from Furstenberg's (2020) review, which documents the importance of (and lack of research on) horizontal lineage, involving 'collateral' kin such as siblings, their partners and children. He challenges the assumption that the 'standard' nuclear family is in some way 'traditional', citing ethnographic studies in low-income US communities in the 1940s which observed that 'family boundaries were not nearly as tightly maintained as appeared to be the case among more privileged families in the middle class' (Furstenberg, 2020, p 366). Ashley's narrative shows how both nonconventional kin relationships *and* traditional family practices are incorporated in her understanding of who family is and what family means in her life.

Of course, family structures are not necessarily large and complicated. A contrasting example, also from the Pause evaluation, reminds us not to essentialize an imaginary of the large, complex or 'troubled' family in care experienced lives. Jasmine's account of family in her life chart comprised her mother, aunt and young child (who lived with Jasmine's mother on a Special Guardianship Order (SGO) and stayed with Jasmine regularly). She commented: "I've haven't got any brothers or sisters. I've only got a small family. […] Mum and Aunt. That's all of the family I've got, that's the same." Jasmine was in residential care as a teenager and said she moved placement multiple times, subsequently becoming homeless on leaving care. She spoke little in her interviews about this period, but it was clear that her placement experiences were not conceptualized as relating to 'family'. But her small intergenerational family was very visible in her everyday life: her home was full of toys, her child was present during the first of our interviews and she saw her mother and aunt frequently. Again, geographic proximity was an important facet of connectedness. By the time of her second interview, she had moved to a flat very close to where her mother lived, and said: "It is perfect. So I've kind of come on my feet with this flat, and it's next to my mum's. I couldn't get any closer." While Jasmine's experience is very different from Ashley's, her account also entails 'double think' about the extra/ordinary family. In addition to the rupture to family life associated with her care biography, Jasmine also observed that it was "very rare" for someone in her position – with a child living in the legally permanent arrangement of a Special Guardianship Order – to have the level of contact she had. Her narrative highlighted her hard work and achievement in securing that unusual arrangement:

Jasmine:	I've worked towards it. Like I had to go against my mum and go to the social services and get the meeting, you know. I had to do the work.
Interviewer:	'So your mum didn't want to do that.
Jasmine:	No, she didn't, because she was scared that she would get into trouble. So, I had to kind of put these boundaries in place myself and I had to work towards it, you know, and it took a long time. It was baby steps. [Child]'s [age] now, so it's taken [several] years. It hasn't been a thing where it's been overnight. It has taken like a long time to prove myself.

In terms of biography and living arrangements, Jasmine's family can be recognized as 'extra-ordinary', but her interviews were also full of descriptions of 'ordinary' family practices such as planning her child's birthday party and going on outings to the seaside. This juxtaposition of the extra/ordinary in quotidian life was most starkly visible in Jasmine's first interview when she began to talk about her previous social worker:

'She took my child away from me and she made up a lot of lies about my Mum. She wanted my child to be adopted. *[Louder voice]* [Child's name], don't do that on the teddy bear, you're going to ruin the teddy. Don't put the slime on it, you're going to ruin it. […] [Child's name] stop! You're meant to put the slime in the pot, you're not meant to put it all over the house. […] *[Quieter again]* What a disaster, why did I buy that for her? I can see there's slime everywhere.'[3]

Following this interjection to discuss the slime, Jasmine continued her narrative (edited here for confidentiality):

> 'She made a load of lies up about my Mum. She made false accusations. Luckily Mum fought for [child] because she wanted [them]. She [social worker] wanted [child] adopted, she did my pre-birth assessment, and she just gave me hell. [...] The fact is that she told lies about my mother. She caused a lot of aggro. She wanted my [child] adopted. She said that if my Mum had [child] that I would ruin [child]'s routine and it wouldn't work, and it's worked out perfectly. My [child] is [age] and as good as an angel.'

Jasmine's story of her and her mother's fight to keep her child is critical to their family biography and so to her understanding of what family means to her. But it is also because of their successes – her mother's in securing the SGO arrangement, and Jasmine's achievement in securing permission for unsupervised contact – that we see the mundane practices of parenting that interrupt the story. For Jasmine, telling her child off for getting slime on the furniture is simultaneously ordinary and extraordinary. Again, this can be recognized as a practice of family display (Finch, 2007). Jasmine shows her engaged parenting to the interviewer, as she monitors the child's behaviour and also notes that the slime was a gift from her – reinforcing her later statement that "it's worked out perfectly". When she ends the narrative by describing her child as being "as good as an angel", she bookends both the story of the social worker and the resolution of the slime incident, illuminating how ordinary and extra-ordinary aspects of family lives are interwoven in the everyday.

Enduring kinship?

In understanding the complexity of kin connections – and what 'counts' as family, or not – it is important to recognize that for several people across both samples, biological family was associated with significant risk. Some people had changed their names to avoid being followed up or identified by biological relatives.[4] And for many, as discussed further in Chapter 5, family was simply unreliable or even absent. As Alicia (Pause evaluation) commented: "I don't know, my family are quite (...) they're important me but I don't care, like it's mad. They're not there for me so I kind of had to cut the strings from a few aprons and that." She explained that she had not spoken to them for more than two years and that relationships she described as "always rocky" had broken down completely since her child had been removed. In Chapter 5, we go on to discuss care and connectedness, thinking about the possibilities and limits of support from family. For Alicia, this kind of caring connection was unequivocally absent. As she said: "I've got friends but not *(long pause)* I don't have anyone that I trust my life with." Similarly, when presented with the life-chart task, Louise (Pause evaluation), observed, "'to be fair with family, my biological family is next to non-existent in my life". She did highlight a former foster carer as someone who felt like a mum to her – a woman who had been her sibling's foster carer and had looked after Louise for a few months as a teenager – but it was not apparent from our interviews over time that this relationship was significant in her everyday life. At the time of our first interview, following issues with non-payment of benefits, Louise was reliant on a relatively new partner to provide financial and housing security. Asked how she managed financially, she said:

'That would be my boyfriend. He gets a decent amount of money from his job at [workplace] so with me staying with him until the flat's sorted [...] he sort of provides for both of us food-wise and otherwise. He basically buys food and keeps us both stable and in good living condition. [...] Thank goodness I have a lovely boyfriend.'

As we have written elsewhere (Boddy et al, 2020b; Boddy and Wheeler, 2020), it was common for women in the Pause evaluation to be living with housing and financial insecurity and this was often a key focus for their work with their Pause practitioners. However, in the context of our present discussion of what 'counts' as family, the experience of women such as Louise and Alicia makes clear the limits of 'corporate parenthood'. This was also starkly apparent in the experience of James (*Against All Odds?*) who had multiple placements before leaving care and spent a year living in hostels before ending up in a young offenders' institution. His description of his time there highlighted his need for practices of care: "And as much as I hated it, I also liked it because I was getting fed, I was getting a routine, I got clothes, I got washing done for me, a bit of education." This structure disappeared abruptly, as James was released with a sum of cash, a 'discharge grant', on a bank holiday weekend:

'And I had a discharge grant (.) which was just spent on drugs and alcohol. I didn't have any accommodation to go to. I was being released with no fixed abode. [...] I went to social services and I asked them for help. I asked them for £70 for a key, for a deposit for a key at a YMCA hostel and they said, we don't owe you anything, James. So they turned me away. And I won't forget it (.) the lady, the duty social worker said that to me. And I don't know (.) I think (.) I probably (.) I don't know how I asked her. Maybe I didn't ask her in the best of ways. But it did feel to me after that that was her response.'

Wilson (2018, p 1214) writes of 'the violence of the "seething absences" associated with several participants' disorienting experiences of leaving care', and this is vivid in James's narrative. His hesitant caveat – "Maybe I didn't ask her in the best of ways" – begs a stark question. Whose responsibility is it to ensure that the functions of family are fulfilled for care experienced young people such as James? Was it *his* responsibility, to be the right sort of young person, asking in the right way? The Department for Education's statutory guidance on the Children Act 1989 suggests otherwise: 'The objective of planning for permanence is therefore to ensure that children have a secure, stable and loving family to support them through childhood and beyond and to give them a sense of security, continuity, commitment, identity and belonging' (Department for Education, 2015, pp 22–23). This guidance implies that the state has responsibility *beyond childhood*. But that responsibility was not apparent in the experience of people such as James, Alicia and Louise. While the rhetoric of corporate parenthood refers to 'acting as any good parent would' (DfE, 2018, p 8), their narratives show that there is no automatic or ineffable affinity of kinship that endures beyond the limits of legal provisions for leaving care support.

Ineffable connections and boundary moves

Mason's (2018) conceptualization of 'ineffable kinship' considers the ethereal nature of connections and questions about relatedness. She writes of 'questions that can be seen to be fascinating and troubling about family resemblance, heredity and relatedness, and where matters of affinity are central' (Mason, 2018, p 60). Questions of kinship are especially complex when relatedness spans placement and biological kin, as in Ashley's account. They were eloquently addressed by William, who was 30 years old when we first interviewed him for the *Against All Odds?* study. He entered care as a toddler and grew up in a long-term foster placement; he lived with his biological siblings and the biological children of his foster carers and had very little other contact with his birth family (although one of his older siblings did have some contact for a period). In his first interview, he spoke about his foster mother's "belief in treating me like her son", and noted that: "In a way I didn't feel like I was in foster care as a 14-year-old or a 15-year-old or a 13-year-old. I knew that [foster mother's name] wasn't my birth mum but I just chose to not think about it, but then actually I just blanked it out and I think for me that's probably dangerous that I just denied it." At the time of our first phase of interviews, William was trying to learn more about his birth family, including his mother who is no longer alive. He took a photograph to show how 'family' is positioned in his sense of self (Figure 4.1).

Figure 4.1: William's picture of 'Two Moons'

His explanation of this metaphorical image in his second interview evokes Smart's (2011) conceptualization of the imaginary as a resource for making meaning:

> 'I was just walking down the road and I looked up and it looks like there's two moons. This is the [street]light. So it looks like there's two worlds. [...] So this is like, this is the [street]light which is man-made by a person. For me that is about my foster family [...] I don't know where that [actual] moon is, and I can't get there cos it's ... you'd need a rocket to get up there. You can't touch it. I can see it – it's there! *[laughs]* I can see it, but I can't be there. [...] I'm happy not to get there, but I'm happy to see it. I'm happy to see it as much as I can, and think about it and write about it and look at it. [...] This is a person who was raised, by people. The nurture is here *(streetlight)* and my nature's here *(moon)*. [...] And that's who I am right now.'

William's reflection on the image shows how he makes meaning of complex family history. In his depiction, the two light sources are equally visible: his man-made foster family and his biological family. The poetic timbre in his narrative – in his repetition, "I'm happy" and the rhythm of his words "to see it […] and think about it and write about it and look at it" – reinforces the critical point that he makes. He does not need to take a rocket to reach the other world of his biological family, but it is nevertheless important to be able to see the two lights and keep the metaphorical moon in sight and in mind. Writing about adoptive identity in young adulthood, Neil et al (2015, p 165) discuss the sense of unease and dislocation that some young people feel at the point when 'the sense of connectedness to the adoptive family and the birth family come together'. They quote one young man in their research describing this as feeling like 'a jigsaw with a missing piece'. William's metaphor of the 'two moons' in his life directly addresses this potential source of tension; the visibility of both enables him to understand "who I am right now".

Across the two studies, family connections were sometimes literally marked on the body through participants' tattoos – for example, documenting names of children for women in the Pause study (see also Morriss, 2018). In the *Against All Odds?* study, Rebecca had a tattoo which simply bore the word 'family':

'I had the idea before care and then I came in care and then the whole time I've been in care I've thought, "Yeah, I'm definitely going to get something that shows that and represents family comes first for me". And I was thinking of different things that could represent it, like song lyrics because my family's into songs a lot, or sort of, you know, just like a tattoo of the different animals that my family likes and stuff. And then I just thought, "Actually it seems very complicated, why not just have the word 'family'?" That is simple and it's exactly what it is, straight to the point. So I got "family".'

Her observation that the tattoo is "simple and […] exactly what it is" is particularly striking because Rebecca's interviews document boundary shifts over time in her understanding of what family is to her. Rebecca was 18 years old at the time of our first interview and had lived with the same foster family since entering care early in her secondary school years. Her younger two siblings had been placed separately to her – initially both together, but this had changed over time as she explained (edited for confidentiality):

'[First sibling] lives in [town] and [second sibling] lives in [another town] but only recently moved there. […] [Second sibling] changed placements a lot so actually it's been a bit difficult. *[Describes second sibling's placement moves]* Right, so they were both in [town] in a foster placement so, you know, a home with a family, and [second sibling] couldn't cope with that. [...] You know, it was too much of a family environment for [them], whereas [they] needed something that wasn't a family environment and wasn't going to be, you know, like a replacement family, whereas [first sibling] sort of more needed a replacement family to make up for what [they] felt [they] was losing. So it was really good for [first sibling] but really bad for [second sibling]. And [second sibling] hated it because [foster carers] were very much sort of "Oh yeah, this is, come into our family, be a part of our family". Which, you know, that would never have worked for me either, I couldn't have someone trying to be my family, you know, if somebody said, "This is your new family," I'd be like, "No, you're fucking not," I'd be really highly offended if someone said that to me, whereas [first sibling] quite liked it. And I think it is a bit of an offensive thing to do for anyone, though I understand that some kids actually like that.'

Rebecca's comment that the idea of a *replacement* family is "offensive" is particularly striking given her account of her foster family relationships later in the same interview. As she wrote her foster carers' names in the 'family' section of the life chart, she explained:

'Oh yeah, no, when I first came in care they weren't (.) I wasn't looking for a family but actually they really are part of my family now, like I really consider (.) Like [foster carers] are almost like aunty and uncle sort of figures, like I am actually really close to them. I very much consider [foster carers] as my family now and like they've been so there for me and they've just been so amazing. And like they never tried to be anything they weren't, they never tried being my family, but they were always still supportive and everything. So yeah.'

Rebecca's description shows the significance of time, through what Wilson et al (2012, p 125) term a 'boundary move', shifting the parameters of family. As these authors note, it is important to recognize the emotional significance of such shifts, highlighted by Rebecca's linguistic turn in the first interview: from "no, you're fucking not" to "actually they really are". But we also see from her narrative that the foster carers were able to *become* family because "they never tried being my family, but they were always still supportive".

By the time of her third interview, Rebecca was 19 years old and living away at university. She showed photographs from the wedding of her foster carers' biological child, pointing out that she was the only one of the family's foster children to attend the wedding. Rebecca's interviews show that she has incorporated her foster family in her understanding of 'family', although she does not see them as parents and they are not a 'replacement family': their relationship does not negate the strength of her connection with her biological kin. In line with Wissö et al's (2019) research in Sweden, Rebecca did not present herself as feeling 'torn' between her biological and placement families; her account is differentiated but there is no ambivalence or ambiguity. The single word 'family' tattooed on her skin encompasses this reconciled duality – evoking William's metaphor of the two moons in his life.

To understand Rebecca's boundary move around 'family' it is important to consider what enabled her change of perspective. In her first interview, she explained that she was initially placed through an emergency arrangement. Until a court order was in place – which took a year – "I didn't really know if I was coming or going, didn't know if I could settle or not". She said that feeling settled took another year and a half:

> 'Just building a relationship with them and actually realizing they weren't going to just drop me, that I wasn't just going to move on to another placement if they got bored of me. It was very much just learning that I always had a place there. Which they told me, when I come back from uni I've got a place there, you know, if I ever need a home I've got a place there, so it's nice.'

Her account resonates with Biehal's (2014, p 964) observation that a sense of 'belonging' for children in foster families is enabled when 'foster carers not only expect that their relationship with the child will endure, but also act accordingly'. Biehal's analysis shows how this expectation is enacted through family display and family practices, and that was also evident in Rebecca's account, exemplified by an extended narrative about one of her photographs (see Figure 4.2), of her electric toothbrush. Introducing the photo, Rebecca explained:

> 'So this is my electric toothbrush and toothpaste, and something to keep my teeth clean (.) and just like hygiene in general. So at home I was never taught to brush my teeth. And I really had to learn that when I came into care. And now (.) and I had to have (.) I was actually put to sleep to have two teeth taken out and I had two fillings or three fillings about a year after I came into care. So it's sort of, I really do (.) I mean I'm very focused on keeping my teeth clean and everything. Yeah.'

Rebecca's opening explanation highlights the significance of picture, given her pre-care experience. She went on to detail the different facets of the

Figure 4.2: Rebecca's picture of her toothbrush

toothbrush – the function of different brush heads, when she used what, and how the dentist "really went for it" to teach her "what people take for granted, because they learn at a much littler age". The narrative of the toothbrush ended by revealing its significance as a practice of care on the part of her foster carers:

> 'And my foster brother and sister thought it was really weird 'cos my [foster] sister asked for a new phone and my foster brother, I can't remember, he asked for something else that's more expensive, I think he asked for a phone as well, something. (.) We all had like one big gift and then there was a few little ones. Mine was an electric toothbrush as my gift. And then they went, oh, yeah, have one more to go with it 'cause it wasn't like as expensive as like [foster sister's] phone and everything and […] I went with this as well, so it's a step counter. So yes I didn't really go for, you know, these fun sort of entertaining gifts I was just like, right I want a toothbrush and step counter. Like for my oral hygiene and one for my health in general.'

This 'ordinary' family practice, of giving a young person something they want for Christmas, reveals multiple facets of care: the foster carers' generosity with all the children *and* their efforts to ensure fairness through the extra gift of the step-counter watch because the toothbrush cost less than the presents for the other children. The gift of a toothbrush – seen as 'weird' by her foster siblings, but important enough for Rebecca to photograph and explain in depth during her interview – demonstrates her foster carers' respect for her wishes and for the importance she attaches to care for her dental and general health. Her account is consistent with the conclusions of Schofield and colleagues' studies of long-term foster care (for example, Schofield and Beek, 2009; Schofield et al, 2012) and their observation that carers' capacity to reflect and put themselves in the child's shoes was key to ensuring that unrelated foster care could offer the qualities of permanence (Schofield and Beek, 2009). In this sense, we see how Rebecca's boundary move – becoming settled and establishing a sense of family – is enabled through traditional family practices *because* these are practised with a lifeworld orientation (see discussion in Chapter 3 and Grunwald and Thiersch, 2009). This distinction also helps understand the difference between Rebecca's experience and her earlier criticism of her siblings' foster carers' exhortation to "be a part of our family". Through the gift of the toothbrush Rebecca's carers afford dignity to her lifeworld rather than simply seeking – however lovingly – to absorb her into theirs.

Family and 'not-family'

In line with Rebecca's critique of the idea of the 'replacement family', other participants in the research similarly highlighted their discomfort in relation to assumed intimacy on the part of foster carers. For example, Louise (*Evaluation of Pause*) described a placement that was intended to be long-term, but ended at her request after a short time:

> 'I then moved to another placement that I had for two months, that was meant to be long term. That one didn't last, that was more I requested a move, the placement wasn't a good fit I don't like the (.) I'm not really into the whole pet name stuff that people do, the honey and darling and stuff like that. The foster carer they put me with was really into that. That didn't go well so that one was a few months.'

Karen (*Against All Odds?*), who entered care as a young teenager, explained that she had never wanted to be in foster care, because she did not want to live with a substitute family. But she moved through multiple foster placements and placement breakdowns, which led to suicide attempts and a period living in a mental health unit, before eventually she was placed in a residential unit. Her narrative highlights the contrast between her experience of this residential unit where she felt like she was "worth the best" and her earlier experiences after entering care:

'Well, the management there, the staff were so real with you. They didn't give you crap and they didn't enforce the rules all the time. And I mean silly rules (.) some people get on power trips unfortunately (.) I don't know. It just (.) it was clean, and I lived in lots of homes that weren't. I had my own bedroom and I had a lock on my bedroom door so no one was coming in in the middle of the night and stealing things, which happens in some children's homes, the ones I was in. So for me it was like amazing. *(Interviewer: You had your own space that was secure.)* Yeah. And it was my first own space really. [...] And when I moved in, I was allowed to paint my bedroom. And then I had a furniture allowance so I could buy a desk and stuff. And that was really important. So it was good in that kind of thing. And it felt like I was worth (.) the best (.) I don't know how you'd say it, but I lived in horrible places that they put me in. I was put in foster care for ages and I never wanted to be fostered. I hated foster care. [...] And they just constantly moved me from foster care to foster care to foster care, trying to find a placement that would work and not break down. So when they put me in there it was the first time I felt that they'd listened to me and listened to what I wanted, which was accommodation in a home actually, in a children's home, not a family. I didn't want to live with a family.'

As indicated in Karen's comments here, the sense of belonging and the family practices that Rebecca described were not universally experienced by participants who had lived in foster care. Karen gave an example from one of her 15+ placements which highlighted that the markers of 'not-family' were sometimes beyond control. In this case, racist perceptions of her Black foster carers' relationship with Karen, a White child, drew public attention. As was true of all her other foster placements, Karen was clear that she "really didn't want to be there":

'There was loads of foster kids there and it was just (.) I just hated it; I did hate it. And I also really stood out. And I don't mean this in a racist way at all, but because she was Black, if we went to shops and stuff, people would look at us, like why is there a Black man and a Black woman with a White girl; and it was embarrassing. And in the end the foster father, he started wearing a blooming ID badge whenever we went out because the amount of times, we would be in like a chip shop – I remember being in a chip shop and a woman asked me if I was OK and did I need the police, because I was with this older Black man. And he started wearing his ID to say that he was a foster carer. And things like that were so embarrassing, so embarrassing. I just didn't want to be there.'

Her example shows how the possibilities of relational connection through an ordinary family practice – the child going with the adult to the shops, or to get fish and chips – are subverted through the racism that the foster carers experience. The foster father's decision to start "wearing a blooming ID badge whenever we went out" is understandable, defending his position through a public signifier of legitimacy, but in doing so he marks Karen as not-family, reinforcing the stigma she feels as a child in care.

Several participants gave examples of what might be termed 'not-family practices' in foster care – practices that functioned to reinforce the foster family's boundaries in ways that positioned the young person as explicitly other and outside. This was exemplified by Max's narrative of starting university. Much like Rebecca, he had entered care early in his teenage years and had lived continuously in the same foster placement until he moved out to go to university. He explained:

'I was there until I was nearly nineteen, so (.) […] Nearly eight years, yes. In comparison to a lot of children I've had a fairly stable teenage upbringing I suppose. That was good (.) somewhat (.) The way it ended kind of (.) it summed up the whole (.) their feelings towards me. What they did at the end I'll never forget. […] Obviously going to uni as a looked after child is quite an achievement (.) according to statistics. And they offered to take me to uni, but they charged me. They wanted me to pay them for them to take me here. Which some people are like, it's a lot of money. But I lived there for seven years, I grew up with them. And then they charged me £125 to take me here, to cover petrol and to stay in a hotel overnight. And they didn't even stay in a hotel overnight, so actually they made a profit for taking me here. Which is an insult because they took their son to uni (…). Yeah, I'm not their son and I don't want to be their son; but they took him to uni a few years ago and they didn't charge him. […] But to do that to me, it just made me realize what I meant to them. I was just money.'

Residential care does not preclude a sense of family, or family practices of care. In the Pause study, Skye described significant instability in her early care experience, before she became settled in a residential placement that felt like home:

'Been [where I live now] for a year, but before I've been there, I've been around the world. Well, not all around the world, but when I first came into care, I was about 12, 13. [*Detailed account of multiple placement moves which culminated in repeatedly running away from out-of-area placement*]. So, they did find me a placement. This was in [*home town*] again, but it was like a bigger care home with more children. There were about seven children in a house, but it was nice because we used to have, like, a shelf full of [*inaudible: nice things?*], and she used to cook, like, all the Caribbean dishes. So, everyone used to be home for dinner, type of thing.'

Skye's description shows how family may still be practised in a residential home with seven children; we again see how a sense of home is evoked by 'ordinary' family practices – full shelves, familiar cooking and everyone home for dinner. But in contrast to Biehal's (2014) observation that a sense of belonging in foster care that was founded on carers' expecting and acting as though their relationship with the child will endure, Skye's experience in her residential home proved less resilient to change in her life. She continued the narrative with a turn in the story:

'That was (.) until I got pregnant. They said I can't stay there anymore. I think I had to go to the mother and baby unit. So, they said I might as well go on the mother and baby unit before the baby came so I get used to it, type of thing.'

Skye's account was typical of many women in the Pause study where the transition to parenthood starkly demonstrated the ways in which placement may be not-family. As Roberts (2021) observes, for women with care experience, becoming a mother commonly initiates the withdrawal and disruption of intergenerational support (see also Chapter 6). Skye's move to a mother and baby foster placement initially seemed positive – she was living with a "lady and her husband" who also cared for their daughter's child. Skye explained that the grandchild and Skye's child got on well and, illustrating the ways in which she was treated as part of the family, she told the story of being taken on "a big family holiday" with the foster carers and her child: "So, they did take us on a big family holiday, but I don't think [my child] would remember because [they] was about nine months, but we went to [describes holiday destination] and then we got our hair done, our nails and whatever. Eventually, we came back to England." However, as Skye continued her narrative, she explained that this initial "nice holiday" led to the foster carers making more travel plans which did not include her and her child:

'So, yes, that was a nice holiday, but eventually, she started booking different holidays to, like, [long-haul destination], but social services were saying that we can't stay in the house while she's on holiday to [place], type of thing, because before, we went with her. She didn't want us coming with her this time.'

As a result, Skye was told that she would have to move:

> 'So, she was explaining that her daughter [...] would supervise us in the house, or whatever, because she is [mid-20s], but they didn't want to allow it. So, they said, "We'll have to move you from there". They didn't want to put me in a mother and baby unit because where I've been fostered for so long, it would've just messed up the whole assessment thing.'

At this point, Skye said she started spending more time in her old neighbourhood (where family and friends lived) and started to come home late with the baby:

> 'So, yes, they were saying I'm coming home late with my baby, and they started taking court proceedings and stuff, and then after a while, they did want to put [child] in foster. Because I had loads of support from my family and stuff, we was like, "[Child] doesn't need to be in foster care". Well, maybe on my mum's side, like, we have a reason not for [child] to be on my mum's side, but on [child's] dad's side, there's not really no problem, do you know what I mean? [...] So, yes, they were just looking for things why they didn't want them to be in the family, but eventually [child] stayed in the family. [Child]'s with [grandmother] now, and that's when they put me in [...] this, shared accommodation, flat-type.'

Of course, it is not possible to draw conclusions from Skye's narrative about the reasons for her child's placement, but her story of the holiday signals how an apparently stable family-like arrangement can be destabilized. The key decisions that shape her life in this narrative – the foster carers who "just kept booking loads of holidays" but "didn't want us coming", and the social services staff who decided she needed to move – make clear that this is *not-family* and not her long-term home. In this context, it seems understandable that a young woman with an uncertain future might be drawn back to the kinship and connections of her old neighbourhood.

The limits of family in care were also illuminated by 16-year-old Charlotte (*Against All Odds?*), who had lived for several years in the same residential home. Completing her life chart, she described two of her residential care workers in the language of family. She asked:

> 'If they're not my biological family but I class them as family, can they still go in family? (*Interviewer: Yeah. Who would that be?*) [Name 1] and [Name 2], they're two people that work at [residential home].

I class [Name 1] as like my second mum and I class [Name 2] as my second dad.'

As consistently positive as she was about these two residential workers, Charlotte's account also starkly indicated how the structural constraints of the residential care system produced instability. At the time of the interview, she had moved out of the residential home and was staying with her boyfriend's family while studying for her GCSEs. She was very clear that this was not an alternative family *or* a long-term solution: "I'm still 16, I still need my own parental figures rather than his parental figures. And if we broke up, where would that leave me? It's not a concrete place to stay. And plus it would probably strain our relationship after a while." Despite these concerns, Charlotte had moved into her boyfriend's home because, she explained, the level of disruption in her residential home made it impossible for her to maintain her studies:

'Every kid we've had for the last year has gone into secure eventually. But that's not a solution. So they said, yeah, we'll move [name of other resident] instead. And they secure her, so she's secured, so I'm all right in [residential home]. Then they bring in another kid, the kid's exactly the same. So it's another two months of that, then they secure her. Then they secure another one and they secure another one. It's not going to fix the problem, it's just going to be a new (.) there's going to be a few weeks' gap and then there's another face doing the exact same thing. But it's not (.) this little situation, it's the bigger picture that's the problem. Kids who are disruptive who are allowed to have severe behaviour problems, mixing them in a home with settled, calm, sort of (.) undisturbed children, which shouldn't happen. But it does happen. But EBD [emotional and behavioural difficulty] homes should be more specific. There should be homes for children who act like that and there should be homes for children who don't act like that. You can't mix a settled, calm, composed kid who's trying to do their GCSEs with a disturbed, troubled maniac. It don't work. It shouldn't be like that, but it is. *(Interviewer: Moving her out and moving another one in isn't going to make your life any better.)* It's just going to be the same situation with a different face.'

Charlotte's analysis chimes with research on residential care and the secure estate, which has highlighted the 'sufficiency issues' that have arisen as significant reductions in the number of secure children's homes (and beds in homes) have coincided with increased demand for specialist places for children with increasingly complex needs, compromising the safeguarding of highly vulnerable young people (Bach-Mortensen et al, 2022, p 4). Williams et al (2020) highlighted concern about the experiences of young people with highly challenging behaviour who are placed initially in alternative accommodation (most commonly a children's residential home) rather than in specialist provision with the expertise to address their mental health needs. But these studies do not address the critical issue that Charlotte highlights. However much the two residential care workers she describes might feel like a second mum and dad, it has become impossible for her to continue living in the placement because of the continuous disruption she describes. The erosion of specialist residential care provision does not only impact the most vulnerable children in the system, as Bach-Mortensen et al (2022) observe. It also erodes the potential for residential care to offer a sense of family, permanence and stability for young people like Charlotte – studying hard, planning A-Levels and aiming for university.

Shifting boundaries and 'chosen' kin

The examples presented through this chapter so far have focused in particular on biological kin or placement relationships. Queer theory's disruption and decentring of the 'conventional heterosexual family' recognizes that 'more and more people live outside its boundaries for significant parts of their lives, and friendship, non-conjugal and non-cohabiting intimate relationships become more important' (Roseneil and Ketokivi, 2016 p 145). This broader attention to relationality is particularly helpful for understanding who counts as family in care experienced lives. This is illuminated by the diverse meanings of family encapsulated by Jo (*Against All Odds?*). Her interviews over time are emblematic of the multiple ways in which family can be recognized and practised, from biological kin to 'furry children' and 'chosen' family. Jo entered care aged 11 years, placed in a kinship arrangement. She had continuing contact with her mother and explained that when she was younger "like I always wanted to go back to my mum. And my aims in life was to get a good job, [and] put her in rehab so she could be my mother again. [...] And even growing up that was what I wanted to do, 'cos I knew she wasn't well". Over time, she said, their relationship had deteriorated and this was in part associated with her mother's repeated suicide attempts, which, Jo said, her mother blamed on the children. Jo had lost contact with her biological father when she very young, but on her life chart she recorded finding him again as a teenager. She commented that this, "probably saved my life to be honest, because I was very depressed then. [...] It gave me somewhere to escape to", from a foster home that was often "chaotic". However, she also suggested it contributed to the subsequent breakdown of her foster placement, despite her foster carers having been the ones to find her father. She said of her foster placement: "I never felt, as a child growing up, that I belonged there.

[...] Because my mum had rejected me, so I didn't feel like anybody kind of wanted me, but then, I found my dad, and to me that was the perfect family." By the time of our interviews, Jo was in her late 20s and the people who she counted as family in earlier life continued to be present, in predictable and less predictable ways. Her relationship with her mother remained very challenging and by our third interview they had limited contact. Jo explained:

> 'And I had spoken to her last year as well and said, look, if you're going to send me these emotionally manipulative messages I'm not going to reply, I'm not going to have communications with you. It's not going to work like that. Which is hard to say to your mum, that actually, you're not my mum.'

Jo's relationship with her father remained very positive and by the time of our interviews Jo had also restored the relationship with her foster mother, which had broken down in her late teens, and when we first interviewed her, she was helping with preparations for a wedding in the foster family. Over her life, Jo also developed new relationships that she described as family. The parent of a college friend, she described as her "chosen mum", and she joked in her first interview that "she knows she is my mum-mum". She lived with them for a few months at one stage and her "mum-mum" helped Jo choose the dress for her own wedding. Of the wedding itself, Jo said: "She was just the superstar of the weekend. There's some pictures of her here as well. So she did the mum thing. [...] she did the mum pictures and (...) [...] And she gave me a foot massage on the Saturday as well when I couldn't walk any more." This account, from her third interview, tells of the other key change in Jo's family relationships – her marriage. At the time of our first interviews, she was living with her partner and his parents while they saved for a house. She jokingly described their pets as their "furry children", and – as was true for other participants who had pets – included their photos in her documentation of their everyday family practices, evoking Gabb's (2011a, p 4) observations about the crucial role of cross-species connections in intimate social networks: 'This may not be the same kind of love one feels for a partner, parent or child, but it is nevertheless experienced as love.' By the final interview, Jo and her husband were in their new home, with "real space to ourselves", establishing the habitual practices of their new family life as "us":

> 'So we choose what's on our television, we choose when we clean up; we choose when we do the washing. Sometimes washing up does get left for a couple of days, but that's just life and it's fun. We don't feel like we're in someone's way if we've left washing up out or there's a pile of washing that hasn't been tidied. It's just not in our routine to

have it all done in one day. We've got a lot going on. So it's nice. We just make it fit around us and our lives.'

Among participants in the two studies discussed in this book, Jo's account was not unusual in the number and variety of relationships that mean 'family' to her. Her relationships with her biological parents and with her foster family endure over time, but they also change. Notably, she describes a critical shift in her relationship with her biological mother, from wanting to help her "be my mother again" to finding the strength to tell her "actually, you're not my mum". The support she draws from her *chosen* family – both her partner and her "mum-mum" is clear. The nuanced distinctions she draws – such as "not my mum" and "chosen mum" – correspond with McCarthy's (2012, p 85) observations about the ways in which the language of 'family' and family relationships is 'invoked precisely to convey that they comprise "something more" than a network of relational individuals, which other terms fail to capture'.

Conclusion

In the epigraph that opened this chapter, Mason (2018, p 111) observed that 'ordinary' people are remarkably good at 'traversing and experiencing everyday life connections between, for example, what we might think of as the genetic, the biological, the social, the cultural, the spiritual and so on, and understanding that there are no walls between these'. That is certainly true of the people whose narratives have been shared here, and their accounts illuminate the complexity of their relational lives. They show the importance of 'family' – and attention to 'what counts' as family – but their diversity gives lie to any notion of the single story of the care experienced family. Instead, we again see the significance of the ostensibly mundane. We see how a sense of family can be engendered through practices of care, enabling boundary shifts over time (see Wilson et al, 2012). But equally, experiences such as Max's underscore how *'not-family'* practices can reinforce stigma and marginalization in young people's lives in placement. This analysis has important implications for policy and practice. The narratives shared here raise critical questions about the extent to which the 'corporate parent' practices family beyond childhood, with the starkest absence most visible for people in their most vulnerable moments – such as when becoming a parent, leaving care, or being released from secure custody. We continue to interrogate questions of inter- and intragenerational responsibility in Chapter Five, as we discuss care and connectedness.

5

'How Can We Not Talk about Family When Family's All That We've Got?': Care and Connectedness

Now Leon has a good system. It took him a few weeks to get it just right but now he could tell anyone what to do to look after a baby in the mornings. Change the nappy (remember to use the white cream or by the second morning the baby's bum is sore). Feed the baby but be careful going downstairs because babies move around in your arms and sometimes they're heavy; if you haven't made the breakfast bottle quickly enough, the baby will start crying again. Put six scoops of baby milk powder in the bottle and fill it with warm water from the kettle. You better taste it to see if it's not too hot. Sometimes if the baby is really hungry, you have to mix in some extra powder and a spoon of sugar. The worst thing is when the baby is sick. That makes a lot of mess and it can take ages to tidy up.

Kit De Waal, My Name is Leon, 2016, p 22

Introduction

We are inherently interdependent beings, reliant on other bodies and networks of support, as Butler (2016, p 16) reminds us: 'Part of what a body is ... is its dependency on other bodies and networks of support'. Participants in both studies gave accounts of family practices of care within and across generations. This chapter draws on these accounts to think about the sharpened significance of family connections for care experienced people, focusing in particular on caring responsibilities.

Thirty years ago, Finch and Mason (1993) observed that the responsibilities attached to adult kin relationships have not been legally defined in Britain since the Poor Law system was formally abolished in 1948. And yet, they noted, social policy continues to assume 'that the strength of family ties, and the sense of responsibility which they incorporate, will be sufficient in most cases to ensure that people's needs are met' (Finch and Mason, 1993, p 9). Since Finch and Mason published this study, a long period of political austerity has changed the shape of the welfare state in England. Cuts to universal and targeted welfare provision have disproportionately impacted families who are already disadvantaged in other ways, as a narrowing of support has coincided with cuts and restrictions on other welfare benefits, increasing rates of material deprivation, labour market insecurity and income inequality for families (see for example Carey and Bell, 2020; Stewart et al, 2021; Rehill and Oppenheim, 2021). In such times, the dividing line of responsibility shifts further away from state obligation towards family as the first line of assistance for financial and practical support. Intergenerational experiences of poverty and precarity are also known to heighten young people's sense of responsibilities to family (for example, Skattebol, 2011).

Finch and Mason (1993) noted that experiences of giving and receiving help within families were common and unremarkable in their research: 'They were seen as a characteristic part of family life. They form part of people's image of what constitutes "a family" and most people in our study wanted to claim that they were part of "a family" of this type' (Finch and Mason, 1993, p 163).

Caring responsibilities were also a common experience for participants in both of the studies considered in this book. This chapter discusses their accounts of the help and support that they give and receive in their everyday lives. The chapter title – 'how can we not talk about family when family is all that we've got?' – is taken from the lyric of a song chosen by one of the participants in *Against All Odds?*.[1] As discussed later, Frank chose this song to represent the importance of family in his life – and particularly, his relationship with his younger siblings. Thinking about the support that people such as Frank provide (and have provided) for siblings and for parents, as children and into adulthood, highlights their agency and responsibilities as young (and young adult) carers and illuminates the significance of family connections in their lives. This in turn has important practice implications for how relationships characterized by complex caring responsibilities might need to be managed and professionally supported, both after a placement is made and after leaving care.

The interdependence that Butler (2016) describes is heightened when the 'protective carapace' of the welfare state can no longer be assumed (Thomson and Østergaard, 2021, p 9) and intergenerational resources become increasingly important for young adults who can rely on them

(Bucx et al, 2012; Toft and Friedman, 2021). In contexts of austerity, giving and receiving help is not only common and unremarkable in family lives, but is essential to everyday survival in times when precarity has been systematically established through contemporary welfare structures for the most economically disadvantaged (Lorey, 2012/2015), such that crises and reliance on help from others becomes routine in everyday lives (Hall, 2019).

Normative neoliberal discourses of an individual biographical transition to independent adulthood are of increasingly questionable relevance for young adults who have been disproportionately affected by the sequelae of the global financial crisis in 2008, including the impacts of austerity politics (see Shildrick et al, 2012; Furlong, 2015; McDowell, 2020; Farrugia, 2021) . As Nilsen and Brannen (2014, np) observed, contemporary young people are not a 'lost' generation; they 'exist in relation to other generations ... they are not free floating isolated age groups in society'. But in hard economic times, when relational interdependence is inescapably important, young adults who are care experienced face distinctive challenges in their relationships with family and the state. They depend on the functioning and entitlements offered by care systems designed to substitute for, or supplement the role of, family, during and after their time in placement (for example, Burns et al, 2017). Their lives may also be shaped by experiences of insecurity and disruption that are specific to the care experience, such as placement instability and associated educational disruption, or abrupt and unstable transitions out of care (for example, Stein, 2012). Their pathways through childhood and into adult lives are also influenced by pre-care experiences such as childhood trauma and loss (for example, Stein and Dumaret, 2011). As we will discuss in this chapter, those pre-care experiences also correspond to complex caring responsibilities for care experienced adults, linked to family characteristics and difficulties that led to their placement – such as parental mental health difficulties or substance use (see also Wade, 2008; Havlicek, 2021).

Throughout this chapter, we will examine practices of care and connectedness within familial relationships – thinking about support *for and from* the people that our participants count as family, and looking back at memories of childhood as well as more recent experiences in early adulthood. Again, we look across the ordinary and extra-ordinary aspects of lives in time, considering everyday practices of care as well as exceptional times.

Sibling connections

In discussing 'who counts' as family in Chapter 4, participants highlighted the importance and complexity of sibling connections. Their experience resonates with a wider literature which documents the significance of sibling relationships for young people in care (see Iyer et al, 2020). Yet Monk and

McVarish (2018) noted a critical neglect of sibling relationships in decisions about placement and contact. They cited research by the Children's Rights Director for England (CRDE 2014 in Monk and McVarish, 2018) which reported that 71 per cent of children in care were separated from siblings who were also in care, and their own research highlighted a lack of attention to ensuring adequate contact between siblings who are placed separately. In the words of one of the young people they interviewed: 'It's like siblings don't actually have rights to see each other but they should have. ... Again, it's all about our rights as a young person, our sibling right' (quoted in Monk and McVarish, 2018, p 45).

Monk and McVarish commented that the lack of attention to sibling relationships for looked after children is mirrored by a wider neglect of the importance of sibling connections in both sociological and psychological literature on family lives. As Edwards and Weller (2014) observed:

> Young people are regarded as passive vessels and power within families is assumed unproblematically to flow from parent/s to child/ren. As a result, in a context where sisters and brothers often spend more time together in childhood than they do with their mothers or fathers, there is a neglect of the complex ways in which children and young people actively shape the gendered and other aspects of their own and their siblings' identities over time and in different spaces. (Edwards and Weller, 2014, p 3)

These authors argue for the need to recognize the significance of siblings' interactions with each other in space and time. The importance of sibling relationships was repeatedly emphasized by participants in our study. Claire (*Against All Odds?*) remained close to her sibling, even though they had never been placed together when in care. The first song she chose to share (see also Chapter 3) was 'Home' by Gabrielle Aplin,[2] and she said this described their relationship:

> 'It's just about being at home not being about the physical things. (...) [...] We've never been in the same placement but we've always been really close and kind of just (...) OK, we may not be at home, but (.) we still get to see each other and we're still together. [...] I don't class myself to have a mum or dad (...) but [my sibling] would, but that doesn't matter. Just because they're part of [their] life doesn't mean it has to be part of my life.'

For many people, including Claire, the significance of sibling relationships was linked to early caring responsibilities. As powerfully evoked by Kit De Waal in the novel *My Name is Leon*, quoted in the chapter epigraph, these participants had either cared for, or been looked after by, siblings prior to entering care. Maria (*Against All Odds?*) commented on the adjustment entailed in no longer having to be the primary carer for her baby sibling after she entered care – moving into a kinship arrangement with her two younger siblings – in her early teens: "I was used to being the adult. I looked after my [sibling] up until [they] was nine months. So I spent all my free time looking after [them] and feeding [them] and stuff, but suddenly [in the kinship placement] I wasn't allowed to do that." Louise (*Evaluation of Pause*) described her experience as a young child, being cared for by her older siblings and helping to look after her younger sibling; the detail of her account echoes Leon's list in the epigraph taken from De Waal's book:

'I was left in my parents' care for eleven years which obviously given they can't […] they weren't able to look after me, they weren't able to reach the requirements of actually providing for a child. I mean, for the better part of my childhood while I was living with my parents, they weren't even looking after me, it was my older [siblings] and for at least half of that when I was actually old enough to start realizing well, this shouldn't be happening, other kids aren't like this […] other kids get better treatment, erm, I ended up helping my older [siblings] look after my little [sibling]. My little [sibling]'s three years younger than me and, you know, for me to look after [them] before I was even a teenager, that says a lot. I mean, we ended up having to bottle, give [them] bottles of milk, you know, literally milk, had to end up getting milk from a carton and warm it up with a bit of hot water so [they] had some, like, warm milk […] because my mother wasn't looking after [them], we ended up having to give [them] baths, change [their] clothes, but it's a case of baths are all warmed up but you need the stuff to go with it, you know, you need […] you still needed the shampoo and conditioner, you know, body wash.'

Frank (*Against All Odds?*) had similar caring responsibilities for his young siblings. He was a teenager, already living in care, when they were born, but in order to look after them, he increased contact with his mother, including staying overnight:

'And she continued to drink with my [siblings]. I brought my [siblings] up myself up until [the older sibling] was five and the youngest was two. It's like, I was there, changing their nappies. I fed them, bathed them (.) I did (…) I used to have sleep contact with my mum. […] So when my [siblings] were born I saw my mum a lot more often. Not because I wanted to see her, but because of my [siblings]. So I basically brought them up myself. […] And then they got taken away from her.'

Frank's siblings were eventually placed in foster care before moving to a kinship care arrangement which was subsequently made legally permanent through a Special Guardianship Order. He said he feels they are only alive now because of the care he gave them, but he also said that it is because of his relationship with them that *he* is alive today:

> 'They are my pride and joy. You know, if it wasn't for them I wouldn't be alive. They are (.) they are (.) I know I've talked about my flat and my job being important to me. But it's those [children] that make me up. It's them that made me who I am today.'

In his second interview, Frank summed up the significance of this relationship through his choice of music,[3] explaining that he chose this song (the lyrics of which title this chapter) because it articulated his feelings for his younger siblings:

> 'This is a song from over the years of me and my [siblings]. [...] They're going to go through dark stages, but they've always got a home here and I'm always going to be there. They're my everything. [...] It's not just a song about them, it's a song (.) about me and them. It's a song how me and them have both progressed, even though we've been away, apart. [...] So it's a very important song. It means a lot to me and the lyrics as well (.) have a meaning to me. [...] I don't play it a lot. [...] But it's a song that doesn't need to be played a lot, you know. It's like you keep [it].'

He explained that he had a vivid memory of first hearing this song while watching a film, and immediately looking it up on YouTube: "And as soon as it started playing I immediately thought about my [siblings] and I immediately thought about the people that I've lost in my life. [...] And that's when I knew. Everyone has their song for themselves. [...] Instantly it was that song; straightaway because it's true." Frank's vivid memory reveals the significance of the moment, of hearing his story in the song, as he explained by drawing on the lyrics: "We have (.) us three, we have come a long way from where we began. And I will tell them all about it (.) when I see them again." In choosing this song and highlighting the 'long way' that he and his siblings have travelled, Frank centres their relationship in his account of himself, foregrounding his identity as a brother and reinforcing the point he made in his first interview – that all three of them are alive today because of his care and the strength of their relationship. Like Maria, Frank also spoke about the adjustment entailed in no longer having to care for his young siblings, despite being pleased that they were settled with his relative:

Interviewer:	Must be really great to see them doing so well now.
Frank:	It's a relief. It was hard because I had to take a step back. They're mine (…) I was starting to develop this kind of fatherly care for them and then out of nowhere they were, in my eyes, taken away from me. (*Interviewer: That must have been hard.*) It was very hard (…) I was happy they was looked after. I knew with my [relative] they'd be perfect […]. Out of the whole family she's the most stable figure. […] For me though it was hard because (.) it was a big adjustment for me because I'd gone from raising them myself for years and now (.) given it to someone else.

This adjustment was made harder for Frank because, he said, social services initially tried to limit his contact with his siblings. He expressed the injustice of this, saying "I didn't cause any of the problems. I've always been (.) done everything I can for them". Fortunately, his relative fought the decision, as he explained: "Because she was very angry with them, the way that I got treated in that area. She turned round and said to them, 'My [relative] ain't having that. If he wants to see them any time he likes, he's going to see them'." Once the Special Guardianship arrangement had been approved, Frank said his relative "makes up the rules now". He continues to have a strong relationship with his siblings and spoke in his interviews about plans such as spending Christmas together.

The experiences of Frank, Maria and Louise and their siblings can be understood in relation to the literature on young carers (see for example, Joseph et al, 2019; Gowen et al, 2021). As Gowen et al (2021, p 121) observe, statutory guidance on the Care Act 2014 specifically prohibits children taking on 'inappropriate or excessive' caring roles. This description seems apt for the responsibilities that participants in our research were managing during childhood, responsibilities that are recognizable in Gowen and colleagues' description of 'global parenting responsibility':

> The term parenting role refers to those duties and responsibilities normatively held by parents in a household such as looking after children including boundary-setting, physical and emotional care, ensuring economic and food security and the safety of the home. Global parenting responsibilities can be viewed as when a child takes on multiple aspects of the parenting role. (Gowen et al, 2021, p 132)

As Louise observed, "this shouldn't be happening, other kids aren't like this". However, Frank's account also resonates with the concerns that Monk and McVarish (2018) document about the neglect of sibling contact. Frank's experience reminds us that concern for the negative impact of caring responsibilities does not negate the need to recognize young people's agency and their understandable pride in the care they ensure, within sibling relationships that Frank says "made me who I am today".

In *Against All Odds?*, 19-year-old Toby provides an example of caring connections between siblings extending into early adulthood, showing how helping and being helped can intersect and contribute to wellbeing in interdependent family relationships. Both his parents had died when he was younger but he continued to have a strong relationship with his sister. At the time of our first interview, he had recently stopped attending his college course, but he described caring responsibilities for his sister's children as key to structuring his day, saying that he spends "most of my day, now, looking after the children, or sleeping. They're my two things I do, sleep and look after the kids". He collected the children from school each day and stayed with them until late evening, and he explained how much he enjoyed being with them:

> 'It's fun, it's fun. I enjoy it, it's (...) They make me laugh and it's easy. They're old enough to look after themselves, so it's not like I have to do everything for them. I make them do most of the stuff I'm supposed to do. Like when I go in I say, "Ok, look, here's my phone, put it on charge. Go do this, go do that". [...] Like, I go, "can you get the plates out for dinner? Get all this, all the food out from the cupboards", and it's set up for me when I go to cook for them. [...] *(Interviewer: So what do you like to cook?)* Home food. Food that is, when you go home to your parents' house, and you sit there and it's cooked, you don't have to do anything, and it's delicious and (.) That is the type of cooking I do. None of this fantasy stuff that looks (...) *(Interviewer: Tiny, square sized.)* Yeah. A plate that big with a cube of food on it *[laughs]*. Nah. [...] Now don't get me wrong, stuff like hollandaise sauce I do use that as well, it's a delicious condiment [*inaudible*], but I much prefer to have Bisto gravy. I do use Bisto gravy a lot, because it has a nice flavour and it reminds me of home.'

Toby had entered care after his mother died when he was in his teens. He continued living at home by himself for a period before being placed in supported lodgings, a process that he described as being "evicted" into a "gut-wrenching, horrible place". His nostalgic reflection that the flavour of Bisto gravy reminds him of home needs to be understood in this context,[4] and his depiction of 'fun' times preparing dinner with his sister's children also sits in contrast to his narrative of cooking in the supported lodgings:

> 'The other young people there were perfectly fine. It's the rules and the staff. So the staff were not nice to people at all. They were only doing

things to watch out for themselves. For example, you weren't allowed to (...), so once you finished cooking you had to wash up straight away. You couldn't put stuff in to soak, because it would bring a mutant rat to the place. *(Interviewer: Immediately [laughing].)* Yeah. So I put that in the sink and go to my bedroom, a rat would be there by the time I'd get back. That's how, that's how poignant it is. And I wasn't accepting of that, y'know, I put stuff in soak because it's easier to clean. But no, so what they said was "if you leave stuff like that, to cover ourselves we'll put it in the bin", my pots and pans in the bin.'

These small stories of cooking with his sister's children and in the supported lodgings show us that eating well is important for Toby. He had a professional qualification in catering and references his expertise in his narratives – as for example, in his comment about hollandaise sauce and his statement that "I wasn't accepting" that it is inappropriate to soak pans before washing up. His experience also resonates with the discussion in Chapter 4, of how quotidian practices within placement can mark experiences as 'not-family', or not home. His relationship with his sister and his caring responsibilities for her children have additional significance in this context – he is not only providing care, but is able to recreate a sense of 'home' and to share his culinary expertise. This can be recognized as a source of significant pride, as well as pleasure, for Toby.

In contrast to Frank and Toby's accounts, Jade (Pause evaluation) described significant rupture in her relationships with her siblings following their placement, and she attributed this to the escalation of difficulties that she faced in her own life. She described her childhood before entering care as characterized by instability: "I grew up moving a lot. My mum, my dad were always arguing so we were always moving. She was always getting into new relationships and sleeping about." When she was a young child, Jade was placed in foster care with her younger sibling, while her older sibling moved in with a relative. She and her younger sibling stayed with the same foster family for seven years, until they were moved "due to violence", as she explained:

'The foster carers were quite abusive towards myself and my [sibling], more me. I took the blame for a lot of things. And then we were moved to [new foster family] and then I was only there for a couple of months and I got kicked out. I could hear my [sibling] screaming one night. "That's mine, my mum got me that." This was Christmas. I went in there, kicked off and they kicked me out. I got moved out straight away, immediately. *(Interviewer: And did your [sibling] stay there?)* My [sibling] stayed, [they] stayed. We was separated. We wasn't supposed to have been. The courts always said that me and my [sibling] should have stayed together, but no, they removed me, separated me and my [sibling]. Since then everything's kind of gone downhill, violence, drugs, criminal record, do you know what I mean? *(Interviewer: So where did you go from there?)* I was still local to my [sibling], but I moved from the foster carers in [place] to foster carers in [place], from the ones in [place] to [place]. I was with them for about six months. I wasn't allowed to see my family at all. I wasn't even allowed to speak to them. I kept running away so then I was moved to [place]. I was there for three years, I think, always in foster care. Always getting picked on, bullied, always running away. Got involved with people, started smoking cigarettes, then I started smoking weed, then I started drinking, getting involved in drugs, and then I started to rebel against my foster carer. I started smashing her house up, and then she moved me out and I was placed in [place], I think. I was there for another three years, two and a half, three years. Didn't like them at all.'

Jade's narrative starkly demonstrates the lived reality of the connection between sibling relationships and the emotional and psychological wellbeing of children and young people in care (see Iyer et al, 2020). In Jade's opening account of her first foster carers' abuse, she spoke of taking the blame – a description which could either evoke her having been scapegoated as the older sibling, or her taking the blame in order to protect of her younger sibling, or possibly both. Certainly, we see her protectiveness in the subsequent episode in her narrative: her response to hearing her sibling screaming. We also see the immediacy of the consequences for her – losing her sibling, against the guidance of the courts – and the long-term impact in her life. Her experience brings to mind Thomson et al's (2002) discussion of critical moments in youth biographies: 'Objective circumstances can only be made sense of in relation to individual biographies and the extent to which different young people have access to the requisite resources to enable them to respond constructively to events and changing circumstances'(Thomson et al, 2002, p 350). Jade's narrative shows how her actions to try and protect her sister are rooted in their shared family biography and experience of abuse by previous foster carers. But her lack of resources and control is evident in the consequences that follow. Her narrative shows her 'living through the consequences of the decisions, or lack of decisions, of others' (Thomson et al, 2002, p 338), as powerful adult others decide that she should be separated from her siblings and prevented from seeing them, with devastating implications for her stability and wellbeing.

To paraphrase Edwards and Weller (2014), young people are not mere 'passive vessels' in their sibling relationships. Discussing young carers, Gowen et al (2021, p 133) also advocate 'encouraging children's agency and active engagement in situations that directly affect them and their families'.

Attending to the importance and complexity of sibling connections for people with care experience means respecting the contributions that young people make to the wellbeing of their families, even if they have no choice and act in response to fear of not or harm or conditions of significant hardship.

Complex and dynamic connections

In Chapter 3, I drew on the experiences of Natalie (*Against All Odds?*) to discuss the role of the everyday in understanding complex family connections. We return to that theme here to consider how relationships that may be complicated and difficult are also fluid over time and can still provide significant support – sometimes in unexpected ways. In a 2018 paper called *Troubling Meanings of Family,* I quoted a Danish policy advisor who took part in our cross-national *Beyond Contact*[5] study of work with families of children in care: 'The relationship between placed children and their parents is never static – it is dynamic. It's important that as professionals we never say "good enough" or "not good enough". It is a difficult relationship – and a different sort of relationship' (quoted in Boddy, 2019, p 2248). The experiences of participants in our two studies show, unsurprisingly, that these complex (dis)continuities continue beyond childhood. This is exemplified by the experience of Anna (*Against All Odds?*), talking about her relationships with her biological father and mother. Speaking about her father in her first interview, she explained:

> 'My relationship with my dad has always been a challenging one up until now. And it goes through phases. Sometimes it's more challenging than others, but there's always an underlying challenge. The bottom line is I just don't understand his life choices. I just don't (.) because the reason that I went into care was because it was at the hands of his (.) my stepmum. And so I grew up never really understanding why he stayed with her and had more children with her and remained in that relationship (…) *(Interviewer: When she was the reason that you (.)?)* Yeah. No matter how hard he appeared to fight for me not to go into care, I can never get my head around why he was staying with someone like that. But you make your own choices in life, I guess. […] I don't speak to him any more, but yeah, there was ongoing contact throughout my childhood, definitely.'

Anna said she always had contact throughout childhood with her father and stepmother and gave various examples of her father's involvement in decisions about her life (for example, in terms of changes in placement), even though, she said, "My dad was just (.) everything that came out of his mouth was a lie". She had no contact at all with her birth mother through this period and finally met her for the first time when she was a young adult, after she persuaded her father to give her mother a letter. She explained what happened in a detailed narrative (edited here for confidentiality):

> 'Yeah. So I was there and I (.) I remember (.) there was one day that I was going to meet her and then she didn't turn up because she had to go and get her hair done or (.) I don't know. So she didn't turn up and I was like, so all that build up and I was like (.) oh, OK. OK.'

Continuing her story, Anna described a subsequent meeting as anticlimactic, but a more difficult encounter was to come:

> 'So yeah, she came and I met her and (.) as I said it was a bit of an anti (.) it was like (.) oh, OK. But it wasn't emotional. I don't know (.) and the thing is, I wasn't expecting anything. There was nothing that I could tell you that I was imagining. But it was a bit (.) oh OK. [...] And then she came in the sitting room and we sat and spoke and that was that. And it was just (.) oh. *(Interviewer: Did it feel like a let-down?)* That didn't feel like a let-down. What did feel like a let-down was (.) some time after that, a few days after that I went to her house and stayed the night I think. And this was the first time that we could have (.) this was the first conversation that we could have just us. And I grew up always thinking like, ah, if my mum knew what was going on. If my mum knew what [stepmother] had done to me, and all this, my mum would defend me. If there's anyone in life that would defend, it's supposed to be I guess your parents. And my dad didn't do a very good job of that. So I thought, my mum (.) and yeah (.) the first conversation, she asked me for money basically. And that really hurt me because I thought, actually you have no idea what my life is, you have no idea what my life has been. And it's like you don't know, but I have had to work my ass off to get to the position that I'm at. And I pay all my bills, I pay all my rent (.) I pay for everything. I don't go to (.) there's no one for me to go to. And you're going to sit here, after not having seen me for twenty years, and the first opportunity you get is, that's your opportunity. So that was really painful. And I disengaged after that. I was just over her and over the whole (...) I just wanted to talk to my brothers and sisters; I didn't even care about her.'

As Anna continued this story of meeting her mother, there was a twist in the tale, two years after their first encounter:

> 'And then I went back two years later with a fresh (...) I'd done this really cool personal development course and I was feeling really on top

of the world, different mindset and had a better conversation with her (.) conversations about me and about what had happened to me and my life really. And she then I think, just before we left, confronted my stepmum about it. I was, yes! That was one of my dreams had come through. I felt like, I could die happy now. Because I thought, if anyone has the right to confront this woman about what she has done to me, it's my mum. No one else really. [...] Yeah, it was a party actually (.) it was a birthday party that it happened at, my [relative's] birthday party. And we went into this room and (.) my stepmum's a lot more shouty and attitudey and fiery. Whereas my mum is very calm and just quiet and chilled. So I thought, oh my God; this woman's going to kill her. But they came out alive (...) I was really nervous. I was super nervous, I didn't know what was going on in that room. I was just pacing up and down. [...] Nothing happened, they spoke and they came out and it was (.) but at least it happened. *(Interviewer: And your mum knew.)* And she felt that she had to do something. And she cared, exactly. Because at first I thought (.) my first visit I was like, do you even care? She doesn't care.'

Anna's narrative of meeting her mother shows the difficulties of trying to establish a relationship after so many years and is consistent with research on the complex experiences and support needs of adult adoptees (re)establishing contact with birth families (for example, Neil et al, 2015; Wrobel and Grotevant, 2019; Sanchez-Sandoval et al, 2020). Neil et al's (for example, 2015) research on post-adoption contact particularly highlights the importance of professional support for young people. In the absence of any such support, it is striking that Anna notes how a "really cool personal development course" (which she had taken through work) helped give her the resources to manage a difficult conversation with her mother.

While Anna initially says she was not expecting anything, we can discern her image of the 'family she lives by' (see Gillis, 1996) and more specifically, her 'common sense' ideology of what motherhood *should* mean, in her account of the three encounters. As Gillis (1996, p 152) writes, 'We simply cannot believe that in giving birth a woman does not also give birth to herself as a mother'. It is clear (and we might think entirely reasonable) that Anna expects her mother to prioritize their first meeting over a hair appointment and, equally evident in her account, that Anna was not expecting to be immediately asked to provide financial support. The final episode in her story reveals the power of her image of what a mother should be, as one of her "dreams had come through' and she says, 'I could die happy now. Because I thought, if anyone has the right to confront this woman about what she has done to me, it's my mum".

Figure 5.1: Anna's photograph of her stepmother's wax print dress

In the light of these comments, it is striking that two of the six photos that Anna took were, indirectly, of her stepmother (see Figure 5.1) – close-up pictures of an African wax-print fabric. After an exceptionally busy couple of weeks, Anna evidently struggled a bit to remember why she had chosen to take these pictures, but introducing the pictures, she said they represented "my heritage and roots". She went on:

> 'I'm trying to remember if it was (.) because I don't think it's one of my own ones. I just can't remember for the life of me what this pattern is and where it's from. […] I think it's a fabric as opposed to a dress or something (.) I think. And I really liked the colours and the print and […] Oh no, I remember it. It's at my stepmum's house. I was at my stepmum's house, so it's her dress. And I like the fabric and I had the camera in my bag, so I took a picture of the fabric because I thought it was really vibrant and colourful and (.) yeah. […] So like I guess, my home home. […] I feel, although I'm not like super-connected to [country where I was born], I still know within myself that's where my roots lie.'

Her choice of photograph highlights two particular considerations in understanding her ongoing complex connections with family. First, given her earlier account of having entered care "at the hands of my stepmum", her account of photographing the dress while at her house might seem surprising.

But her stepmother's house was also where she would meet up sometimes with siblings that she described as "a big driving force for me". The experience of participants in both our studies show that relationships often endure even if they have difficult histories, and this was true for Anna too.

Second, her picture of her stepmother's dress highlights their shared connection through Anna's country of birth.[6] Across her interviews, Anna detailed the complexity of her understanding of her national and ethnic identity. Of Black African origin, she had experienced several placement moves that she said were linked to attempts at matching foster carers to her ethnic origin. After living for several years with a Black Caribbean family where she said, "I know that they loved me and they wouldn't want me to go anywhere else", Anna was moved to live with a family from the same African country as her biological family, "leaving the only real family that I know in this country (.) and they were the family that saw me through the hardest parts". She was extremely unhappy in her new placement, expressing doubts that the foster carers had been properly approved, and commenting on the impact on her behaviour and wellbeing:

> 'I wanted to run away (.) All I guess the stereotypical makeup of the teenager in foster care, that's how I was in this placement. I was ready to run away, I was rude, I was (.) because I was unhappy. I felt isolated, I felt alone, I felt neglected, I felt (.) like I wasn't wanted (.) all of those feelings in that one placement. It was so unnecessary, but it was OK because they were [from African country].'

After this and subsequent placement breakdowns, Anna eventually returned to her first foster family. Her song choice was one of their family songs (Rockaway, by Beres Hammond[7]), as she explained, "you know you've got songs that your parents listened to". But she also described it in terms of their Caribbean cultural identity, as "a standard Caribbean song that you hear at any Caribbean wedding or party or whatever", and she referenced the nostalgia in the lyrics that speak of "perfect days where we used to rock away". Considering her song choice alongside her photo of the wax print worn by her stepmother, we can see how Anna's understanding of what is important in her life incorporates both her African and Caribbean family identities. Both were complicated – for example, she said her return to the Caribbean family was "bittersweet". Nonetheless, both families were visibly present in her everyday life and were highly significant to her understanding of herself.

Parenting responsibilities?

Unsurprisingly, given the reasons that can lead to a child's placement in care, the 'global parenting responsibilities' (Gowen et al, 2021) discussed previously in terms of sibling relationships were also sometimes apparent in people's narratives about their relationships with their parents, or parent figures, including ongoing responsibilities in their lives today. In the Pause evaluation, Maya's interviews over time revealed complex and changeable relationships with her biological mother. She said both her parents had significant and chronic mental health conditions and that her mother was not at all involved in the first years of her life. She was placed in kinship care as a young child, but subsequently moved because she was being abused by one of her kinship carers.

At the time of our first interview, Maya described a close and supportive relationship with both of her biological parents. She was staying with her mother, having recently been forced to move out of her flat owing to her former partner's violence. Early in the interview her mother called to check she was okay and as we were ending the interview she chatted about the chicken fajitas that her mother was cooking for their dinner. She also spoke of ordinary practices of care on the part of her father, describing him doing "what any parent can do in that situation" when she went with him back to her flat for the first time:

> 'I went there the other day and literally within five minutes of being in the house I was on the floor crying my eyes out and wanting to leave. *(Interviewer: And did you go and do that on your own?)* No, my dad was with me at the time. And obviously, he was really supportive and he just done what any, well, what any parent can do in that situation and it worked, worked perfectly well, you know, I had a good little cry and then I realized life's too short for all this crap.'

Her comment that "obviously, he was really supportive" implies taken-for-grantedness, and her subsequent interviews indicated that this relationship continued to be close. For example, in her second interview, she shared photos from her phone of her new flat, explaining that she and her father had worked together to lay the floor: "Yeah, I basically laid it myself. My dad done all like the jigsaw bits and stuff, and then I done all the laying down of it and stuff." Yet in the same interview, she explained that she had recently realized she needed to end contact with her mother after an incident when her mother became abusive because she had not been invited to the birthday of Maya's sibling's child:

> 'But she basically started calling me a cunt for it. She's a very contradictive woman, very contradictive woman. She's calling me names about it. On my [adopted child's] birthday, where I can't see my child, the next day she rung me all apologetic and going, "I'm really sorry Maya, I'm really sorry, it's not your fault. It's not your fault

that our relationship is like that". And then the next day still calls me more names over it. So at the moment I'm just like, "Do you know what, you can keep your contradictive self to yourself because I've got bigger and better things that I need to deal with". Like I can't keep sitting there and not dealing with what I need to deal with because she's getting upset over certain situations. I'm her child, not her parent. But again as [Pause practitioner] always used to say to me, she always used to say to me, "Maya, you need to remember, your parents don't have the parenting skills that you are looking for and they won't be able to help you like you want them to help you because they don't have them skills", which I understand, but it's still not going to stop me from sitting there and thinking, "You're a fucking idiot". Like do you know what I mean? It shouldn't be a child that's parenting a parent. […] I look at my mum like I have to parent her, I have to be around her to make sure that she's doing things properly. It shouldn't be like that. It should be her ringing me to make sure I'm okay. But I just can't be bothered with it anymore. […]'

Continuing her account, Maya gave a backstory to their relationship which evidenced her lengthy efforts to establish a positive relationship with her mother:

'Don't get me wrong, I fought for that relationship with my mother. […] She didn't bother with me for […] years of my life. […] I was going to Adfam and sitting in group meetings about dealing with family members who are drug and alcohol misusers just so I can have a relationship with her [as a teenager]. No [teenager] should be sitting in a group full of people that are talking about alcohol and drug misuse. No [teenager] should be doing that. If my child ever ends up having to be in that predicament, sorry to say it, I would cuss myself so far down that my depression probably would kick in, because how can you allow your child to feel like that? How can you allow your child to sit there and feel the necessary need to go and sit in support groups in order to have a relationship with you? It's not fair.'

The comparison she draws between herself and her mother – "If my child ever ends up having to be in that predicament" – is particularly important to understand given Maya's efforts to manage her identity as a mother-at-a-distance to her own children. Her oldest child is adopted and she has regular contact in her own home with the younger one, who lives permanently with a family member. She described her flat as full of toys, oriented to her youngest child's visits, but as the following small story illustrates, she also took care to ensure that her older child was part of her regular family practices:

'Last week it was my [older child's] birthday, the one that's been adopted, and don't get me wrong, I had a little cry in the morning, just to myself, and then I got up, I had a few visitors. I had pancakes and bacon for breakfast and made a cake and put, '[child's name], happy birthday,' on it, and took loads of pictures, so then when [child] does come home I can explain to [them], "Okay, look, this is what Mummy's done every year for your birthday. This is what Mummy's done for you every year for Christmas". Or even down to just keeping the letters that I write to [child], so then I can then turn round and say, "Well, hold on a minute, babe, I did think about you. These are the letters that I sent to social services and then these are the letters that I kept for myself".'

In Chapter 6 we will turn to discussing experiences of parenthood for people in the two studies. As with Maya's example here, many women in the Pause evaluation were engaged in practices that situated their relationships with their children within their everyday lives and imagined futures (see also Morriss, 2018). Maya's language shows this future as definite – "when she does come home" – but also emphasizes the intimacy of their connection in her reported talk, as she refers to herself as "Mummy" and her child as "babe". This loving language sits in stark contrast to the way her mother spoke to her and she sums up her understanding of the difference between them when she explains that "it shouldn't be a child that's parenting a parent".

Austerity and interdependence

> We can see here a quite disconcerting aspect of longitudinal study, the impossibility of analytical closure, new rounds of data can provide new perspectives and render earlier interpretations redundant.
>
> Janet Holland and Rachel Thomson, 'Gaining perspective on choice and fate', *European Societies*, 2009, p 460.

Maya's stories over time about her relationship with her mother show the impossibility of analytical closure, as Holland and Thomson (2009) note. We cannot conclude that her relationship with her mother is good or bad, supportive or unsupportive – only that it is complicated and changeable. The longitudinal nature of the material makes it possible to appreciate this dynamic complexity. The experience of Hannah, also in the Pause evaluation, shows how welfare politics intersect with this dynamic process, impacting family relationships that can be simultaneously challenging and supportive.

Like Maya, Hannah described an ambivalent relationship with her biological mother. She listed her as one of the key people in her life, but when discussing her own recovery from drug addiction, she discussed her own struggles in comparison to her mother's difficulties:

'I'd rather, you know, struggle through life with my emotions and whatever and know when I'm older and [my children are] older they'll think like, at least my mum tried, she didn't just give up and feel sorry for herself like my mum did. But I understand why my mum did, I love my mum, I forgive her, but I just don't want to be like her. I want to be better.'

Hannah's relationship with her mother was also tied up in mutual financial and practical support. It is well established (for example, Galloway et al, 2018) that people with mental health difficulties experience discrimination in accessing targeted benefits for chronic health conditions and disabilities, and this is reflected in Hannah's experience. When she started working with Pause, she was surviving on basic benefit entitlements that she said amounted to £170 to £190 on average a month: "I know, it was really like is this for real? I couldn't believe it was right". By the time of our first interview, things had improved somewhat. With the support of her Pause practitioner, she had secured Employment Support Allowance (a means tested out-of-work benefit for people who have limited capability to work[8]), but she had been unsuccessful in an application for Personal Independence Payment[9] (PIP), which provides financial support to people who need help with everyday life because of a long-term illness, disability or mental health condition. Consequently, Hannah and her mother had applied for Carer's Allowance[10] (a means-tested benefit payable to those who spend at least 35 hours a week caring for someone), as she explained: "And that's when I applied to be her carer so that I could at least get some money, yeah".

Hannah's interviews over time revealed the particular demands of this financial dependence and caring responsibility. In her second interview, asked how often she visited her mother, she documented a list of responsibilities:

'Every day near enough, unless like I'm really knackered out. Like today I won't go because I've done too much. But sometimes my mum's got a car so she'll come and get me, which makes it a lot easier. So yeah, I'll either go to my mum's, go to my appointment, and then I will stay there for a couple of hours. If I'm at my mum's, I'll help her with her appointments, shopping, cooking, washing, ghosts, whatever she wants. She's obsessed that she's got ghosts. But yeah, whatever it is she wants.'

The final item in her list of quotidian tasks – "appointments, shopping, cooking, washing, ghosts" – illuminates the demands of this relationship. In the same interview, she highlighted the difference that her experience of professional support through therapy had made in helping her navigate the tensions involved:

> 'It's made me be able to handle my mum and I's relationship a lot better, because she is a difficult woman, she's got her own mental health problems and I'm her carer so I have to deal with her, and I used to get angry and blow up and react whereas now I know how to breathe and like get rid of the tension in my body. I know how to basically calm her down, validate her for her feelings but don't validate her behaviour. So it is helping.'

But by her third interview things had become more difficult again and Hannah's mental health had deteriorated. This was partly related to incidents not detailed here to protect confidentiality, but as the following exchange shows, it was exacerbated by her caring responsibilities:

Hannah:	My mum she's really stressed me out recently, the more I've seen her the less I've gone to therapy and she's really caused me a lot of stress. […] It's just crazy, obviously she's my mum but she is crazy; if I don't answer the phone quick enough sometimes that's the problem.
Interviewer:	So she gets very angry?
Hannah:	Yeah.
Interviewer:	You were seeing her just about every day I think weren't you?
Hannah:	Yeah.
Interviewer:	Are you still her main carer?
Hannah:	I am at the moment but I went to my doctor's and I said I can't do it, she's stressing me out and stuff, I'm starting to hear voices and have hallucinations.

Hannah's account of her conversation with her GP made clear that her financial dependence on Carer's Allowance was complicating the situation: "My doctor said she will help me with that. She basically said that I can stop being my mum's carer and that she will tell them that I can't do that, like not to make me go to work right now." With the support of her GP, Hannah applied for PIP again and by the time of her final interview she had been successful on appeal – "I fought against PIP and I won" – with payments backdated two years. She was supported in managing this lump sum by her mother, who "helped me spend it on the right things, things that are going to last". She was making improvements to her council flat, including replacing her fridge and a cooker that had long had only one functioning ring. In this final interview, she reflected on their relationship:

'It's still quite difficult. But it's always been like that, and I think it will always be like that. One minute we're good – like me and my mum we go through an emotional rollercoaster about 20 times a day. When we're together like we'll laugh, we'll have loads of jokes, and then we'll argue. So small amounts. At the moment she's helping me, so I've got to see her a big amount, so it is quite hard, but I appreciate it.'

While Hannah's relationship with her mother "will always be like that", her experiences over the course of our research also shows how effective professional and financial support had helped her to manage the "emotional rollercoaster" – both in terms of her financial entitlements to benefits related to her own chronic health needs, and in terms of the support of key professionals. Equally, her interviews show the negative consequences for her wellbeing when she and her mother were forced by poverty into a position of heightened stress and financial interdependence, because she was not awarded the benefits that, ultimately, it is clear she was entitled to. This is the lived experience of austerity politics (see Hall, 2019).

The possibilities and limits of family support

In a cross-national analysis of data from *Against All Odds?* (Boddy et al, 2020a), we drew on Vygotsky's (1978, p 85) metaphor of 'scaffolding' to think through the importance of kinship connections for navigating biographical transitions that are not specific to care experience – building on his argument that considering 'what children can do with the assistance of others' illuminates capabilities that cannot be understood when focusing only on what they can do alone.

It is perhaps unsurprising, especially given the material discussed earlier in this book, that accounts such as Hannah's and Jade's describe support from family members that was sometimes ambiguous or ambivalent. Participants often relied on support from family members, especially in the absence of formal or professional provision, but the extent to which support could be relied upon was variable. In this section, I present two examples – one from the Pause evaluation and one from *Against All Odds?* – to highlight the how family support enabled young women to navigate through difficulties in romantic relationships.

In the *Against All Odds?* study, 19-year-old Sophie explained that she had spent much of her childhood in a long-term foster placement which was made permanent through a Special Guardianship arrangement. In her first interview, she described "a year where everything fell apart, to be honest". Starting university, she moved out of her long-term foster home into a nearby city and university accommodation:

> 'It was really expensive and [...] I ended up moving in with five other girls, which wasn't great because they were all so bitchy and like they all had like boyfriend troubles and one of them was really horrible and mean and like I was just having the worst year of my life.'

Around that time Sophie broke up with her long-term boyfriend and within a month she had moved in with a new boyfriend, triggering a further period of instability. She described this relationship as a "mess", and they broke up when she found out he had been unfaithful. They had very recently rented a flat together and Sophie described her foster family playing a crucial role in helping her out of a complex and potentially costly situation:

> 'So I just said, "Oh I'm walking away from it, like he's instigated the break-up, he caused like all of the hurt". [...] So I had like a little squad, like my little family, and my [foster] mum and dad and then [sibling] and [their] fiancé, all come up in their cars to collect me and all my stuff.'

After staying with her foster sibling for a while, Sophie moved into a small flat nearby, where she lived with her pets. Because she was cared for under a Special Guardianship Order she was not entitled to leaving care support and so her foster sibling acted as her legal guarantor, and her foster father helped decorate, because "it was disgusting. Because no one will take a student". But by the time of our interviews, Sophie had evidently settled into the flat that she described as a stable "little sanctuary to come back to", commuting to university in the city.

In the Pause study, Michelle, who described herself as having learning difficulties, lived alone with her dog near her biological family. Across her interviews, she emphasized the importance of this geographic proximity in making her feel safe:

> 'I love it [where I live], there's me and my dog that live there. Got a [breed of dog], she makes me feel safe, even though I did feel safe 'cos I'm not far from my granny you see. We all live [name of area] so if there's anything happening to me or anything like that it's just easier for them to run round.'

The repetition in her narrative shows both how important feeling safe is for her and the role of family in that feeling: she mentions her granny but then broadens her frame of reference with the inclusive phrase "we all live". The importance that she attaches to place and proximity is particularly striking because – unlike Sophie, but in common with many women in the Pause evaluation sample – she had experienced multiple placement moves as a child:

'No, I was originally born [place] which is [name of area], I was born up there and I moved to [place] 'cause I was in and out of different foster homes, been in about 35 foster homes and I've been in two different children's homes, one in [another city] and then got moved back to [inaudible] when I was about nine and then when I was about ten I moved to [area]. From there I lived, it's still a part of [area], I lived in [place] so I've been up [area] since 13 and I do like it up there, they get used to you, your home town.'

Across all of her interviews, Michelle described regular contact with biological family members, referring to seeing her siblings and parents as well as her grandmother. In her third interview, Michelle spoke of a new relationship with a boyfriend that she described as a significant and supportive figure in her life. She had stopped working with Pause by this stage and commented that: "I'm not even getting really support from anyone now, just me and my bloke." But by her fourth and final interview, she had broken up with him after he assaulted her. This traumatic experience had exacerbated her ongoing mental health difficulties and it was clear that her nearby family were a crucial source of support, as she explained in a detailed story about her sibling's children (edited here for length and confidentiality):

'But if I panic or like when I go into a real bad anxiety attack, I sort out my dog, and then I go out and I go to [sibling's] and I stay there. And [they] doesn't like me leaving until [they] knows I'm calm. [...] I calm down there, because I'm around people and they're talking to me about different things. And having a laugh and I talk to my niece and nephew and my nephew's only [age]. And he comes up to me and he goes, he's been doing it quite recently, because he knows something's up with me but I'm not obviously going to say, do you know what I mean? Because I don't want to traumatize the poor kid. And he says to me, "Aunty Michelle, are you okay?" I'm like "Yes, I'm okay". [...] And my niece, she's only [age], and she says, "Aunty Michelle, are you sure you're okay?" And I'm like, "Yes, I'm fine". She goes, "Oh okay, would you like a hug?" I'm like, "Oh, yes please". So they sort of understand when something's not okay and someone's sad or angry. [...] And then they'll say to me, "You're not going home". [...] No, they wouldn't let me go home. Like sometimes I'm saying, "I'm going now" and [niece] goes, "No, you're staying, you're coming upstairs and coming in my bed, sleepover".'

Michelle's detailed reported conversation with the two young children evidences and emphasizes to the interviewer how she is cared for by her family, even as she shows her responsibility in not revealing the reason for her distress to them. Like Sophie, she documents how her family stepped in to support her in this moment of crisis. But Michelle's account, across her four interviews, was also more ambivalent than Sophie's. Her account of her sibling's support following the assault contrasts with her comment in Interview 3, that she was not getting support from anyone apart from her boyfriend. Other material in her interviews indicates the limits of family support in other areas of her life. At the time of our second interview, she was waiting for an appointment for an operation and expressed anxiety about how she would manage the short hospitalization without help:

Michelle: I don't even know no one that can help me with my dog while I'm like this. [...] I've asked and obviously my family can't because they're busy, so.

Interviewer: Yes, so will you just leave her some food or something, what will you do?

Michelle: I don't know because I have to go in the back garden and pick up dog mess and I've got to be bending down and stuff like that and I can't keep bending down, so I've got really no one.

Both Michelle and Sophie rely on support from family when they cannot draw on any professional resources to help them through difficult periods in their lives. But Michelle's experience shows how complicated and variable that can be. Family is a critical source of emotional support following the assault, but at other times, family support cannot be assumed. The contrast in Sophie and Michelle's experiences also highlights a critical question for policy and practice. Sophie's 'squad', her Special Guardianship family, enables her independence as a young adult, scaffolding her move from a vulnerable situation into the 'sanctuary' of her flat. Her experience accords with evidence in the wider youth studies literature of the importance of parental support in young adult lives (for example, Majamaa, 2011; Bucx et al, 2012; Nilsen and Brannen, 2014; Nilsen, 2021). Michelle's biological family is also supportive, but within limits. Her anxiety about managing her operation is focused on the care of her dog; this could be seen as trivial – although it is not for her – but it reveals wider questions. If corporate parenting is 'acting as any good parent would' (Department for Education, 2018, p 8), where are the limits? In her mid-twenties, Michelle was beyond the age of leaving care provision, and by the time of her surgery she was no longer working intensively with Pause, so could not assume their help. Is it fanciful to imagine that supporting a care experienced adult through hospitalization is an area where we might expect the state to provide support? Who will support young adults who have been in care at times when they cannot rely on friends and family?

Conclusion

Nilsen's (2021) analysis of three-generation families in Norway drew attention to the ways in which privileged background is taken-for-granted and unspoken, 'part of the silent discourse' by which 'intergenerational support can serve to maintain ideals of independence in notions of adulthood' (Nilsen, 2021, pp 134–135). Perhaps this 'silent discourse' explains the historic lack of policy drive to recognize the complex, interdependent, intra- and intergenerational caring responsibilities that people with care experience must navigate through childhood and beyond. The analyses presented in this chapter resonate with the messages of the Care Experienced Conference held in England in 2019 and with their subsequent 2021 survey of care experienced people, published in the *Our Care, Our Say* report, which emphasized that support should be determined by need across the life course, not limited by age-specific entitlements (*Our Care, Our Say*, 2021).

The analyses presented in this chapter indicate that support may or may not relate directly to care experience. For example, in Hannah's account of the importance of specialist therapeutic support (helping her manage complex mental health problems and a complicated relationship with her mother) and Anna's evident lack of support (in navigating changes of placement and a new relationship with her birth mother in her 20s), we can recognize needs that are specific to their care experience. The same is true for participants such as Frank and Jade, who specifically needed recognition and support for their caring role in relation to their siblings. But the experiences of Michelle, Maya and Sophie show that even when support needs are not directly related to having been in care, there are factors associated with care experience – notably, the capacity of families to provide support – which have critical implications for young adults' interdependent lives. In their classic text, *Inventing Adulthoods*, Thomson et al (2002, p 343) commented that 'the capacity of the individual to access and to take advantage of resources is implicated in processes of social inclusion and exclusion'. Yet this in turn depends on the capacity of friends and family to provide the resources that young adults need.

In the English government's recently published Independent Review of Children's Social Care, MacAlister (2022) argued for the importance of ensuring that people leave care with 'a loving network of people' around them, with relationships that are clearly much more than just 'nice to have' (MacAlister, 2022, p 144). But – as I will discuss further in Chapter 7 – this may not be enough, especially in a context of political and welfare austerity, when the affordances of professional support are constrained. The experiences discussed in this chapter show the possibilities *and* the limits of loving networks, demonstrating why flexible professional support is necessary into adulthood and what it means when intergenerational support *cannot* be taken for granted.

6

Understandings and Experiences of Parenthood

> The subjective experience of pregnancy and birth is dependent on the personal and economic circumstances of expectant mothers, their positions within families and the intergenerational legacies that come into play as maternal subjectivities are formed. Bodily situations combine with personal histories to locate women differently in relation to norms and discourses.
>
> Rachel Thomson et al, *Making Modern Mothers*, 2011, pp 6–7

Introduction

Phoenix et al's (1991) edited book *Motherhood* set out a conceptual distinction between the *meanings* that motherhood has for women (whether or not they are mothers); the *practices* of mothering, within the circumstances in which they live, and the *ideologies* of motherhood, which they describe as commonsense ideas which shape theoretical work and discourses and which 'help construct what motherhood is considered to be' (Phoenix et al, 1991, p 5). This distinction is useful in thinking through the understandings and experiences of parenthood for the people who took part in our research.[1] It seems obvious to note that, even when separated from their children, parenthood still has significant meaning in people's lives (see also Morriss, 2018). This chapter will also consider how family is displayed and mothering practised at a distance by women who have lost custody of their children. The analysis also addresses ideologies of care experienced motherhood – considering intergenerational support (and the role of professional support and the 'corporate grandparent') alongside experiences of stigma and future imaginaries of family lives.

The chapter is organized temporally and begins by considering experiences of becoming a parent. For the most part, I will talk about mothers, drawing on examples from both studies. All of the women in the Pause evaluation had at least one child, as did four participants in *Against All Odds?*, one of whom became a mother during the course of the study. Only one respondent in *Against All Odds?* was a father and the chapter includes his experiences, while attending to other participants' accounts of fathers' roles and involvement. The second part of the chapter draws on earlier discussions of family display and practices (Finch, 2007; Morgan, 2011) to consider how family is practised *at a distance* by women who have had children removed into care or adoption, considering how they manage and maintain identities as mothers separated from their children, taking account of different permanence, placement and contact arrangements. The concluding section of the chapter will turn to future imaginaries of family and parenthood and includes perspectives from male and female participants (from *Against All Odds?*) who were not parents.

At the outset of this discussion, it is important to emphasize two caveats. First, the participants whose experiences are shared here are not typical of care experienced parents: all the women in the Pause study had children who were living in care, special guardianship or adoption, and two of the four parents in *Against All Odds?* were not living with their children. As discussed later, parents in and leaving care are at increased risk of having children removed from their care, but this is far from an inevitability. Second, in analysing experiences narrated by people in our research whose children had been removed into care or legally permanent arrangements, it is of course impossible to comment on the decision-making about child removal – we only have the women's accounts of their experience. Nevertheless, and in line with other research (for example, Barn and Mantovani, 2007; Chase et al, 2009; Roberts, 2021), our findings clearly demonstrate both their support needs and the stigma and lack of support that they faced on becoming parents.

The state as 'corporate grandparent'?

In the epigraph that opened this chapter, Thomson and colleagues (2011) observed that experiences of becoming a mother depend on personal and economic circumstances, family positions and intergenerational legacies. While recognizing that care experienced parents are diverse, we might add that experiences of becoming a parent depend on the ways in which the state functions within the intergenerational space. The examples in this chapter may not be typical of the population of care experienced parents as a whole, but they help with understanding what happens when the state – mandated to act as any good parent would for a child in care (DfE, 2018) – becomes, in effect, a corporate *grandparent*. To paraphrase Thomson et al (2011), what is the intergenerational legacy of corporate parenthood for people with care experience who become parents? How does the state – through the professionals and systems that are mandated to provide support and/or intervention – shape what it means to become a parent and how parenthood may be practised? How is professional support shaped by 'common sense' discourses of what care experienced parenthood can be? These questions are addressed in the pages that follow.

Intergenerational support has become increasingly important for low-income families in recent years, as the dividing line between family and state responsibilities has shifted in line with the shrinking of the welfare state (see for example, Webb and Bywaters, 2018; Hall, 2019; Hill et al, 2021). Informal support from wider social networks (and particularly family) plays a critical role in buffering against weaknesses in institutional provision and state support: 'With low income households bearing the consequences of this 'risk shift' from social protection to individualised responsibility, they have to rely more on their own resources when faced with difficulties' (Hill et al, 2021, p 20).

For families living with poverty and economic insecurity, the needs fulfilled by grandparental support are not the same as in more affluent families. In the UK, Tarrant (2021, p 117) highlights class-based distinctions in grandparenting practices, contrasting 'being there for children' but 'not-interfering' in middle-class families, and 'rescue and repair' grandparenting in low-income contexts. Citing the example of kinship care, she comments: 'Vulnerable and marginalised themselves, these grandparents provide supplementary and time-intensive care that is often invisible beyond the family and often results in complex and difficult engagements and dependencies'(Tarrant, 2021, p 117). Writing about the US, Dolbin-MacNab and Few-Demo (2018) also discuss this marginalization, arguing that, 'what is needed are critical conversations about the historical and contemporary patterns of oppression that result in grandparents fulfilling a caregiving role within their families' (p 203).

If supportive grandparenting fulfils different functions depending on family resources, this has critical implications for the conceptualization of an appropriate role of the state for care experienced people who become parents. What kind of grandparent is the 'corporate grandparent'? A distinction noted in Chapter 2 is helpful here: Sjöberg and Bertilsdotter-Rosqvist's (2017) Swedish study of young parents contrasted 'be-there-no-matter-what' grandparental support with an 'inhibition' repertoire, characterized by grandparental 'power and control' and assumptions of the 'riskiness' and insufficiency of the young parent (2017, p 325). For young parents, such assumptions are also gendered, racialised and classed; for example, Thomson (2020, p 6) argues that feminist activism has been complicit in the problematization of 'too-young' motherhood, because it privileges 'a particular version of classed and racialised feminist freedom'.

Stigma and intersectionality

> Intersectionality has proven to be a powerful critique of debates, policies and practices that rely on a fiction of mutually exclusive categories, such as 'woman' or 'black', which in fact mask intersecting and interacting relations of domination and inequality, power and privilege.
>
> Leah Bassel, *The Politics of Listening: Possibilities and Challenges for Democratic Life*, 2017, p 18

It is not possible to consider meanings and experiences of parenthood – and support for parenthood – for care experienced people without attending to stigma. As Bassel's (2017) comments here imply, this also requires attention to intersectionality. She argues that attention to intersectionality can help challenge the inaudibility of minority experiences. Naming intersections draws attention to power, privilege and inequalities and thus provides a way of 'speaking against stigma' (Bassel and Emejulu, 2018, p 93). These arguments are highly relevant to thinking through meanings, practices and ideologies of parenthood for people with care experience.

Young people in or leaving care are more likely to become young parents (for example, Barn and Mantovani, 2007; Chase et al, 2009; Roberts et al, 2018; Roberts, 2021); they are also likely to experience a clustering of factors that make life more challenging as a young parent – all of which are also associated with teenage pregnancy and parenthood. As noted in Chapter 2, young people in care disproportionately come from backgrounds of relative poverty (see Elliott, 2020); they are likely to face disrupted education both before and during their time in care (for example, Jackson and Cameron, 2012; O'Higgins et al, 2017); and if they become young parents, they are more likely to experience poverty, because welfare systems such as Universal Credit disproportionately disadvantage young parents. Such inequalities are likely to have greatest impact on parents who cannot rely on intergenerational support from family. Young care experienced parents are also likely to face intersectional stigmatization, associated with being in care and being a young parent, as Roberts (2021) warns in introducing her book, *The Children of Looked After Children*:

> Readers are encouraged to continually consider if the support responses or expectations placed upon parents in and leaving care differ from those of other young parents supported by their families. This includes examining the potential for parents to be stigmatised because of their care status and discriminated against because of their care histories. (Roberts, 2021, p 10)

As discussed later (see also Morriss, 2018; Broadhurst and Mason, 2020), the intersecting stigmatization faced by young care experienced parents is intensified for women – such as the participants in the Pause evaluation – who lose custody of their own children. As Morriss (2018, p 819) writes, 'parenting is collapsed into failed mothering; an intersectional shaming process involving imagined moral flaws of class, gender and sexuality'.

Failure to think about care experienced parenthood in intersectional terms is not only a failure to understand complex, relational lives, it actively contributes to stigmatization: essentializing 'common sense' ideologies of the 'riskiness' of the care experienced parent. Bassel and Emejulu (2018, p 94) quote from the 2013 book *Femmes des quartiers populaires: En resistance contre les discriminations* [Women from working class neighbourhoods: In resistance against discriminations], written by a group of women from the working-class neighbourhoods of Blanc-Mesnil, a Paris suburb, in collaboration with the sociologist Saïd Bouamama. While referring to a very different context, their words are apposite in introducing this discussion of the experiences of parenthood for people who have been in care: 'Our lives are already violent enough for us not to be further insulted. ... This violence of words that we experience does us a lot of damage. It hurts our dignity and barbarises us' (Bouamama and Femmes du Blanc-Mesnil, 2013, p 180; quoted in Bassel and Emejulu, 2018, p 94).

Becoming a parent
Stigma and instability

> An understanding of the social contexts in which particular women live is ... crucial to an understanding of how (and why) early motherhood affects their lives as it does.
> Ann Phoenix, *Young Mothers?* 1991, p 246

Thomson et al (2011, p 92) write that 'new motherhood incites new forms of sociality', and a reconfiguration of relationships. This was apparent for mothers in our sample, but overwhelmingly – and in line with Phoenix's (1991) observations – their narratives of reconfiguration were shaped by the implications of being care experienced, both in terms of possibilities for stability (and requirements for changes of placement) and in terms of the expectations they faced as care experienced women.

In Chapter 4, Skye (*Evaluation of Pause*) discussed her required move, after becoming pregnant, from a residential home characterized by family-like practices (like everyone coming 'home for dinner') to a mother-and-baby foster placement. Skye's narrative had similarities with that of many other mothers in our research, who described losing stability and support after becoming pregnant or having a baby, whether they became pregnant during or after their time in care. Stigma and instability coincide in their accounts. In the *Against All Odds?* study, Rosa said, 'Social services thought I was going to neglect my [child] like my mum neglected me'. She spoke of her experiences as she and her child – who was eventually placed in kinship care – were moved into a mother-and-baby foster placement:

> 'They moved me into a mother and baby placement and she [the foster carer] was going on about how she wanted to adopt [them]. And I said it's not going to happen. So we were there for six months pretty much under the look of that horrible woman, and then we moved into my flat, well, our house, me and [child] and they gave me three months instead of two years. They didn't even give me a chance. I did everything they said and (…) just (…) there's no way I could be like my mum.'

Professional support – the corporate grandparent – was crucial for Rosa in becoming a mother, because she could not rely on informal support from her family. She described a difficult relationship with several family members, who she said just ask her for money. She was closer to one sister, but this relationship could not be relied on for support: her sister had a large family and in fact Rosa tended to help her, for example with babysitting. Rosa's recognition that she needed support is reflected in her later observation that her child's eventual kinship carer had offered for her to move in at the same time as her child, but this suggestion was rejected by the social worker:

> '[Child's relative] offered me to move in with them. I said yes but the social worker said no. *(Interviewer: So it was about having a stable place?)* If they'd have said yes, I would still be with my [child] right now. That is a guarantee. I might have even been here with my [child] by myself. But I never got that chance.'

Of course, we cannot know more than Rosa says about the decision-making in this situation, but her description of 'living under the look of that horrible woman' evokes the 'inhibition repertoire' of grandparent care focused on risk and insufficiency (Sjöberg and Bertilsdotter-Rosqvist, 2017). Her contention that living with her child's kinship carer would have been successful shows that she recognized other forms of support were possible, and she saw the curtailed possibilities for a stable life with her child.

In the Pause evaluation, Alicia's transition to motherhood was also characterized by stigma and instability. She also had to move after her child was born, when she was 16 years old, and it took quite some time and a number of forced moves before she and her child had a secure place to live:

'Yeah, it's been alright, I've always had like a roof kind of over my head with my [child], but with me and my [child] I always had. (...) Because I was 16 and in care they gave me a semi-independent but I couldn't move in there straightaway because I'd just had a baby, so. [...] But they assessed me in hospital and then I lived with [family friend], because before I lived with [family friend], my mum chucked me out when I was five days overdue. But that's irrelevant. *(Interviewer: So you were back living with your mum at that point, yeah?)* Yeah. And then got my own little place. And ever since then, yeah, we've always had a roof over our head no matter what. *(long pause)* It was difficult because when I turned 18 they took my semi-independent off me but they didn't teach me how like what a bidding number was, how to get my own place, so I had to go to a month-only one. Then I went into a B&B, then I went into this place and then (.) a hostel (.) and then I finally got my house. But I've always had a roof over my head. Some people can't really say that.'

Alicia bookends her narrative with a positive framing: "it's been alright" and "I've always had a roof over my head". Yet her account conveys how challenging the insecurity of her living arrangements must have been. In her first interview, she spoke about the stigma she faced as a care experienced mother, and commented: "But I can kind of tell if people want to get to know me or if they've read about me, both; they look at me completely different when I start speaking and I'm like, 'So you judged me on reading about me and you haven't got to know me'." When she and her child were finally allocated a flat, this was marred by difficult relationships with her neighbours from the outset: "From when I walked in everyone was like, 'Oh it's a young person, de, de, de'." She gave a variety of examples of neighbours calling the police for what she clearly saw as unjustified reasons (such as her child crying when she left them with someone so she could go to work). They were subsequently placed in a mother and baby assessment unit, and from there her child was removed into care.

Broadhurst and Mason (2020) observed that the trauma of child removal in the absence of support exacerbates risk in other aspects of women's lives, both in terms of the immediate psychosocial crisis that follows the loss of a child, and in enduring and cumulative effects. The psychosocial impacts of intersectional stigma were evident in Alicia's account, for example, when she spoke of "the smirks on Social Services' faces when they're taking your child off you". A young care experienced mother of mixed White/Black Caribbean ethnicity, she also spoke in her interviews about being seen as "angry". While Alicia did not relate this to racism explicitly, her comments accord with Hamilton's (2022) discussion of the controlling hegemonic construction of Black women, and Black motherhood, through the racist stereotype of the 'angry Black woman'. Alicia's narratives showed how being seen as angry made her vulnerable to the power of professionals, as in the short story she told of an 'argument' that took place at the time of the breakdown of the placement in the mother and baby unit:

> 'As I talk, like I talk a lot with my hands, so [social worker] was like, "Stop pointing," and I said, "How dare you. You know I'm not pointing, you know this is me just talking". I had to show her what pointing was. And then she was like, "Yeah?" "Yeah, I'm not staying here now". And it was just like the power. And that's where I fell a lot because I didn't have a great social worker, the social worker was against me. It was a new social worker, so I felt they had something to prove. No one knew me. And it's crazy because you're dealing with someone's life. Like "I carried my [child] for nine months, I went through [describes serious complications during childbirth] and everything to keep my child and I fought to keep my [child] when I was 16, and now you lot come in and you just take [them] away".'

In this example, Alicia talks of her physical expressiveness being misrecognized as aggression – she is seen as angry because "I talk a lot with my hands". Elsewhere she spoke about being seen as "angry" when she was expressing frustration at not being listened to – evoking Bassel's (2017) comments about the inaudibility of minority experiences. Alicia explained this in the context of a very positive description of her child's current social worker, whom she described as "worth his weight in gold":

> 'And he's learnt to know how I am; I'm very loud, I'm very passionate. People say angry; yeah, it's easy to look at me and say, "Oh she's angry". No, if you listen to what I'm saying you'll actually understand what I've been saying, you'll get to know that I'm not angry. I'm pissed off to be honest with you but [...] if you're not listening then I'm going to get angry. But I'm not angry because I'm just an angry person, I'm angry because you're not listening to me. And when I get angry and then you start listening (...) Okay, so I might as well just be angry so you can listen to me, no? Like put two and two together.'

Alicia's narratives recall Lorde's (1984) writing on anger in *When I Dare to Be Powerful*:

> I know how much of my life as a powerful feeling woman is laced through with this net of rage. It is an electric thread woven into every emotional tapestry upon which I set the essentials of my life – a boiling hot spring likely to erupt at any point, leaping out of my consciousness

like a fire on the landscape. How to train that anger with accuracy rather than deny it has been one of the major tasks of my life. (Lorde, 1984, pp 18–19)

We can recognize Alicia, from her narratives, as a 'powerful feeling woman' with reasons to be angry. And she also spoke about learning to train her anger with accuracy, in discussing how she would like to help other young parents in the same situation:

'I've lived it, been through it, still living it, but I want to be able to help other young women, or just parents anyway, especially young parents. Just don't get angry, get even. You do certain things that they don't expect you to do. They always expect you to get angry. The more angry you get, the more they can go to a judge, "Look how bad this parent is". Don't do that. Stay humble. When you have meetings visualize your child on that person that you want to punch [in the] face. That's what I do, I have to think of my [child]. Oh, I'd have beat up so many people by now and I'm not going to give them the satisfaction of it. So yeah, so. *(Interviewer: So you don't automatically just know those kind of strategies, do you, you have to learn them?)* Yeah, no, you don't, you have to learn them, and it's taken me a long time. But that's all I wanted to do, was beat everyone up when I got my [child] taken off me, just fight the world, it just seemed easier, but it wasn't.'

We will return to Alicia's experiences later in this chapter, as her narratives of her ongoing relationship with her child and their carers show how she continues to navigate motherhood in the context of intersectional stigma.

Misrecognition of motherhood?

As discussed in Chapter 2, Pause as a service is focused on reducing the likelihood of repeated child removal. All of the women in the Pause 'care leaver pilot' (see Chapter 2) had experienced the loss of at least one child into care, special guardianship or adoption.[2] Broadhurst and Mason's (2020) research shows how stigma 'plays out in multiple settings for this group of women – who feel discredited in both interpersonal and professional encounters' (2020, p 15). Within our research, stigma, disruption and the discrediting of women's motherhood was starkly apparent in their narratives of their experiences with later-born children. Ashley's experience exemplifies this, resonating with Broadhurst and Mason's analysis.

In her first interview, explaining her living situation, Ashley told the story of losing her (insecure) accommodation just days after giving birth and having her child removed from her care. The accommodation was tied to a voluntary role with a homelessness charity (who had supported her when she became homeless after the removal of her older children). She was able to stay there while she was pregnant, but as she explained, the arrangement broke down because of their expectation that she would return to work within a week of her child being born:

> 'I moved out, well what it was they wanted me to work three days after I had [child] and two days after I lost [them]. [...] I said no, because of me being upset as well as having [post-birth health complication], I said no. And they said, "Well you're out then. If you can't work down here, then you are out". And I said, "Fair enough then I will. I'll pack my bags and get out". And she goes, "Well that's fine then, blah, blah, blah".'

Ashley's needs as a mother who had recently given birth and experienced the significant trauma of losing a child were rendered invisible in her experience with the charity that had been housing her. We can understand this as *misrecognition,* in line with Fraser's (2001 p 24) definition of the term (see Chapter 1), as her motherhood is rendered 'inferior, excluded, wholly other or simply invisible'. As noted in Chapter 4, Ashley had a complicated relationship with her former adoptive family and it would have been impossible for her to turn to them for support. In the end, she and her partner moved between different homeless hostels for a period, before moving in with her biological mother, where they stayed until they were finally allocated more secure accommodation.

Zoe was one of two women who had a child during our longitudinal *Evaluation of Pause.* Her first child was living in a kinship arrangement and they had regular contact. Shortly before our first interview, she withdrew from the Pause intervention because she wanted to switch to the contraceptive pill instead of using a long-acting reversible method of contraception.[3] At that time, she and her partner (who both had learning disabilities, she said) were living in a local authority flat where they were very settled (discussed briefly in Chapter 3). In her second interview, she explained that she was now pregnant, after a family emergency (not detailed here for confidentiality) meant that she missed taking the pill. During her pregnancy she took part in parenting classes and after the birth she and her partner moved into a parent and child assessment unit where they spent four months. By the time of our third interview, the child had been placed in foster care, following a care order with a plan for adoption.

In her account of what happened, Zoe described the assessment unit as 'intense'; she spoke of rules (such as when it was permitted to cook, and curfews on going out even if the child's other parent was there) and monitoring, noting that their room "had a camera in it so they can monitor us and it was quite (...) I would say it was quite intense with the cameras". Zoe explained that she felt "betrayed" by the people in the placement, "because they said that they had our backs and they go away and say something different in court", and it was evident from her account that she and her partner felt unsupported while living there. For example, she said, "they said that we would need 24-hour support looking after our child when we done it all on our own for four months all they did was observe us".

In common with Rosa's narrative (related earlier), Zoe's account implies her acknowledgement that she and her partner need help to manage parenthood. But her narrative of surveillance without support – exemplified by her use of the word "observe" and her reference to the camera – highlights a wider point she made about how they were seen through this process, as parents who had previously lost custody of a child:

> 'They're going on the basis of the old case, my [older child]'s case and some very minor things that happened. *(Interviewer: What kind of things?)* [...] They used my partner was half-asleep and he sort of like jolted and accidentally kicked me [...] I was trying to wake him up and he jolted out of his sleep and kicked me by accident, so they took that as domestic abuse. They took that quite seriously but it's quite minor it wasn't on purpose if you know what I mean. [...] He didn't mean to do it and if he done it on purpose I would have reacted, but they took that quite seriously as they would and they used that mainly to take my [child] off me, it wasn't exactly the co-sleeping it was mainly that.'

Of course, we only have Zoe's perspective and cannot judge the safeguarding implications of the incident she describes, or the decision-making of the court. But when she opens this story by explaining that "they're going on the basis of the old case, my [older child]'s case", she describes the experience of misrecognition (see Fraser, 2001): for her, the stigma of her older child's removal shapes how they are seen as a family. Her narrative evokes Tyler's (2020, p 211) writing about the ways in which 'shame lives on the eyelids', as stigma functions as a disciplinary source of power.

And fatherhood?

Zoe went on to explain that, at the time of the court case, it was recommended that she was referred for therapy. Several months later, by our final interview, this support was yet to appear. Their final pre-adoption contact with the child was impending and she mentioned that she was thinking of bringing a relative to provide support:

'Just to make it easier for [partner], easier for us and me and stuff because it's really hitting [partner] now, he's got no support whatsoever and I've been trying to get him to have support and it seems to be only me that's doing it. None of the professionals want to help him, you know what I mean? They haven't looked at therapy for him but they've done it for me, but they haven't done anything for him and it's a bit rude, you know what I mean? […] Yes. I have been trying to help him but it doesn't seem that I can be the only one to help him. […] He needs professional help, from a professional person, someone who can help him professionally, but I can help him other ways.'

Zoe's analysis of her partner's support needs chimes with evidence on gendered conceptions of parenting and family in children's services (Bedston et al, 2019) and the corresponding ways in which fathers become 'absent from view' except in terms of risk within child protection interventions and care proceedings (Bedston et al, 2019; Philip et al, 2020; Critchley, 2022, p 595). Philip and colleagues (2020) conducted the first large-scale study in England of fathers involved in repeat care proceedings. In line with research involving mothers who experience repeat removals of children into care or adoption (for example, Broadhurst et al, 2017), fathers in their study often described complex histories of adversity which 'reverberated throughout childhood, into adolescence and adulthood' (Philip et al, 2020, p 8). Alongside ongoing issues with mental health, alcohol and substance use, the fathers in Philip and colleagues' research highlighted the lack of support at key times in their lives. Zoe's observation that "it's a bit rude" that "none of the professionals want to help" her partner speaks to another form of gendered misrecognition – of his support needs as a father and of his commitment and involvement to their family. As Tarrant (2021, p 195) writes, we need to shift towards 'compassionate and context aware' approaches to work with fathers, 'to listen with empathy and to acknowledge what impinges on men's efforts towards their families and drives them in such circumstances'.

James (*Against All Odds?*) spoke only briefly in his first interview about being a father. His experience chimes with Tarrant's (2021) arguments about the need to critique deficit-focused assumptions about absent fathers, which neglect 'the complexities and dynamics of their family lives, identities and relationships (Tarrant, 2021, p 10). James had multiple placements during his time in care, followed by episodes of homelessness and imprisonment, related to drug addiction. He became a father in his late teens. He mentioned his children for the first time towards the end of our first interview, as part of a longer narrative about overcoming adversity, reflecting on "people that have come into my life very temporarily but have given me positives that have never left me". He went on:

'I have [...] children. I don't see them. They were born in my active addiction when I was committing a lot of crime and in and out of prison. Their mum was very angry with me, and she had a lot of her own issues so I don't see them as a result of that. [...] I was selling a lot of drugs, she was with me; I was taking a lot of drugs, she was with me.'

Asked if he would like to have contact with the children, he said:

'Having their mum in my life and what that entails, that's not what I want. And she just presented a lot of obstacles and challenges to see the kids and be a part of their lives. It was very, very difficult. And I just don't think that would be a healthy thing to do. I just don't think it would be healthy for me to have that in my life.'

His comments here – about what would be healthy for him – reflect James's recognition of his own vulnerability as a recovering addict, something he discussed in depth during his interviews. He told a small story of the last time he had seen the children, saying:

'I'd just come out of rehab, I was full up with all this recovery stuff and just trying to stay clean. I couldn't say that I loved these kids because I didn't know what that meant. And I guess that's an area of my life that I struggle with, is relationships, romantic relationships. That's probably the most challenging area of my life so far. I wish it wasn't, but it is. It's all that attachment stuff.'

This context makes clear that for James, attempting to establish a relationship with his children would depend on rekindling a relationship with their mother that feels deeply unsafe for him, given their shared history of addiction and conflict. Having been supported to stop using drugs in prison, he described his fears of relapse on his release: "All I wanted to do was just not use drugs that day. I just wanted to make sure I could stay clean and I just wanted to know that I was going to be safe, because I didn't ever feel safe when I came out of prison." In line with his comment about "all that attachment stuff", James spoke a lot about feelings of (un)safety in relationships, observing that he never felt safe with his mother, and also noting that he has just one close friend who has "never felt unsafe to care about" (see Chapter 3). Looking more closely at James's account of his fatherhood and of relationships, we can see that while he has been absent from his children's lives, this is not due to lack of care. Rather, his account reveals the complex ongoing effects of significant childhood trauma and the constant effort involved in keeping himself safe and maintaining his recovery. It is striking that James, who started using drugs at 15, was only supported in his recovery when in prison for an extended period. Perhaps it is unsurprising, given the research discussed previously (for example, Bedston et al, 2019; Philip et al, 2020; Critchley, 2022), that James made no mention of any professional support for his young fatherhood. But the critical question for policy and practice remains: what kind of support, and corporate grandparenting, would have enabled someone in James's position to have a paternal role with his children, and to feel safe in doing so?

Support and recognition

Zoe's family's experience contrasts with that of Christie, the other parent in the Pause evaluation sample who had a child during the course of our research. Christie had her first child when she was 16. She was first placed in foster care early in her secondary school years and said she lived in almost 30 foster homes during her time in care. She spoke very little about this period in her life, but identified no supportive professionals (such as social workers or foster carers) from that time. Her experience of professional involvement changed when she started working with Pause and she explained that "No one has ever approached me the way [Pause practitioner] has, to help me".

A discussion of Pause support is beyond the scope of this book and has been reported in detail elsewhere (see Boddy et al, 2020b). While Christie's experience was exceptional within the study as a whole, her account, across all four of her interviews, shows the value of consistent and timely support for both her *and* her partner, and this evidently made a crucial difference in the decision to return her youngest child to her care. By the time of our second interview, Christie had a new baby and by our third interview she said that social services had signed off their case. The family were supported by Pause and by other agencies, accessed with the support of Pause; this included specialist therapy for Christie and targeted support for her partner in addressing his cannabis use and re-engaging with work. Over the course of the study they faced significant challenges, including serious issues with a private landlord, but by the end of the research they had recently moved into a secure three-bedroom local authority property and her partner was settled in full-time work. Christie's final interview reflected the quotidian practices of family life with young children. She described her oldest child attending a new nursery – "[they're] doing really, really good now. [They're] really settled, and [they] just runs in now with no problem" – and the youngest "trying to walk now" and "just a little terror at the moment". Like so many people in our research, Christie had complex relationships with her extended kin network – some of whom were caring for older children – and she commented that while her partner was very supportive, she did not have family help nearby. Professional support, rather than informal help, was crucial to the changes in her family life. Her experience shows the difference that holistic professional scaffolding can make for care experienced parents who face challenging circumstances with few intergenerational resources – and invites the question, is this what corporate grandparenting could achieve?

In *Against All Odds?*, Megan's experience of becoming a mother highlights the value of supportive foster care. Megan was a mature student and her child was at primary school when we first interviewed her. She first entered care as a toddler and moved between five different placements during her time in care. When she first became pregnant, she was in a relationship with someone she described as "only there for the physical". She said at the time she experienced a lot of pressure to have an abortion – from her boyfriend, who threatened that "he will kick the baby out of me or something", as well as his mother and her leaving care social worker. Phoenix (1991, p 91) wrote that '"young mothers" have their own views about early motherhood, which do not always accord with outsider perspectives', and this was true for Megan. She explained in her interview that she felt "really pressured" to terminate the pregnancy; while she did not want to, "there was no one supporting me to have the baby [...] My friends were, but the people who needed to weren't really". Megan took steps to arrange an abortion, even going to the clinic, but on the day, "I just ran out the place". Immediately, she called one of her former foster carers.

She had lived with this foster carer for four years, until the age of 16. The placement had broken down when Megan started running away – something she attributed with hindsight to rebelling against the rules of a strict Christian household – but she also described her foster carer as "strict with love", and described being fully involved in significant family practices, such as attending church and travelling abroad with the family to a relative's wedding. When she called on the day she ran out of the clinic, her foster carer gave Megan the reassurance that she was seeking about whether to continue the pregnancy: "And I told her about it, and she advised me to (...) because she always said to me that she doesn't believe in abortions. And that the baby is meant to be for a reason." Like others in the study, Megan did not have informal support networks apart from friendships to scaffold her through a pregnancy that she wanted to continue. Her narrative described the challenges that she faced and she noted that her circumstances meant that social services "had to" put a child protection plan in place:

> 'They had to do a child protection plan from when I was pregnant because of all my history and because I was still [under 18]. [...] And they kept the child protection plan in place until after [child] was born, after I proved that I can look after [them] etcetera. [...] And they could see that I had bonded to [child] straightaway – because they were worried I wouldn't because of my relationship with my mum. But I bonded to [child] straightaway and they could see that I really

loved [them] and that I was meeting all [their] needs. And they would have unannounced visits sometimes to see that I was OK with [child]. But they were very impressed with me.'

She continued by talking about her struggles to manage the relationship with the child's father, who never attended any of the child protection plan meetings but started to want "more of an involvement" in the child's life after they turned three. Discussing his unreliability in keeping contact arrangements, she emphasized that 'I always wanted [child] to have consistency with him, so even if he only wants to see [them] once a month, just stick to it once a month. But he could never provide that'. She went on to explain:

'And all the stuff I was asking for, which wasn't much, was just normal things to me. And I only learnt all of this through my foster mum. Like basic just consistency in [child's] life and to provide something positive as well in [their] life. Teach [them] things, be [their] parent, be responsible as well.'

Discussing the support she has now, Megan spoke of supportive friends and referred again to her "foster mum", who she said, had offered to be present for the birth:

'And she took me to a couple of my hospital appointments as well. And I think when I was going into labour she said, do you want me to come? But at the time I said no, it's OK, because [close friend] was there. And I didn't want too (…) when you're pregnant so many people want to be in your life and it's just too much sometimes. So I just stuck with [close friend] being there.'

The close friend was someone she met at school, during the period when she was living with her foster mum, indicating that – despite the strictness of the household rules – the placement had allowed her to establish enduring relationships. Moreover, the foster mother's offer of being present during labour is a practice that signifies an enduring family-like connection, evoking Sjöberg and Bertilsdotter-Rosqvist's (2017) characterization of 'be-there-no-matter what' grandparental support.

Megan described her foster mother as her role model. Her narratives also show how the support of the foster carer provides recognition, in Honneth's terms (see Fraser et al, 2003; Honneth, 2012). He delineates three components of recognition: *love*, which can be understood as relating to care, and having one's physical and emotional needs recognized and met; *rights*, in terms of reciprocal recognition of the other as a bearer of equal rights (the converse being legal and social exclusion within society); and *solidarity*, which refers to recognition of strengths and social contributions, and which Honneth frames as essential to the development of self-esteem. While her former foster carer was not actively involved in helping Megan with the day-to-day practices of pregnancy and motherhood, her reassurance and role modelling enabled Megan to make meaning of her impending motherhood and to establish ideologies and practices of mothering rooted in her foster mother's values, which she understands as "normal". These observations in Megan's first interview were echoed when she was interviewed for the third time a year later. Still at university and midway through a work placement, she gave a detailed account of a "strict and regimented routine", which recalls her earlier memories of her foster mother's strict and consistent family practices.

> 'Well my daily routine is I wake up at 6.20, so that gives me an hour-and-a-half, so I leave at 7.50 exactly. I drop [child] to breakfast club for eight o'clock and then I travel to my placement to start at nine. [...] And then I work until five usually [...] get [child] for six in the after-school club, come back, do dinner and do reading (.) and just talk about [their] day. And then get [them] ready (.) [child] usually goes to bed for eight. And then when [they're] in bed at eight I then do the ironing for the following day and get [their] book bag and my bag ready. And (.) and then by nine o'clock I'm hoping to start (...) maybe make a hot drink and then start studying between nine thirty and ten. But sometimes I have to (...) maybe fold up clothes or do housework instead. So it is a very strict and regimented routine that kind of (...) it's the same thing every day.'

Megan's narrative of their daily routine can be seen as an act of family display (see Finch, 2007; Heaphy, 2011), detailing practices of care and highlighting the labour and organizational skill involved in being a working single parent. Following Gillis (1996), her narratives also show the connection she maintains between the foster family values that she lives by, and the family that she lives in, and has created with her child.

Practicing family-at-a-distance

For women such as Megan and Christie who had custody of their children, narratives of motherhood contain rich accounts of quotidian family practices of care. Yet, the narratives of women who did not have custody of their children also offer insights into the meanings, practices and ideologies of motherhood (see Phoenix and Woollett, 1991). Drawing on Morgan's (2011) theorization of family practices and Finch's (2007) conceptualization of family display, I write here of practicing *family-at-a-distance,* to recognize 'the ways in which women actually mother within the circumstances in which they live' (Phoenix and Woollett, 1991, p 5).

Our analysis of interviews across the Pause sample as a whole (Boddy and Wheeler, 2020) considered the ways in which women's possible subjectivities as mothers are shaped by the regulatory power of the state, in ways that constrain their possibilities for grief and their recognition as mothers (Morriss, 2018; Broadhurst and Mason, 2020). Drawing on Fraser's (2001) conceptualization of (mis)recognition (as set out previously) we considered the recognition of motherhood for women who have children removed into care or permanency arrangements. In that article, we noted that Pause documentation, including the Pause framework (Pause, 2017) consistently refers to women rather than mothers, and – particularly in the context of the programme's contraceptive requirements – this could be seen to raise a question about the ways in which women's motherhood is recognized. The focus of the programme is not on working with women's parenting capacity, with the aim of securing children's return from care. Instead, it is focused on work with each woman's own needs and priorities, based on 'genuine interest in her life and a change from how other services may have worked with her' (Pause, 2017, p 27). The framework also highlights the need for practice to recognize that women's potential stories of themselves as mothers have often been '"problem saturated"' (Pause, 2017, p 18). As such, the programme's focus on the woman need not obscure recognition of the mother, but rather can be seen as intended to enable alternative narratives: recognizing women's motherhood without reducing them to a problem-saturated and stigmatized maternal identity.

Family display

Morriss (2018, p 821) writes of 'haunted motherhood' for women who have experienced child removal, highlighting the ways in which children are 'there and not there at the same time'. This idea is relevant to our analysis here, for the women we spoke to foregrounded their identities as mothers. Our interview fieldnotes often documented children's visible presence in their quotidian lives – for example, with names tattooed on forearms, photographs displayed on walls and mantelpieces, and pictures visible on the lockscreens of smartphones. These practices can be seen as 'as the active demonstration of commitment' (Heaphy, 2011, p 23) – a means of sustaining maternal identity and relationships with absent children through family display. This was exemplified by Rosa's response to the photography task in *Against All Odds?* She shared 32 photos in her second interview, taken to represent what is important in her everyday life. These included multiple pictures of her child's artwork on the walls of her home (see Figure 6.1), and she explained: "[Child's] artwork means a lot to me but I don't get much of it.

Figure 6.1: Rosa's picture of her child's art

So, when I get it, I put it up straightaway. [...] They have to stay there. Even if I repaint and I take them down, they have to go back up."

Rosa's photographs of her child's art were followed by pictures she – and her child – had taken of the child and of the meal they shared at their last contact. These prompted her to speak more about her child:

> '[They are] gorgeous. [They're] very photogenic. I used to be when I was younger as well. *(Interviewer: [They're] very smart looking as well.)* [...] Oh yeah. [They've] got a brain. [...] [They're] very well advanced. [They] knows everything. [They] knows more than a [preschool aged child] should. [They] knows the name of every single animal, [they] knows [their] alphabet, A to Z, [they] knows how to count up to a hundred. You ask any [child that age] to count up to a hundred or go through the whole alphabet or name more than five animals, none would do it. [They] would. [They'd] name every single animal that are their favourites starting from the giraffe to a zebra to a snake (...) *[continues listing animals that the child knows, with details such as where they live in the world]*. [They'll] sit there and give you a geography lesson. I don't know any other child that's as smart as [them]. [They're] smarter than I am, and that's saying something considering [they] gets [their] brains from me.'

Rosa's narrative and photographs here are doing the work of family display. Her detailed narrative emphasizes her maternal pride, but also shows her knowledge of the child and their active position in her everyday life. In opening and closing the narrative, she points to connections between her own and her child's characteristics. Gabb (2011b) has written about the challenges of displaying family when family forms do not fit readily into the heteronormative social categories and familial lexicon available to them, arguing for the importance of foregrounding 'context and the personal motivations that may impact on encoded displays of family, sensitizing us to individual circumstances' (Gabb, 2011b, p 52). Rosa's photographs and narrative can be recognized as part of a culturally familiar lexicon – the proud mother displaying her child's work and narrating their beauty and intelligence – but understanding its significance depends on attention to the context of her storytelling and her particular circumstances. This allows us to recognize how her family display provides a strategy for resisting stigma and reclaiming a positive social identity in her motherhood (see Phoenix, 1991), as she explains that the qualities she highlights – her child's beauty and intelligence – come "from me".

Women who took part in the Pause evaluation consistently highlighted ways in which work with the programme could help with the ongoing reconfiguration of their loss, establishing identities and supporting their practices as mothers at a distance. This can be seen as a form of recognition (following Honneth, for example, 2012), enabling alternative narratives of ongoing motherhood that allowed women's expertise in their children. For example, Leila, whose children were adopted, talked in her first interview about how sad she felt to be restricted to letterbox contact once a year, but she also spoke with pride about choosing cards for her children with the help of her Pause practitioner and showed the interviewer the cards they had selected:

'I'm seeing [Pause practitioner] on I think Monday, yeah, I think Monday at twelve to do with letterbox contact. That is going to be a sore subject but, yeah, and (…) *(Interviewer: She's helping you write the letters, yeah?)* Yeah, she got [children's names] from me and [partner], we're going to write this up, this is [one child's] card, to approve it […] And that one's [other child's]. She got these, I chose them, I told her what kind of cards they love; [one child] likes, [they] likes sparkle and stuff. You know at first you don't really know your kids and then you get better with them. (…) And then I told her to pick these, so she picked these up and I said, they're quite nice and we're going to write it up on Monday.'

Leila's story of the cards was echoed in her third interview, when she spoke again about planning cards for her children's upcoming birthdays:

'Yeah. I know [children's] birthdays are coming up. [Child] is first. It's surprising, people say how do you know even though your kid is gone. I said the birthstones. The truth is [their] birthday is coming up, so I want to write [them] a really nice card. I'm going to make it. They said it shows more appreciation or something. It shows more effort that you're making a card.'

These stories show how Leila acts to maintain a positive identity and practice mothering at a distance, within the confines of letterbox contact. The account of her practitioner's support – choosing cards, coming to help write them – resonates with Vygotsky's (1978) metaphor of scaffolding, as discussed in Chapter 5, and his argument that the assistance of others reveals capabilities that cannot be understood when focusing only on what someone can do alone. But as the practice of family-at-a-distance, letterbox contact is unavoidably emotionally complex. In Leila's second interview, she spoke about how much she worries about her children's wellbeing, "because I kept worrying … at one point I kept worrying; I'm not judging on the [adoptive] parents, I kept worrying on that, they're not fine". She also spoke about the reassurance and complicated emotions that she experienced on reading the letter from the adoptive parents:

'And then when I read that letter I was shocked, I was like they're doing fine, they're doing fine and that made me happy and emotional and then, I'll be honest, I started having them memories when I looked after them. [...] And I think that's what got to me a little bit. But I didn't want to break down, that's the thing, because when I break down it upsets [partner], he don't mean to get upset but he don't like me crying in front of him, because it hurts him.'

Leila's third interview also addressed the complexity of contact and connections:

'[Child's] very independent. [Child] does his own shoes. I'll be honest, the only reason why I get upset over the letters is because I think it makes you emotional. [...] Last time I read that letter, it made me cry and it made me happy at the same time. I just want to make sure that they're doing fine. When I saw the letter I was shocked that [other child] has taken after me singing. [Older child] is having pasta. [They] loves mango. [They] loves football. "Where are all these talents coming from?", I said to [partner]. [Child]'s independent. Every time the adoptive parents say to [them] do you want me to do your shoes (…) because [child's] starting to talk more and more now. As [they're] getting older, [they] wants to do it [themselves]. [Child] just does it [themselves]. [They're] walking.

[They're] doing really well so far. [...] They're saying that they're very nice kids. They love them to bits, which I'm happy about. The truth is I'm glad that they're looking after our kids and giving them a good life, it's just hard the fact that they're not with us. It feels weird that they're with adoptive parents and not us. *(Interviewer: It must be hard.)* I am glad. I do like them, and I do try to get along with them. I'm doing it for [children] because I don't want [children] to say why didn't you get along with my adoptive parents when they find out.'

Like Rosa, before, Leila comments on intergenerational connections – "where are all these talents coming from?" – and particularly highlights similarities between her older child (the one who sings) and herself. Welch (2018, p 205) has discussed how accounts of biological connections provide 'irrefutable links' to adopted children in birth mothers' accounts, often highlighted through descriptions of family resemblance. Leila continued her narrative, saying: "Apparently, [child's] very friendly. [They've] taken after me in a way because I used to be like that. [They're] very friendly and [...] loves everyone. [They've] made new friends and [...] makes little jokes up now. [They've] got a really funny personality." In this and in the detailed telling of her children's strengths and characteristics she not only highlights resemblance. She also displays her expertise in her children's lives, in spite of the enforced limits on their relationship. The information in the letters makes it possible for Leila to situate herself in relation to hegemonic ideas of engaged motherhood – she can speak of knowing what one child likes to eat, that the other has new friends. Yet her final comment reveals a distinctive challenge for practicing parenthood at a distance, as she reflects on how her children might see her in future, and the corresponding need to ensure that – via the constraints of letterbox contact – she and her partner are seen to 'get along' with the children's adoptive parents.

Alicia (whose experience was discussed previously) also spoke a lot in her interviews about her child, with whom she had regular contact. By the third interview, the child had moved to a new foster placement; she had regular unsupervised contact and aspirations that they would in future be able to return home. In her fourth and final interview, no longer working with Pause, she demonstrated her care and understanding as a mother in a detailed account of her concerns about her child's wellbeing and happiness in the foster placement, documenting a number of specific issues including the following:

'I think [child] is getting bullied, [child] keeps talking about how [they] don't like [their] colour. I'm not being funny, they have taken a Black kid basically and stuck [them] in the Whitest place ever with a fully White family that doesn't know how to maintain [their] skin, doesn't know how to maintain [their] hair.'

Alicia's account made clear that the lack of professional recognition of her worries added significantly to her concern about the situation. She had not been able to make contact with her child's social worker, despite several attempts and, unable to talk to any professionals about her concerns, she commented that "I'm definitely nearly on the complaint making base". She explained that her confidence to raise a complaint was linked to her experience of participating in training for social workers while she was working with Pause. She explained: "I got a platform to speak out […] to say, 'How can we get this better for next time?'." Arguably, Alicia's work with Pause helped her recognize herself as someone who has the power to speak out, entitled to be heard as a mother of a child in care. But her account of her concerns, alongside the lack of response from the social worker, simultaneously reveals the lack of power and 'voice' inherent in her positioning. If professional narratives of women are 'problem-saturated' (to paraphrase the Pause framework) through intersectional stigma, this is likely to obscure recognition of them as potentially knowledgeable or caring in their motherhood. While of course we only have Alicia's account of the situation, her experience suggests that the failure of her child's social worker to respond to her concerns as a mother could have an adverse impact on their professional understanding of her child's needs and wellbeing.

Enabling the practice of motherhood when children are in care

Experiences such as those discussed are a reminder that part of the complexity of 'disenfranchised grief' (Broadhurst and Mason, 2020) relates to the ongoing practice of parenthood through different forms of 'contact'. Analysis of Pause monitoring data for the main evaluation indicated that about three-quarters of women had contact with children and this proportion remained fairly constant between baseline (161/215) and endpoint (168/215) (see Boddy et al, 2020b). Within the evaluation sample as a whole, children lived in a wide range of situations, from adoption through to informal kinship arrangements and there was a correspondingly variable picture of contact. Some had no current contact, some only letterbox contact and some only supervised contact arrangements, while others (particularly those such as Jasmine,[4] with children living with relatives in kinship arrangements including Special Guardianship) described high levels of contact, and even overnight stays. For women with children in kinship arrangements, improved contact was often linked to improved family relationships, and support from Pause was described as significant in achieving this.

Chapter 5 discussed Hannah's account of how professional support – from Pause and a specialist therapist, as well as from her GP – had made a difference to her relationship with her mother, and she also discussed how this support had helped her with managing contact. At the time of our first interview, she had ceased letterbox contact with her younger child when things were at their worst, and she explained:

> 'I stopped writing for a while because I didn't have anything positive to say [...] so I left it especially when I was taking drugs and stuff so recently me and [Pause practitioner's] been talking about it and me and [older child] are going to write a letter to [adopted child] and start it back up again, yeah, and get [older child] writing to [adopted child]. [...] So I'm going to definitely start writing that soon. We were only talking about it yesterday, [Pause practitioner] was here actually, yeah.'

By the time of our second interview, letterbox contact had been re-established, including the older child, as she had hoped, and this was ongoing at the time of our final interview. She also described significant improvements in her relationship with the older child's kinship carer. In her second interview, she observed:

> 'We wasn't getting on because I thought she was a bitch, but she wasn't, you know. She was just responsible and going by the rules. I was being irresponsible and disrespectful, so I can see that now and I can try and make up for what I've done, you know.'

Reflecting this improvement in relationships, at the time of her second interview Hannah and her mother had recently attended a birthday celebration for the child, hosted by her child's carer, and she commented on the carer's recognition that things had changed:

> 'It's an honour, you know what I mean? Even she pulled my mum to the side and said, "Hannah's doing really well. I've seen the changes that she's making. I'm really proud of her". And I was like, "Oh!" *[laughs]* You know? Because [kinship carer and other relative] used to be like that when I walked in, yeah. *[Tone implies, talking about her as a problem]* It feels wicked, like. It's mad. When I look back, at 19 years of age, I would never have saw this in the future. I would have been really thinking like it could never happen, which would make me suicidal. But now when I look back, I'm like, "Woah, imagine my 19 year old self seeing this". I couldn't, I couldn't, I couldn't ever think that, "Oh, the [two relatives] was doing good". I used to see them as the devil, like.'

Our *Evaluation of Pause* (see Boddy et al, 2020b) concluded that support from Pause practitioners had a positive impact on quality of diverse forms of contact and relationships with existing children. This corresponded to three (often interrelated) facets of change: stabilization and improvements in other aspects of women's lives (for example, mental health and substance use); support in reconfiguring loss and maternal identity; and help with managing the emotional and practical complexities of contact itself, in all its fluidity and diversity. Assessment of the impact on children was beyond the scope of the evaluation, but examples such as Hannah's illuminate the potential for this. Through effective professional support, she managed to re-establish letterbox contact with one child, and an extended intergenerational kin network with a difficult history were able to come together and celebrate with her child. The potential future significance of these changes is indicated by an established body of research that demonstrates the importance of enabling children in care or permanency arrangements to make sense of complex relationships with birth families (for example, Ellingsen et al, 2011; Neil et al, 2015). In line with that evidence, Iyer et al's (2020) review concluded that enabling positive experiences of contact was key to ensuring child wellbeing and recommended that 'support for birth parents – as well as for children and carers – is designed to enable positive experiences of contact: to support children's reconfiguration of complex and dynamic family relationships, and to mitigate potential risks' (Iyer et al, 2020, p 39).

Future imaginaries

I end this discussion of understandings and experiences of parenthood by looking to the future. I begin by considering the experiences of women living apart from children who were in care or permanency arrangements, many of whom anticipated future changes in contact with their children – whether in terms of increased closeness or a child's return home, or in imagined reunions when adopted children have turned 18. Subsequently I turn to narratives of imagined future families for people in *Against All Odds?* who did not yet have children. Their future imaginaries were of course very varied and I have not attempted to convey that diversity here. Rather, I focus on three examples which help fulfil the intention set out in Chapter 1, of disrupting the 'single story' of care experienced lives by highlighting the ways in which future imaginaries of family are shaped by a constellation of factors which may include – but are not restricted to – care experience and which also reflect the normative uncertainties of young adulthoods in contemporary times (for example, Leccardi, 2005).

Children growing up

Morriss (2018, p 822) writes that mothers who have experienced the state-ordered removal of their children are often 'living for an imagined future when their child reaches adulthood ... thus, their past, present and future are intertwined'. This was certainly true for some women in the Pause evaluation (see Boddy and Wheeler, 2020), although – as the examples given here and earlier in this volume show – many had direct contact, to varying degrees, and some were very actively involved in their children's present lives. Variations in their relationships with children in the present inevitably shaped women's projected narratives of future family, in relation to existing and possible future children.

Jasmine, who had frequent unsupervised contact with her child (see Chapter 4) was quite emphatic that she had no plans for further children. She commented:

> 'I don't think I'll ever have any other babies, to be honest, ever. It's just going to be drama. They won't let me have children anyway *[laughs]*. They'll probably just take it away, and I don't want to go through it all. It's long. I have to go through assessments again and all that. I can't be bothered.'

Her account is shaped by her past experience of social work intervention, underpinning the expectation that "it's just going to be drama". But her perspective was also evidently informed by her strong existing relationship with her child, as she half-jokingly observed:

> 'Yeah, I've got one anyway [...] it's not like I don't have [them]. Yeah, and [they're] hard work anyway and expensive. I don't want kids. When you're with someone, you're just tied down to them anyway and then you're left with a screaming baby. I don't want that, no. I don't think I even want kids again. I'm happy with just one. I did though, but it's weird. That's another thing [that Pause] helped me – because I did want another baby to get back at my partner because he had another kid, and then now I've realized it and I've thought, "I don't even want another kid. What am I wasting my – no, I don't want it".'

Jasmine's imagined future is also shaped by her past relationship experience, of being left to look after "a screaming baby" by an unreliable partner. Later in her interview she softened this position, saying that it was something she might consider in a few years "if I met the right guy".

This shift from definite short-term plans to a more tentative sense of longer-term possibilities was also evident in Leila's account. The imagined future return of her children was evident in the narratives quoted here, as she discussed needing to show her children that she got along with their adoptive parents and she also spoke of her partner having set up a savings account for their children, where he put £5 away whenever they could afford it. Like Jasmine, she referenced the probability of social work intervention if she was to have children in future, in this case, while reflecting on her decision to use long-acting reversible contraception:

> 'This is how we decided, we decided this, right, it took long but me and [partner] decided not to have kids no more because we don't want our [future] kid to go through the pain that [children] went through, taken away from their parents. So we decided (…) we was talking about the future, like not now, but we decided once we settle down we'd like to have kids, but right now focus on getting out of here and settling down and focusing on my skills, but maybe soon, not now maybe three years, two years later we'll have a kid but not now.'

Leila's emphasis on "settling down and focusing on my skills" before she considers having more children has commonalities with some participants in the *Against All Odds?* study (see the following examples), whose narratives indicated a normative linear progression, where having children is preceded by establishing a home and career. But her emphasis on moving from a hostel into secure housing ("getting out of here") and her repetition of "settling down" could also be interpreted in relation to James's observations, discussed earlier in this chapter, about having learned to recognize his own needs and prioritize self-care. Leila's comments also evoke the words of a Norwegian participant in *Against All Odds?*, who spoke of her desire to live a "do-able" life: "'I won't have a fantastic childhood or know what that is, but at least I can make my life do-able'" (quoted in Bakketeig et al, 2020, p 6).

Like Leila and Jasmine, Ruby also spoke about not wanting more children. At the time of her second interview she had limited contact with her child, who was settling into a new arrangement with a kinship carer, having moved out of a foster placement that Ruby was unhappy with. She explained:

> 'Well, I'd be happier if [they] was with me but, yes, I think my [relative] is the second-best person to have [them], so I'm happy about it, I know that [they're] in my family, so if I wanted to go there, like if something serious happened, I know that she'd let me know, she tells me at night-time when [they're] sleeping [...] she's really, really nice and open.'

Earlier in this interview, Ruby mentioned that her social worker had advised that she might be able to secure her child's return home if she could demonstrate that she is sufficiently settled and could manage. But as she continued her description of the kinship placement, Ruby's narrative showed how her hopes for this possibility were situated in relation to her concern to ensure the best for her child:

'Yes, so that [arrangement] applies for a year and then after if I wanted to, I can appeal, but I'm going to wait a year and a half, just so I can say I'm settled enough, but [...] I don't want to obstruct [child's] life. I just want to give [them] that time, let [them] be in a normal routine, get myself in a routine, and get all my stuff sorted out. [...] It's hard to do because sometimes it's like, oh, I miss [child] so much, I want to go there to get [them], because obviously I've been to [kinship carer's] house, I know where [child] is and everything, but I know that's not what's best for [them] right now so (...).'

Like Leila's, Ruby's narrative shows her investment in her child's present and future wellbeing, as she balances her hopes for an imagined future where they are reunited, with her more immediate happiness that her child is being cared for by someone that she likes and trusts. What's most important is "what's best for [them] right now".

Taken together, the experiences of Leila and Ruby – one with adopted children, the other with a child in kinship care – show that, for these women, the intertwining of past, present and future is not driven by an imaginary future of reunification but rather by contemporaneous concerns for the wellbeing of their children and a desire to enable that (now and in the future) by being 'settled' and 'sorted out'. That interpretation would accord with the Pause intervention's emphasis on helping women to focus on themselves and their own needs, rather than simply being seen, or supported, in terms of their parenting capacity (Pause, 2017).

Uncertain possibilities?

Finally in this chapter, I turn to thinking about the ways in which people who were not (or not yet) parents talked about future families. For some, their imaginaries of future family lives were framed in relation to concern about repeating history, as Natalie put it in the *Against All Odds?* study. Her account of her mother in her first interview (see Chapter 3) included the reflection that she carried a "little fear" of repeating circles and "changing really into a person I don't want to be", as her mother had also been in care as a child. In all three of her interviews she emphasized her focus on her education and career plans and in her first interview she contrasted herself to care experienced people who "want to do well and have a kid just to show that they won't mess up as their parents did". In her final interview, asked to imagine what life might be like when she was 45, she said:

'My own house. House (...) [lists close relatives] (...) possibly my own family. *(Interviewer: So have you thought about if you want to have kids and stuff like that?)* Not really. I'm more I want to have a job first before I have kids; that's all that I've thought about really. [...] Because I want to be able to – if I end up having kids I want to have a secure job where I have maternity leave and that. I don't want to be like I'm pregnant and then when I'm on maternity leave they employ someone else and I'm out of a job.'

While her earlier comments situate this future story in relation to 'breaking the circle' of intergenerational care experience, Natalie's account can also be recognized as a normative narrative for a young woman focused on education and career who can 'leave the future for the morrow' (Brannen and Nilsen, 2002, p 523). But in the twenty years since Brannen and Nilsen conducted their study in England and Norway, normative futures for young people have become increasingly complex, uncertain and insecure (for example, Cuzzocrea, 2018). As Leccardi writes: 'contemporary social uncertainty is part of the biographical constructions of young people' (Leccardi, 2005, p 125). Recognition of this uncertainty is apparent in Natalie's reference to the structural and gendered insecurity of her future plans: the challenge of establishing a secure job where she can take maternity leave without being replaced. Jack (*Against All Odds?*) also expressed uncertainty in his future imaginary of family life, but in contrast to Natalie, this was primarily relationally, rather than structurally, configured. At the time of the conversation about the future in his final interview, a long-term relationship had very recently ended, after a "stressful period" when he moved in with his girlfriend and her parents after he finished university and the tenancy ended on his flat, a situation he described as "a bit of a disaster really". The hesitancy in his account shows how difficult it was to imagine a different future in this context. Discussing the future-life chart, the interviewer asked how Jack would like things to be in five years' time:

Jack:	Don't really know.
Interviewer:	What would you like things to be like?
Jack:	I suppose it would be nice to have a girlfriend then. *(Laughs)* I don't know, I suppose a partner. *(Long pause)* So a partner. But, again, family just stays the same, doesn't it, family life, I suppose?
Interviewer:	So partner, is that engaged, married, or (...)?
Jack:	No, just a partner then, I think; I don't think I want to be married that early. *(Laughs)*

After discussing other domains of the life chart, the interviewer moved on to ask about life when he was 45:

'So, 45. *(Laughs)* I'd like to be in my house by 45, hopefully. I'd say married with kids maybe, so I'll put 'children'. Sounds a bit ahead of myself. *(Laughs) (Interviewer: At 45, or (...)?)* No, no, just in terms of where I am now. [...] Yeah, married with children by 45, hopefully.'

In his hesitant laughter and his final comment "hopefully", we can imagine how the break-up has disrupted Jack's certainty about his future plans. In the context of our analysis in this book, this experience also acts as a reminder that future imaginaries – and uncertainties – about family for care experienced young adults are not necessarily defined by care experience. Romantic break ups in young adult lives are not unusual (for example, Nico, 2016). Although the stress that contributed to the breakup can be understood to have been influenced by Jack's care experienced status, in terms of his need to find somewhere to live during a gap between tenancies as a student, he described being "lucky" with Social Services, which agreed to his new private landlord's demands for six month's rent in advance. Future family imaginaries are shaped by complex constellations of structure and biography, and this includes – but cannot be reduced to – care experience.

In contrast to Jack and Natalie, Daniel, who had recently started seeing someone after being single for a while, set out more definite aspirations for establishing a family. At the time of our third interview, he was living alone for the first time in his life, having finished university and been allocated a flat by his local authority. His biological mother – whom he described as "unpredictable" – had recently surprised him with the gift of a kitten. As discussed in Boddy (2019), this (unexpected) gift was significant for Daniel in addressing his potential loneliness in a new biographical phase of early adulthood. Asked to complete the future life chart, the kitten also featured in his imagined family life in five years' time: "I would say living with like my partner, I'd say, because if I'm not by then, then God help me. *(Laughs)* Now, I'd like to have two cats by then *(Laughs)*." As he went on to imagine life at 45, he queried the interviewer:

Daniel: And then when I'm 45. (...) God. I think I might come back to the 45. [...] Family. (...) What do you mean in terms of family, like do you mean however I interpret it?
Interviewer: However you interpret it.

He carried on discussing other domains in the life chart, before returning to his long-term family plans in an extended narrative:

'I want to get married quite young, like I'd say probably like in the next five years maybe, so I kind of have to meet someone now. *(Laughs)* No pressure. So I would say "think about settling down" because then if I'm not married by 29 I won't feel that bad. *(Laughs)* [...] So I would be living with my partner and cats, if they're still here. *[Exchange about the possibility of kittens] (Laughing)* So I'll say living with my partner and cats and children, if possible. *(Interviewer: So are you still thinking. (...) Because previously[5] you mentioned that you might foster or adopt yourself, you were thinking like that, is that still?)* Yeah, like it sounds stupid because me and [boyfriend] have only been seeing each other for [a few] months but we have like spoken about children. I think it's something that you do when you're first starting it, and you just kind of like see, kind of, if they're on the same page as you. He wants three. No, he wants four, I wanted three. And we both want to get married like in the same place, we both want to get married in the woods. [...] So I definitely would adopt like all of them if I have to, I honestly don't mind. And there's obviously like the option of a surrogate parent as well so either/or. But I definitely would adopt one of them just because it's like nice and like obviously I've been in that situation as well. So like I know kind of what it feels like to feel like you're not wanted as a child and it's obviously not the nicest thing, but obviously my foster parents were really nice and took me on and I don't think I turned out too bad. [...] Family, I'd say have my own family. *(Extended pause)* And I guess it's kind of like at that age when you kind of like start to see more of your siblings, if that makes sense, and like spending more time with them and they're bringing the children round and like your kids play together. I don't know how I'd write it. "A family guy"?

The importance of family for Daniel is summed up in his closing description of himself as "a family guy". As was true for Jack and Natalie, Daniel's narrative also shows that the dynamic constellation of influences on his future family imaginary includes – but is not defined by – his care experience. Some ideas have emerged from his new relationship and living situation (including the cat), while others have been established for a longer period – as with his aspiration to foster or adopt, which he mentioned in his first interview. He connects the latter to his own positive experiences in kinship care, which was something that he spoke a lot about across all of his interviews, including sharing many photos of his extended kinship family. His plans are also shaped by his sexuality – as when he talks about the possibilities of surrogacy as well as adoption. His account of marrying in the woods brings to mind Carter and Duncan's (2017) description of the repurposing of tradition to give contemporary weddings a distinctive 'edge' (see Chapter 3). Overall, his imaginary of family evokes Heaphy's (2018) discussion of the ways in which traditional and post-traditional understandings of family can be combined.

Conclusion

This chapter has drawn on Phoenix et al's (1991) distinction between the meanings, practices and ideologies of motherhood, in order to consider the understandings and experiences of parents in the two studies and the possible ways in which care experienced people who were not parents imagined their future family lives. While noting the caveat that the people included in our analysis cannot be considered typical of care experienced parents, there are nevertheless strong resonances with existing research (for example, Morriss, 2018; Philip et al, 2020; Broadhurst and Mason, 2020; Roberts, 2021). Dominant ideologies of stigmatized parenthood – of young and care experienced mothers and of absent or invisible fathers – shape structural experiences of instability and lack of support for people navigating transitions to parenthood. These impacts were heightened for women having babies after the state-ordered removal of an older child; as Broadhurst and Mason (2020) have written, the collateral consequences of child removal in the absence of adequate support exacerbate future risk. Yet our analysis also demonstrated the difference that positive experiences of support can make – both in terms of professional support and specialist intervention, as for Christie and her partner, and in terms of supportive caring relationships, such as Megan's experience with her former foster carer.

The final part of this chapter, addressing future imaginaries of family, makes clearer than ever that there is no single story: aspirations for future family are not defined by previous care experience. The accounts of mothers in the Pause evaluation and non-parents in *Against All Odds?* are inevitably very different. But they share a recognition of uncertainty and a corresponding concern to ensure stability and security – whether for participants themselves, or for existing or imagined future children. Again, questions of professional support – and the appropriate role of the state as 'corporate grandparent' – arise. I will turn to those considerations in Chapter 7, which concludes this book by drawing together learning from the diverse experiences that have been shared throughout.

7

Thinking Through Family: Implications for Theory and Practice

> Attempts to fathom the depths of life by examining our flesh and blood create new imperatives for the state.
> Sue White and David Wastell, *Families, Relationships and Societies*, 2017, p 441

Why 'thinking through family'?

This is a book about family, based on the narratives of 35 young adults with care experience. These individuals are not typical, or statistically representative, of care experienced adults in England. They took part in one of two studies, which were very different in focus: *Against All Odds?* was a cross-national project focused on people who were in education or employment at the time of joining the research; the *Evaluation of Pause* examined the work of a programme of intensive support for women in England who had been identified as being at risk of recurrent child removal. This book is focused on the experiences of two subgroups within those studies: *Against All Odds?* participants who were living in England, and participants in the *Evaluation of Pause* who were part of a 'care leaver pilot'. The population of people with care experience is diverse and, inevitably, there are striking similarities and differences in people's experiences within and between the two studies. But my aim in bringing the studies together was not to compare, nor have I tried to identify pathways to risk or protective factors. Rather, the purpose has been to illuminate the diversity of experiences and narratives of family for people with care experience, and to enable the recognition of care experienced lives as varied, specific and socially and biographically located, avoiding the dangers of a deficit-focused 'single story' of the care experienced family. The overarching objective of the book has been to *think through family* in the lives of care experienced people, in order to:

- extend the theorization and conceptualization of 'family', challenging the politicized binary of the 'ordinary' and the troubled 'other';
- inform family-minded approaches to policy and practice that respond to the enduring dynamic complexities of family relationships for young people, during childhood and into adult lives.

Conceptualizing family: thinking beyond the 'single story'

I began this book by discussing the dangers of a 'single story' of family, borrowing the metaphor from Adichie's (2009) discussion of the Igbo concept of *nkali*, meaning 'to be greater than another'. Writing about a very different context, Jamieson (1998) similarly warns that stories of the conventional modern family are never 'just stories', but have political power. They contribute to the stigmatizing judgement conveyed in the term *nkali*, through reductive politicized constructions of some families as 'ordinary' and therefore greater than the 'troubled' and abject 'other'. The diverse narratives included in this book reveal the impossibility of assuming any notion of any 'single story' for the 'care experienced family'. Instead, participants' stories illuminate the multifaceted fluidity of 'family', disrupting its reification as a static and unitary concept. The analysis shows the value of a sociological lens, including attention to family practices, for challenging the myth of the 'cornflakes packet' family (see Morgan, 2011 and Chapter 1). In this, our conclusions reinforce the arguments made by researchers who question the ways in which some families are constructed as 'troubled' (McCarthy et al, 2013; 2019) and as the 'the objects or abjects' of disgust (Tyler, 2013, p 26), through the sociopolitical machinery of stigma (see also Gillies et al, 2017; Crossley, 2018; Tyler, 2020).

By recognizing the 'care experienced family' as one distinctive but diverse category of unconventional family form, the work also resonates with efforts within queer theory to expand the parameters of the concept of family, challenging the presumed deviance of 'family configurations that run counter to … hegemonic structures' (Allen and Mendez, 2018, p 76) while recognizing the enduring significance of family in people's lives (see also Gabb, 2011a; b; Heaphy, 2011; 2018; Roseneil et al, 2016). Care experienced families *are* unconventional: they are statistically unusual within the population as a whole (see Chapter 2) and they are distinctively (and unavoidably) complex, because care is a fundamental intervention into family and household structure and family practices. As the child moves from one set of regular and taken-for-granted family practices to another household, whatever the form of placement (whether family-based or institutional care), the practices of everyday life will differ and cannot be taken for granted. In common with other studies of complex or nontraditional family forms (for example, Heaphy, 2011; 2018), the narratives shared in this book illuminate the value of attention to family *practices* and family *display* for understanding how people navigate the conventional and unconventional aspects of their family lives.

Family practices and family display

The stories of family shared in this book include accounts of family practices of 'everyday life' in both of the senses that Morgan (2011) sets out: regular and taken-for-granted practices of family living, and significant family events, experienced by a large proportion of the population. Narratives of quotidian practices in childhood – such as playing, sharing meals, watching TV and listening to music – act as a reminder that memories of family for people with care experience are not restricted to problems, or even the experience of being 'in care'. In Chapter 1, I drew on Phoenix's (for example, 1987) discussion of 'normalized absence and pathologised presence' in research with families from minoritized ethnic groups. I argued that these dangers were also present in research with care experienced people, if they are only studied and discussed in terms of vulnerability or risk. Through their narratives of family practices of love and care, participants in our research make the 'unremarkable' remarkable and resist reductive, stigmatizing imaginaries of the care experienced family. In sharing narratives of everyday childhoods, participants in the two studies also underline the significance of the ordinary for understanding what family means to them. They highlight that fond memories of family life can be part of a childhood which included significant trauma and hardship. Recognizing one does not negate the other. Nonetheless, participants' narratives also illuminated the ways in which quotidian family practices such as mealtimes and swimming lessons could be closely juxtaposed with experiences of significant adversity. Taken-for-granted practices are not necessarily benign.

Participants' description of traditional family practices – linked to key lifecourse events such as birthdays, weddings and funerals – evoked Heaphy's (for example, 2018) conceptualization of 'double think' in his research with same-sex couple families. His work highlights the ways in which families may be recognized as simultaneously conventional and non-conventional, drawing on tradition in order to legitimate their status through family display. In our research, this was apparent in accounts of both quotidian and traditional practices – even when the re/configuration of family practices was forced by circumstance, rather than a chosen rejection of norms. A close analysis of narratives of everyday family practices also revealed accounts of family and relationships that might superficially be seen as inconsistent or contradictory, but are in fact indicative of dynamic complexity, in lives that often seemed to 'change gears and directions, along with its rules, every day' (Carver, 1997, p 35).

Practicing family with a lifeworld orientation

Chapter 3 introduced the social pedagogic concept of lifeworld orientation (following Schutz, 1932/1967 and Grunwald and Thiersch, 2009). Schutz conceptualized the lifeworld as both individual and socialized, shaped by societal structures as well as by life histories and relationships over time. The conceptualization of lifeworld orientation as a framework for practice is concerned with understanding how these different factors interact. It is also about recognizing the practice of social work (in the broadest sense of that term) as a social justice project, as Roets et al (2013, p 539) observe: 'The theoretical framework of lifeworld orientation was developed as a radical social criticism, challenging taken-for-granted institutional problem constructions that are wielding an alienating and colonizing influence on people's everyday experiences.'

Linking a lifeworld orientation with a family practices lens has particular value in thinking through family for people with care experience: helping to understand complex experiences at the intersection of biography and society and highlighting the importance of recognizing and respecting relational subjectivities. This in turn helps to illuminate why lack of recognition and respect for children's existing relationships and caring responsibilities could contribute to placement breakdown and spiralling difficulties.

Welch (2018, p 200) observes that 'when children are removed from their parents, the alternative care arrangements they are provided with often seek to reconstruct a normative family through "family-based" or "family-like" care', highlighting questions about how this normative family is conceived. In line with previous research (see Biehal, 2014), our analysis indicates that narratives of everyday practices illuminate the subjectivities of what makes a placement feel 'like family' – or not. It was also apparent that the presence of 'family-like' quotidian practices in placement were not confined to foster care. Some participants spoke of residential care feeling like home or family – for example, with residential care workers described as a second mum and dad, and memories of familiar cooking and shared mealtimes. Morgan (for example, 1996; 2011) argues that a family practices lens allows a sense of the active. In the context of our analysis of care experience, this enables thinking about what families *do* and how positive and valued family practices might be replicated within placements of different kinds.

Equally striking across the two studies were examples of practices within placement that could mark experiences as 'not-family', which signalled to participants that they did not belong. These ranged from the quotidian to practices linked to key lifecourse transitions, such as starting university, or having a baby. Thinking about (residential or foster) care in terms of family practices – and recognizing how these function to configure the boundaries of family (see Morgan, 2011) – makes it possible to recognize, and seek to avoid, those practices that reinforce for the young person that they are not family and cannot rely on family-like care.

Finally, as will be discussed further, this perspective also helps with understanding what it means to practise family-at-a-distance, for parents living apart from their children. Our samples across the two studies meant inevitably that we focused mainly on the experiences of mothers, but the examples given in Chapter 6 also indicated the complexity, and professional neglect, of the experience of fathers (see also Philip et al, 2020). Our analysis shows the importance of maintaining support for, and the recognition of, practices of parenthood, even when permanency arrangements mean it may be many years before direct contact is possible.

The value of the concept of family

As discussed in Chapter 1 (and see also Boddy, 2019), concern about the political and normative implications of reifying 'the family' has led some researchers to argue for a move away from the concept altogether, opting instead to focus on 'personal life', kinship or intimate relationships (for example, Jamieson, 1998; Smart, 2011; Roseneil and Ketokivi, 2016). The narratives shared in this book reveal the importance of 'chosen' and biological kin, but they also show why it is important to retain the concept of 'family', while recognizing its multifaceted diversity and fluidity. As Finch (2007) observes, 'The need to establish positively the contours and character of 'my family' is further reinforced by the obvious point that families are subject to change over time, as individuals move through the life course and change their mode of living' (Finch, 2007, p 69). The enduring significance of family was underlined in participants' family display: in their music choices and the photographs they took for *Against All Odds?* and, across both studies, in pictures shared on phones, in visible markers such as tattoos, and in their reflections on who counts as family and what family means in their lives. As Edwards et al (2012, p 735) observe: 'People can use the language of family in their everyday lives in a way that is a vital cultural and personal signifier of deep and ambivalent desires for and fears about togetherness, belonging and connectedness.'

Attention to family and family practices illuminates the ways in which temporality and spatiality intertwine. Participants' narratives extend temporally across multiple generations as well as through the individual life course and into imagined futures; they extend spatially across households, connecting in turn with quotidian and habitual practices which are situated in the practical and emotional time and space of everyday lives (see Morgan, 2011; 2020).

The ways in which participants navigate emotional space and time in their family relationships was perhaps especially vivid in the narratives of women living apart from their children. They described practices that cross households and imagined future reunions, drawing attention to concrete signifiers such as photographs and children's artworks that functioned to situate the absent child within the home, and sharing narratives of maternal knowledge (of children's preferences and characteristics, for example) and intergenerational resemblance. In these ways, participants were able to practise *motherhood* at a distance in their everyday lives, even when living arrangements and legal restrictions mean that it is not possible to practise *mothering* more directly.[1] Kinship endures beyond placement and permanency decisions, but the ways in which family may be practised are configured by wider factors, including legal status and the decisions of more powerful others, as well as participants' own needs and vulnerabilities.

The research discussed here also highlights why family cannot be conceptualized as coterminous with household, or with the mother–child dyad. The importance attached to siblings, fathers and grandparents in narratives of family was striking, across both studies. While relationships with mothers were discussed more often, we also heard several examples of fathers playing a significant and supportive role in young adult lives – an observation that challenges the stigmatized imaginary of the absent or invisible father (see Tarrant, 2021). The discussion of care experienced parenthood in Chapter 6, albeit predominantly focused on mothers (reflecting the profile of participants in the two studies), also highlights the ways in which experiences of fathers can be marginalized – resonating with messages from other research (for example, Philip et al, 2020; Roberts, 2021).

Grandparents were significant in several respects. Some participants shared memories of grandparents which were distinctive in their contrast to quotidian hardship. Some highlighted the importance of intergenerational connections in terms of understanding themselves and their families, even in contexts of intergenerational difficulties. Extended kin, including grandparents, great-grandparents and others, could play a crucial role in family configuration as kinship carers – for participants in both studies during their own childhoods, as well as for children of women in the Pause evaluation. Consistent with other studies of kinship care (for example, Kiraly and Humphreys, 2016; McCartan et al, 2018; Hunt, 2020), our research illuminates both the complex challenges and the importance of these ongoing connections. Longitudinal analysis in the *Evaluation of Pause* also showed how these relationships could change – often enabled by professional support – generating new possibilities for positive developments in family connections.

In discussing 'who counts' as family, participants from both studies highlighted the importance and complexity of sibling connections. This emphasis on *intra*-generational connection reinforces the arguments that Monk and McVarish (2018) make about the significance of sibling relationships in children's lives and the critical neglect of sibling relationships in decision-making about placement and contact. The implications for policy and practice of our findings in relation to sibling relationships will be discussed further. However, in terms of the focus in this section on the conceptualization of *family,* the research lends weight to a body of literature that argues for attention to siblings within family studies (for example, Punch, 2008; Edwards and Weller, 2014; Davies, 2015; Gulløv and Winther, 2021). Particularly relevant are Gulløv and Winther's (2021) arguments for moving beyond normative and household-specific understandings of siblingship, to a more open-minded recognition of the variety and fluidity of relationships that can span households and diverse parentage. Sibling relationships within our two studies certainly reflect this range. Across diverse family lives, participants' accounts show the importance of recognizing children's mutual love and care in childhood, the significance of sibling relationships for understandings of self and the ways in which intragenerational support and connections between siblings can endure in young adult lives.

The longitudinal design of the two studies – linking past, present and imagined futures – also illuminates the fluidity of families over time, as participants' narratives reveal the changeable dynamics of relationships with kin, in childhood and adulthood (see Finch, 2007; Morgan, 2011). A narrative analytic approach, with its attention to multiple and multifaceted stories, also helps with this understanding of family fluidity. Discussing traditional oral storytellers, the cultural critic Walter Benjamin illuminates this point, contrasting their practice with the artificial endpoint of the novel. While the novelist 'invites the reader to a divinatory realisation of the meaning of life by writing "Finis"', the storyteller knows that 'there is no story for which the question as to how it continued would not be legitimate' (Benjamin, 1955/2015, p 99). This understanding is particularly valuable in a context where much research (and research funding) involving care experienced people is focused on understanding 'outcomes' (see Chapter 2). In social research, outcomes are not endpoints, but are snapshots of a moment in space and time (see Bakketeig et al, 2020 for a further discussion in relation to *Against All Odds?*). It is not our place as researchers to write 'Finis' on people's lives, and this is certainly true when we research the concept of 'family' – in care experienced or any other lives.

Reflections on family-minded policy and practice

> The notion of the child as a separate entity, an island, also discounts the potential the family may offer.
>
> Brid Featherstone et al, *Re-imagining Child Protection: Towards Humane Social Work with Families*, 2014, p 139

By thinking through family, the analysis in this book supports arguments for a family-minded humane social work developed by Featherstone et al (2014). White and Wastell (2017, p 441), in the epigraph to this chapter, highlight the imperatives for the state that arise from attention to 'our flesh and blood'. Our research illuminates why family-mindedness matters – for recognizing, along with other forms of kinship, the enduring importance of 'what is understood as an immutable biological family' (Welch, 2018, p 213) with all of the complexity and challenges that entails. Participants' narratives also demonstrate why a family-minded approach needs to be maintained *after* leaving care, why the dynamic dis/continuities and ambiguous complexities of family relationships over time must be recognized. It is hardly surprising that experiences of family relationships in childhood shape participants' understandings of those relationships into adult lives. Our research has shown that their narratives document both change and consistency in their relationships over time, showing how they may be both important and troubling, simultaneously difficult to manage *and* crucially supportive. To understand the implications of these findings for work with care experienced families, we need to consider how wider policy and welfare contexts shape possibilities for practice.

Family-minded approaches in precarious times?

> Despite practitioners having sophisticated understandings of assumed and acceptable familial constructs and practices, when the conversation shifts from description to action, these intricate understandings quickly modify to fit institutionally defined priorities, and categories of entitlements.
>
> Julie Walsh et al, 'How do you solve a problem like Maria? Family complexity and institutional complications in UK social work', 2019, p 1056

Walsh and colleagues' (2019) analysis of social work responses to a case vignette noted the ways in which '*family* is reduced to a set of problems; a "type" of a family' (p 1059), caught in complicated organizational structures that undermine relational practice. The narratives shared in this book show why 'sophisticated understandings of assumed and acceptable family constructs and practices' (Walsh et al, 2019, p 1056) are essential for policy and practice concerned with care experienced family lives. Understandings and experiences of family were varied, complex and dynamic. Approaches to policy or practice that are reductive, based on a homogenizing imaginary of the problem family, will inevitably fail to meet people's needs.

Such tensions are heightened in contemporary times, when 'austerity' has become an ideological norm and the public sector has shrunk dramatically (Boddy, 2023). The desiccation of the public sector is evident in Harris and colleagues' (2019) fiscal analysis of local authority funding in England. Analysing a ten-year period commencing 2009/10, they found that the most economically deprived municipalities have experienced the most significant fall in resources. Over the same period, local authority spending on children's social care increased, as rising demand for statutory safeguarding services coincides with dramatic cuts to non-statutory, universally accessible and/or early intervention provision (see also Webb and Bywaters, 2018). These patterns reveal a wider context of constant uncertainty and ongoing change: child and family poverty are increasing at the same time as services to support children and families are diminishing. Any recommendations for improving practice in work with care experienced children or adults, and their families, must account for this policy context.

In his Independent Review of Social Care in England, MacAlister (2022) criticized what he saw as a tendency for children's social care to be 'rigid and linear', arguing that: 'Scarce resources, reactive crisis management and a mindset that does not recognise the importance of family and community are all part of what is keeping services from meeting the needs of families' (MacAlister, 2022, p 11). At a time when the precarization of child and family services *and* family lives has been systematically and ideologically driven by government (Boddy, 2023, following Lorey, 2012/2015), MacAlister's words invite a critical question about whose mindset needs to be changed.

This book has documented the ways in which precarity – in all its intersecting forms – exacerbates pressures and creates risks for care experienced adults (see also Boddy et al, 2020a), leading us to argue that the solution to these problems lies in addressing the welfare policy that drives scarcity of resources and reactive crisis management. Of course, recognizing this wider context does not mean denying the importance of interpersonal relationships, nor does it negate the importance of professional practice. Across the two studies, participants' narratives consistently highlighted the difference made by supportive professionals and time-intensive skilled relational work, helping them to navigate both welfare insecurity and complicated family lives over time.[2] But in considering what the research means for professional work with care experienced families, we must recognize sociopolitical contexts and the corresponding constraints on possibilities for practice.

Supporting relational interdependency

The narratives shared in this book add to a body of scholarship which illuminates the relational interdependencies of adult lives, demonstrating the diverse ways in which young adults support (and are often supported by) family members in their lives over time. This was evident in accounts of the everyday and in key moments of crisis and transition. Of course, interdependence was not confined to kinship; the analysis has also shown the importance of chosen family and friendships. Nevertheless, thinking through family is important in making interdependencies visible, challenging the 'silent discourse' of socio-economic privilege (Nilsen, 2021, p 134), within which intergenerational support can be taken for granted, while fostering the neoliberal myth of autonomous independent adulthood.

We live in a period when young adults (or at least, those who are able to do so) increasingly rely on family for informal, housing and financial support, as youth transitions have become 'increasingly protracted and complex' (Furlong and Cartmel, 2003, p 138; see also Woodman, 2022). Furlong and Cartmel's (2003, p 143) theoretical framework for understanding youth transitions highlights the importance of family as part of the 'resource base' for 'mobilisation of capacities'; they highlight the family's economic resources; its knowledge, assumptions and connections; and its support and encouragement. Arguably, these resources become particularly important in times when the external context is more challenging and uncertain and the welfare state is shrinking further. One consequence is that inequality widens, between those who can take familial resources for granted and those who cannot.

Young people in care experience these social changes more sharply. They often face abrupt and accelerated transitions on leaving the system (for example, Stein and Ward, 2021; Palmer et al, 2022), despite consistent evidence that timely and flexible support makes a critical difference in scaffolding young adults through key periods of transition (for example, Paulsen and Berg, 2016; Bakketeig and Backe-Hansen, 2018; Boddy et al, 2020b; Glynn and Mayock, 2021). The national charity Become, which supports and advocates for children in care and care leavers, terms this experience a 'Care Cliff', launching a campaign in 2020 to remove 'the #CareCliff and the expectation of "independence" asked of young people as they approach 18'.[3] Many care experienced young people will now face this cliff-edge at an even younger age, as changes to requirements for regulated settings means that semi-independent, independent and supported accommodation settings are no longer required to provide day-to-day care for young people aged 16–17 years (see Chapter 2).

The Independent Review of Children's Social Care (MacAlister, 2022) has arguably addressed these considerations, in proposing a shift from 'corporate parenting' to 'community parenting'. MacAlister writes:

> Whilst the state can never provide love for a child, it should obsess over creating loving networks of people around them, to provide the support and care that every one of us needs as the foundation for a good life. Any young person leaving care without a group of loving adults around them is a signal that the care system has failed. It can be easy to consider relationships as a 'nice to have' or a marginal issue. However, you need only consider the importance placed on relationships in an extensive body of research on promoting good childhood development and mental health. Or imagine for yourself what it would be like to live in a world where you struggle to define yourself in relation to others and where your search for belonging and connection is unreciprocated. (MacAlister, 2022, p 144)

Undoubtedly, our analysis shows the enduring importance of loving networks. Many care experienced people do not navigate early adulthood alone; they are loved by family and friends and often rely on their help in the absence of more formal support. However, our research illuminates what this aspiration for loving networks might mean for policy and in practice. In the discussion that follows, we look across different kinds of kin connections discussed by our participants, considering the implications for supporting care experienced people through childhood and beyond.

Supportive siblings?

The importance of sibling relationships, through childhood and into adulthood, was discussed earlier in this chapter. Sibling relationships were clearly emotionally significant, but provided much more than that. Several participants shared accounts of providing significant care for their brothers and sisters in childhood, consistent with Gowen et al's (2021, p 132) description of children taking on 'multiple aspects of the parenting role'. This agency, love and care must be respected in making decisions about placement and best interests. That's not to say that siblings should *inevitably* be placed together – as discussed in Chapter 4, sometimes they may want and need different things. But equally, the analysis shows that, when sibling relationships are ignored, the implications for a child's immediate and long-term wellbeing can be devastating. Supporting sibling relationships *in childhood* is also important because siblings were very often a critical source of emotional and practical support *in adulthood*, spanning quotidian practices such as helping with childcare as well as major responsibilities in significant lifecourse events. As Monk and McVarish (2018) observed, sibling connections are a neglected area of policy and practice for children in care; our analysis shows that they matter enormously, both in and beyond childhood.

Chosen family

The analysis also highlights the importance of 'chosen family' in young adult lives, enabling positive relationships that can endure, with foster carers, residential care workers and other professionals, as well as with friends. Across the two studies, participants' narratives highlighted the significance of these relationships in key lifecourse events such as weddings, funerals and becoming a mother. Their experiences invite the question of how such relationships can be supported, through childhood and beyond. The Lifelong Links programme established by Family Rights Group in England has addressed this issue, working with a child in care to identify important people (who they know, and who they might like to know) and then working to establish contact and supporting the development of a network for the child. Holmes et al's (2020) independent evaluation documented that the programme helped children and young people to build safe and positive relationships and to establish their own understandings of identity and experience. In a reflection that carries echoes of William's metaphor of the 'two moons' of his foster family and his unreachable biological family (see Chapter 4 and Figure 4.2), one of the participants in their study observed:

> It's [Lifelong Links] made me a happier person. It's made me stronger because I now realise that there are going to be family members out there that I have no clue about and that I'm never going to be able to see, but it's made me realise that even if I can't see this family, doesn't mean there's no one there. They're still there; they're still a part of me. (Young person quoted in Holmes et al, 2020, p 43)

Participants in our research also highlighted the importance of geographical proximity for enabling enduring connections, indicating that a family-minded approach to supporting young people in and after care, as they navigate their everyday lives, entails finding out who people want and need to be close to. That understanding depends on thinking through family with a lifeworld orientation (Grunwald and Thiersch, 2009). It means attending to relational subjectivities in people's priorities and decision-making in order to understand, for example, why a young person might run away from a placement, or why a young parent might jeopardize decisions about custody of their child by visiting friends and family.

The limits of loving networks – and the need for continuing professional support

Alongside evidence of the importance of family in early adulthood, the narratives discussed in this book documented the limits, contingencies and unpredictability of familial resources, care and support. Many people had significant, and complicated, caring responsibilities for other family members, including parents and siblings. It seems hardly surprising that when family difficulties are sufficient to necessitate a child's placement, they might continue to constrain possibilities for familial support in adult lives. But this has implications for the role of the state. In times when young adults routinely and increasingly rely on familial resources, there are critical questions for policy and practice about the extent to which the intergenerational contract with the state as 'corporate parent' extends into adulthood for people with care experience. Statutory guidance on the Children Act 1989 stipulates that the state as corporate parent should act 'as any good parent would' (DfE, 2018, p 8). But our research did not show the state engaged in normative patterns of parenting for young adults, ensuring the 'resource base' necessary to 'mobilise their capacities' (see Furlong and Cartmel, 2003). Rather, our analysis indicates that the kinship of the state does not endure beyond the constraints of legal provisions for leaving care support.

To sum up, the narratives shared in this book provide robust evidence of the importance of enabling children in care to maintain and develop loving networks. Yet the research also shows why loving networks are not enough. Young people in care need professional support, through childhood and into adulthood, to manage and (where desired) to maintain family relationships that will endure, in various ways for better and worse, into adulthood. Given the differences in focus of the two studies, the consistency of this finding is striking.

Professional support – continuing into adulthood – was shown to be important in multiple ways. First, the research documented the difference that skilled trauma-informed relational support could make to people who were managing complex relationships with family members, including significant caring responsibilities that threaten to override their own needs. Moreover, there were inevitably limits to the support that loving networks could provide – for example, a sibling might be supportive in some ways, but unable to step in at critical times. The analysis also showed the importance of flexible access to financial, emotional and practical support, relating to events that are both ordinary (not distinctive to care experience) and extra-ordinary. That might simply involve help looking after a much-loved pet during a short hospital stay – which could be seen as trivial but which caused significant anxiety. The striking examples of organizing and paying for funerals illustrate the way in which an 'everyday' lifecourse event (in Morgan's (2011) terms), becomes an extraordinary responsibility for a young adult without financial and practical support from members of older generations. In line with other research with care experienced parents (for example, Barn and Mantovani, 2007; Chase et al, 2009; Roberts, 2021) the lack of timely support, combined with evidence of stigma and destabilization following a pregnancy, highlights critical questions about the state's responsibilities as corporate *grand*parent: to 'be-there-no-matter-what' (Sjöberg and Bertilsdotter-Rosqvist, 2017) for both care experienced mothers *and* fathers at such a crucial time.

In an evidence review of contact and wellbeing, conducted with Padmini Iyer and colleagues (Iyer et al, 2020, p 43) for the Nuffield Family Justice Observatory (FJO), we argued that 'contact' would be better conceptualized as 'safe and meaningful involvement' of the people that matter in a child's life. The experiences discussed in this book reinforce that argument, illuminating the need to help care experienced children build positive and secure foundations for long-term inter- and intragenerational interdependencies. Our Nuffield FJO review also noted the importance of skilled professional support to manage complex relationships and avoid potential risks including re-traumatization through contact. The analysis presented here takes that message further, showing why a long-term view is vital in managing those considerations. As McCarthy et al (2013, p 16) observe, it is important to 'avoid using children's best interests in a way that assumes it is simple to know what they are'. Difficult relationships, including with parents who have been abusive or have chronic and complex needs, continue to be challenging for young adults who have been in care. Decisions about the best interests of the child need to be made with possible futures in mind. Thinking through family reveals the need to recognize this extended temporality, highlighting the importance of supporting young adults with connections (and welfare concerns) that reach far beyond childhood. The analysis presented through this book as a whole also reinforces a key message from the *Our Care, Our Say* (2021) report, following up on their learning from the 2019 Care Experienced Conference in England: 'Help should not be limited by age or timelines – people need support at the right time and when they are ready. Care experienced people carry their experience for life and need support throughout their lifetime' (Our Care, Our Say, 2021 p 32).

MacAlister's (2022) arguments for the importance of enabling enduring loving networks are reinforced by the analysis shared in this book, but our findings also highlight why the state needs to maintain a role as corporate parent – and as corporate *grand*parent when necessary – that reaches beyond childhood. The experiences of participants in our research demonstrate that there is no clear 'cut-off' or age when a supportive family is no longer required. Again, that conclusion should not be surprising, given the wider literature on intergenerational support in young adulthood (for example, Woodman, 2022). The Igbo term *nkali* ('to be greater than another') is relevant here again. If corporate parenting is defined in statutory guidance as 'acting as any good parent would' (Department for Education, 2018, p 8), why is it acceptable to tolerate something different, something *less than* that, for care experienced people?

Conclusion

The families discussed in this book were all different. Their varied and complex lives resist any reduction to a 'single story' of the care experienced family. The people who took part in our research were all young adults and they all have care experience in common, but one of the key messages from the research is the need to recognize and respect the specificities and relational subjectivities of their lifeworlds and their families. As Lemn Sissay (2016, p 80) put it in the poem with which I opened this book: 'Different eggs/In the same nest'.

One of the critical dangers of the 'single story' of the troubled family is that it effaces complexity. Family lives that do not fit the imaginary of the 'bourgeois household and the romances of the family and the fairy-tales that lie behind its closed doors' (Steedman, 1986, p 139) are marginalized or misrepresented in public and policy imagination. The narratives shared in this book challenge this normative myth, illuminating 'diverse and negotiable family forms' (Heaphy, 2018, p 161) and revealing how the 'ordinary' and 'distinctive' aspects of family intersect. Participants' accounts document enduring kinship, love and care. They also highlight complex adversities and distinctive forms of disruption, corresponding to placement experiences and reasons for care entry, as well as to stigmatizing and destabilizing professional practices that could persist beyond leaving care.

Sissay, who spent his childhood in foster and residential care (see Sissay, 2019), has described care experienced people as superheroes, commenting that, 'like the superhero, young people in care draw on extraordinary skills to deal with extraordinary situations' (Sissay, 2011, np). These words inspired my choice of the cover image for this book: children in superhero capes running forward together. But our analysis also indicates that the exercise of extraordinary skills depends on support, from loving networks of many kinds, and also from the state – including skilled relational support and flexible access to practical and financial help. These resources are necessary in order to mitigate both the normative uncertainties of early adult lives and the distinctive challenges associated with care experience. Butler (2016, p 14) put it succinctly: 'Freedom can only be exercised if there is enough support for the exercise of freedom'.

Ensuring loving networks for people with care experience is important. But achieving that aspiration depends on recognition of the complex meanings of family in care experienced lives. It does not negate the role of the state as corporate parent, acting as any good parent would to scaffold young adults through interconnected lives – in childhood and for as long as needed. Thinking through family helps us to understand that superheroes do not succeed alone.

Notes

Epigraph
1. Lemn Sissay, *Gold from the Stone: New and Selected Poems*, © Lemn Sissay, 1985, 1988, 1992, 1999, 2008, 2016; reproduced with permission of the Licensor through PLSclear.

Chapter 1
1. Children Act 1989, Part 3, Section 17.1.a. http://www.legislation.gov.uk/ukpga/1989/41/part/III [Accessed 20 December 2022].
2. Pause is a national non-governmental organization (NGO) which supports local practices to work with women who have experienced removal of at least one child into care or permanence arrangements, and who are judged to be at risk of further removals of children. In 2017, Pause was funded through the Department for Education Innovation Programme to scale up and roll out their practice model; this included the development of a 'care leaver pilot' involving care experienced women (aged 16–25) who have had one or more children removed (see https://www.pause.org.uk/ and Boddy et al, 2020b).
3. Published in *The Australian Women's Weekly* 14 December 1960 (TROVE, National Library of Australia). https://trove.nla.gov.au/newspaper/article/46469251?browse=ndp%3Abrowse%2Ftitle%2FA%2Ftitle%2F112%2F1960%2F12%2F14%2Fpage%2F4916717%2Farticle%2F46469251) [Accessed 2 December 2022].
4. https://twitter.com/i/status/1327506558322880514 [Accessed 30 December 2022].
5. I draw on a Norwegian exemplar here to show the persistence of this ideal type imaginary of family across different welfare states. Thanks to Monica Five Aarset for drawing it to my attention.
6. The four UK nations are distinct in key legal frameworks relevant to the focus of this book (notably in relation to child and family welfare and health services) and so throughout, we will normally refer to England rather than the UK unless we are referring to Scotland, Northern Ireland, Wales *and* England together.

Chapter 2
1. Source of all data on looked after children, DfE (2021) *Children Looked After in England Including Adoption*. https://explore-education-statistics.service.gov.uk/find-statistics/children-looked-after-in-england-including-adoptions/2020#dataDownloads-1 [Accessed 2 April 2021].
2. A measure under private law which makes the caring arrangement legally permanent. See https://www.legislation.gov.uk/ukpga/1989/41/part/II/crossheading/special-guardianship [Accessed 3 August 2022].
3. Of these placement changes, 16 per cent are changes in the status of the placement. Examples given in DfE guidance on reporting (2019, p 86) include: a foster carer moving house, a foster carer working for a local authority becomes managed by an independent

fostering agency, a placement for adoption transferring to a regional adoption agency, or a child in residential accommodation moving under the same provider.
4   Participants in *Against All Odds?* in England were aged 16–30 years at the start of the study (across the three countries, ages ranged from 16–32). Participants in the *Evaluation of Pause* were aged 19–28 years at the time of starting the research.
5   https://www.legislation.gov.uk/uksi/2021/161/made [Accessed 12 August 2022].
6   The programme has been associated with a fall in the under-18 conception rate, particularly in areas of higher deprivation (see Hadley et al, 2016; Wellings et al, 2016).
7   In April 2013, the English government reduced housing benefit payments for households deemed to have one or more 'spare bedrooms'; the result was a reduction in housing benefit of 14 per cent for one 'spare' room.
8   Pseudonyms have been assigned, rather than allowing participants to choose, to avoid the risk that a participant might choose the name of someone else in the research. Where possible we have also aimed to avoid pseudonyms that coincide with the names of participants' children, but that cannot be guaranteed as these were not always shared.
9   Norges Forskningsråd; grant number 236718.
10 One woman had an adult child who lived with her, and one woman had a child returned home over the course of the research.
11 In some cases, all interviews were face-to-face (for example, if women requested this); some were conducted predominantly over the phone (for example, if a woman was not available for a face-to-face arranged appointment on long-distance fieldwork, the rescheduled interview sometimes took place by phone).

Chapter 3
1   Department for Education. https://explore-education-statistics.service.gov.uk/find-statistics/children-looked-after-in-england-including-adoptions/2021 [Accessed 1 December 2021].
2   Department for Education. https://explore-education-statistics.service.gov.uk/find-statistics/children-looked-after-in-england-including-adoptions/2021 [Accessed 1 December 2021].
3   ONS population estimates for 2019. https://www.ons.gov.uk/peoplepopulationandcommmunity/populationandmigration/populationestimates/articles/overviewoftheukpopulation/january2021 [Accessed 1 December 2021].
4   'I Believe I Can Fly' by R. Kelly (https://www.youtube.com/watch?v=GIQn8pab8Vc); note, Daniel's selection was made quite some time before the most recent revelations about R. Kelly's abusive behaviour were publicized in the media.
5   Edited for confidentiality.
6   'Oh Daddy', by Fleetwood Mac (https://youtu.be/cDCXuMtIaVw).
7   A detailed discussion of related considerations such as managing endings in intensive support is beyond the scope of this book, but is addressed in the report of the Pause national evaluation; see Boddy et al, 2020b.
8   No date or page number: https://frg.org.uk/lifelong-links/[Accessed 3 December 2021].
9   https://youtu.be/W0UrRWyIZ74 [Accessed 4 August 2022].
10 In Chapter 4, we give two examples of weddings – from Rebecca and Jo (both *Against All Odds?*) – that illuminate how the boundaries of family are re/configured over time, to incorporate a foster family (for Rebecca) and 'chosen' kin (the mother of a friend, in Jo's case). Another relevant example comes in Chapter 5, as Jade discusses her child's birthday. Participants in the Pause study, who were all mothers, often spoke about birthdays and other significant lifecourse events in relation to their own children – illuminating how these significant family practices are navigated at a distance. We will turn to that distinctive context for ritual practices in Chapter 6.

NOTES

11   See https://youtu.be/2RAgVxpyABA [Accessed 4 August 2022].
12   The audio-recording failed in the second interview with Joelle, and so this account is based on a detailed fieldnote completed immediately post-interview.

Chapter 4

1   To take one high profile example, in December 2021, then UK Prime Minister Boris Johnson publicly acknowledged for the first time how many children he had; at the time of writing, he has acknowledged seven children from his three marriages and an eighth child as the result of an extra-marital relationship. While the uncertainty around his paternity has been a matter of media commentary and curiosity, he and his family have not been subject to the stigmatization extended to families such as those discussed by Jensen and Tyler (2015) or Crossley (2018). See https://www.independent.co.uk/life-style/health-and-families/boris-johnson-children-jow-many-carrie-b2117776.html [Accessed 7 July 2022].
2   Her narrative was prompted by the invitation to complete the life chart, beginning with the 'family' domain. Details such as numbers of siblings are edited to protect confidentiality.
3   Ethically, this abrupt shift – as Jasmine moves from the discussion of the child's removal into care to speaking directly to them – makes uncomfortable reading for me (JB) as the interviewer. Was the child aware of what was being discussed? Perhaps this story, of their fight to keep the child – is a 'family story', a well-worn tale within the family. Consistent with that interpretation was the repetition of certain key phrases as Jasmine continued the narrative – saying three times that the social worker "made a load of lies up about my Mum" and twice that she was "sick and twisted". Perhaps Jasmine was accustomed to talking in this way in front of the child, but that cannot be known. Certainly, there is a question of whether I should have done more to avoid sensitive topics given the child's presence. The transcript and fieldnote from the interview show that I was surprised that the child was present, and at the beginning of the interview I rather clumsily try to establish their relationship, asking "Is [this] your [child]?" and then immediately apologising, "Sorry, it sounds like a stupid question but Pause doesn't give us any information. I don't want to come in and start making assumptions". My fieldnote also records that the child was busy playing throughout the interview – with the slime and other toys in the flat and on the balcony – while the CBeebies children's channel was playing at high volume on a large TV. I wrote, 'I didn't ask [Jasmine] to turn the TV off because I felt that she probably thought it would keep her child entertained while we talk'. Jasmine also spoke more quietly to me than to the child – raising her voice slightly when she spoke about the slime – and there was a pause of a few minutes in the interview while I gave the child some paper to put under the slime so they could continue to play. But it is also clear that I followed Jasmine's lead in terms of what she chose to talk about in front of her child.
4   Details are not given here in case this might undermine anonymity in conjunction with other information presented in the book.

Chapter 5

1   'See You Again' by Whiz Khalifa featuring Charlie Puth (https://www.youtube.com/watch?v=RgKAFK5djSk).
2   https://youtu.be/8mVbdjec0pA [Accessed 4 August 2022].
3   'See You Again' by Whiz Khalifa featuring Charlie Puth (https://www.youtube.com/watch?v=RgKAFK5djSk).
4   Of course, gravy – like cornflakes – is also often advertised through an idealized imaginary of home and family, as with the Sainsbury's Christmas advertisement discussed in Chapter 1. For a Bisto-related example from my own childhood, see: https://youtu.be/CFyZ1AylnY8 [Accessed 20 December 2022].

5. Funded by the Nuffield Foundation, the focus of *Beyond Contact* was on work with families of children who live in placements away from their birth parents, through voluntary or court ordered arrangements. The research was conducted in four countries: England, Denmark, France and the Netherlands – chosen to exemplify different welfare approaches and systems for work with children in care and their families. The methods combined professional stakeholder interviews, a documentary review of policy and literature, and stakeholder seminars (see Boddy et al, 2013; 2014; Boddy, 2019).
6. Not specified to protect confidentiality.
7. https://youtu.be/Dj-E-YnyLK4[Accessed 3 August 2022].
8. See https://www.citizensadvice.org.uk/benefits/sick-or-disabled-people-and-carers/employment-and-support-allowance/help-with-your-esa-claim/check-if-you-can-claim-esa/ [Accessed 29 July 2022].
9. See https://www.citizensadvice.org.uk/benefits/sick-or-disabled-people-and-carers/pip/ [Accessed 29 July 2022].
10. See https://www.citizensadvice.org.uk/benefits/sick-or-disabled-people-and-carers/carers-allowance/ [Accessed 29 July 2022].

Chapter 6

1. Of the 35 people in the two studies, 18 were parents (14 mothers in the Pause evaluation, and three mothers and one father in *Against All Odds?*). Three (two mothers in *Against All Odds?* and one in the *Evaluation of Pause*) had primary custody of their children.
2. Women in the 'care leaver pilot' subsample of the Pause evaluation had between one and four children at the time of joining the study.
3. Requirements for use of contraception during the Pause intervention have changed since the research was conducted and women may now choose to use other forms of contraception rather than a long-acting reversible method. At the time of writing, the Pause website states: 'Following the initial 16-week engagement phase, we ask women to commit to a pause in pregnancy if they choose to go onto the Pause Programme. If they are ready to take a pause in pregnancy, women will work with their Pause practitioner and local sexual health service to understand more about their sexual and reproductive health. They will be supported by their sexual health service to make an informed choice about the method of contraception that is most effective and acceptable to them, that will help them to take a sustained pause in pregnancy for 18 months.' See https://www.pause.org.uk/what-we-do/the-pause-model/ [Accessed 9 August 2022].
4. See Chapter 4.
5. In an earlier interview.

Chapter 7

1. Brannen and Nilsen (2006) draw a distinction between father*ing* and father*hood*, commenting that the term fathering is more apposite for the practical and relational aspects of 'hands on' parenting, but equally noting that relational aspects of care were highly valued by fathers who 'by choice or circumstance' (p 349) were not involved in practical everyday care of children.
2. Professional support is discussed in more detail in other publications from the two studies including Bakketeig and Backe-Hansen, 2018; Hanrahan et al, 2019; Boddy et al, 2020a; Boddy et al, 2020b; Boddy and Wheeler 2020; Gundersen 2021.
3. See https://becomecharity.org.uk/become-the-movement/our-campaigns/ending-the-carecliff/ [Accessed 11 September 2022].

References

Abbott, A. (1992) What do cases do? Some notes on activity in sociological analysis. In C.C. Ragin and H.S. Becker (eds) *What is a Case? Exploring the Foundations of Social Inquiry*. Cambridge: Cambridge University Press, pp 53–82.

Acosta, K.L. (2018) Queering family scholarship: Theorizing from the borderlands. *Journal of Family Theory and Review*, 10: 406–418.

Adichie, C.N. (2009) 'The Danger of a Single Story' [Online]. https://www.ted.com/talks/chimamanda_ngozi_adichie_the_danger_of_a_single_story?language=en [Accessed 30 March 2021].

Allen, S.H. and Mendez, S.N. (2018) Hegemonic heteronormativity: Toward a new era of queer family theory. *Journal of Family Theory and Review*, 10: 70–86.

Andrews, M. (2014) *Narrative Imagination and Everyday Life*. Oxford: Oxford University Press.

Arnau-Sabates, L. and Gilligan, R. (2015) What helps young care leavers to enter the world of work? Possible lessons learned from an exploratory study in Ireland and Catalonia. *Children and Youth Services Review*, 53(6): 185–191.

Bach-Mortensen, A.J., Goodair, B., Briggs, E. and O'Higgins, A. (2022) *Commissioning Secure Children's Homes Placements in England*. London: What Works for Children's Social Care.

Bakketeig, E. and Backe-Hansen, E. (2018) Agency and flexible support in transition from care: Learning from the experiences of a Norwegian sample of care leavers doing well. *Nordic Social Work Research*, 8: 30–42.

Bakketeig, E., Boddy, J., Gundersen, T., Østergaard, J. and Hanrahan, F. (2020) Deconstructing doing well; what can we learn from care experienced young people in England, Denmark and Norway? *Children and Youth Services Review*, 118, 105333.

Barn, R. and Mantovani, N. (2007) Young mothers and the care system: Contextualizing risk and vulnerability. *British Journal of Social Work*, 37(2): 225–243.

Bassel, L. (2017) *The Politics of Listening: Possibilities and Challenges for Democratic Life*. London: Palgrave Pivot.

Bassel, L. and Emejulu, A. (2018) *Minority Women and Austerity: Survival and Resistance in France and Britain*. Bristol: Policy Press.

Batchelor, S., Fraser, A., Whittaker, L. and Li, L. (2020) Precarious leisure: (Re)imagining youth, transitions and temporality. *Journal of Youth Studies*, 23: 93–108.

Baumrind, D. (1975) The contributions of the family to the development of competence in children. *Schizophrenia Bulletin*, 14: 12–37.

Bedston, S., Philip, G., Youansamouth, L., Clifton, J., Broadhurst, K., Brandon, M. and Hu, Y. (2019) Linked lives: Gender, family relations and recurrent care proceedings in England. *Children and Youth Services Review*, 105: 104392.

Bekaert, S. and Bradly, J., (2019) The increasingly leaky stigma of the 'pregnant teen': When does 'young motherhood' cease to be problematic?. *Studies in the Maternal*, 11(1): 8.

Benjamin, W. (1955/2015) *Illuminations*, trans. H. Zorn. London: Bodley Head.

Berlin, M., Kääriälä, A., Lausten, M., Andersson, G. and Brännström, L. (2021) Long-term NEET among young adults with experience of out-of-home care: A comparative study of three Nordic countries. *International Journal of Social Welfare*, 30(3): 266–279.

Bernardi, L. and Oppo, A. (2011) Couple formation as a transition between families. In R. Jallinoja and E.D. Widmer (eds) *Families and Kinship in Contemporary Europe. Rules and Practices of Relatedness*. Basingstoke: Palgrave Macmillan.

Berrington, A., Stone, J. and Falkingham, J. (2009) The changing living arrangements of young adults in the UK. *Population Trends*, 138. London: Office for National Statistics.

Biehal, N. (2014) A sense of belonging: meanings of family and home in long-term foster care. *The British Journal of Social Work*, 44(4): 955–971.

Biehal, N. and Wade, J. (1996) Looking back, looking forward: Care leavers, families and change. *Children and Youth Services Review*, 18: 425–446.

Bilson, A. and Bywaters, P. (2020) Born into care: Evidence of a failed state. *Children and Youth Services Review*, 116: 105164.

Boddy, J. (2017) Voluntary placement arrangements: A scoping review of policy approaches in five European countries. In C. Lynch, C. (ed) *Cooperation or Coercion? Children coming into the care system under voluntary arrangements – Findings and recommendations of the Your Family/Your Voice Knowledge Inquiry*. London: Family Rights Group/Your Family, Your Voice.

Boddy, J. (2019) Troubling meanings of 'family' for young people who have been in care: From policy to lived experience. *Journal of Family Issues*, 40(16): 2239–2263.

Boddy, J. (2023) Engaging with uncertainty: studying child and family welfare in precarious times. *Families, Relationships and Societies*, 12(1): 127–141.

Boddy, J., Statham, J., Danielsen, I., Geurts, E., Join-Lambert, M. and Euillet, S. (2013) *Beyond Contact: Work with families of children placed away from home in four European countries*. Brighton: University of Sussex. https://www.nuffieldfoundation.org/about/publications/beyond-contact-work-with-families-of-children-placed-away-from-home-in-four-european-countries-janet-boddy-june-statham-inge-danielsen-esther-geurts-helene-join-lambert-and-severine-euillet [Accessed 3 August 2022].

Boddy, J., Statham, J., Danielsen, I., Geurts, E., Join-Lambert, M. and Euillet, S. (2014) Beyond contact? Policy approaches to work with families of looked after children in four European countries. *Children & Society*, 28: 152–161.

Boddy, J., Lausten, M., Backe-Hansen, E. and Gundersen, T. (2019) *Understanding the Lives of Care-Experienced Young People in Denmark, England and Norway*. Copenhagen: VIVE.

Boddy, J., Bakketeig, E. and Østergaard, J. (2020a) Navigating precarious times? The experience of young adults who have been in care in Norway, Denmark and England. *Journal of Youth Studies,* 23: 291–306.

Boddy, J., Bowyer, S., Godar, R., Hale, C., Kearney, J., Preston, O., et al (2020b) *Evaluation of Pause*. Research Report RR1042. London: Department for Education. https://assets.publishing.service.gov.uk/government/uploads/system/uploads/attachment_data/file/932816/Pause_-_Sussex.pdf [Accessed 11 August 2022].

Boddy, J. and Wheeler, B. (2020) Recognition and justice? Conceptualizing support for women whose children are in care or adopted. *Societies*, 10(4): 96.

Boddy, J., Phoenix, A., Walker, C. and Vennam, U. (2021) Multi-method approaches in narrative family research across majority and minority worlds. In A. Phoenix, J. Brannen and C. Squire (eds) *Researching Family Narratives*. London: Sage, pp 15–36.

Bouamama, S. and Femmes du Blanc-Mesnil (2013) *Femmes des quartiers populaires: En resistance contre les discriminations*. Paris: Le Temps de Cerises.

Brady, E. and Gilligan, R. (2018) The life course perspective: An integrative research paradigm for examining the educational experiences of adult care leavers? *Children and Youth Services Review*, 87: 69–77.

Brannen, J. and Nilsen, A. (2002) Young people's time perspectives: From youth to adulthood. *Sociology*, 36(3): 513–537.

Brannen, J. and Nilsen, A. (2006) From fatherhood to fathering: Transmission and change among British fathers in four-generation families. *Sociology*, 40: 335–352.

Brannen, J. and Nilsen, A. (2011) Comparative biographies in case-based cross-national research: Methodological considerations. *Sociology*, 45: 603–618.

Broadhurst, K., Alrouh, B., Yeend, E., Harwin, J., Shaw, M., Pilling, M., et al (2015) Connecting events in time to identify a hidden population: Birth mothers and their children in recurrent care proceedings in England. *British Journal of Social Work,* 45: 2241–2260.

Broadhurst, K., Mason, C., Bedston, S., Alrouh, B., Morriss, L., McQuarrie,T., et al (2017) *Vulnerable Birth Mothers and Recurrent Care Proceedings.* Final Main Report. Lancaster: Centre for Child and Family Justice Research.

Broadhurst, K. and Mason, C. (2020) Child removal as the gateway to further adversity: Birth mother accounts of the immediate and enduring collateral consequences of child removal. *Qualitative Social Work,* 19: 15–37.

Bucx, F., van Wel, F. and Knijn, T. (2012) Life course status and exchanges of support between young adults and parents. *Journal of Marriage and Family,* 74: 101–115.

Burns, K., Pösö, T. and Skivenes, M. (2017) *Child Welfare Removals by the State: A Cross-Country Analysis of Decision-Making Systems.* Oxford: Oxford University Press.

Butler, J. (2005) *Giving An Account of Oneself.* New York: Fordham University Press.

Butler, J. (1990/2006) *Gender Trouble: Feminism and the Subversion of Identity.* London: Routledge.

Butler, J. (2016) Rethinking vulnerability and resistance. In J. Butler, Z. Gambetti and L. Sabsay (eds) *Vulnerability in Resistance.* Durham, NC: Duke University Press, pp 12–27.

Bywaters, P., Brady, G., Bunting, L., Daniel, B., Featherstone, B., Jones, C. et al (2018) Inequalities in English child protection practice under austerity: A universal challenge? *Child & Family Social Work,* 23: 53–61.

Carey, M. and Bell, S. (2020) Universal Credit, lone mothers and poverty: Some context and challenges for social work with children and families. *Critical and Radical Social Work,* 8(2): 189–203.

Carter, J. and Duncan, S. (2017) Wedding paradoxes: Individualized conformity and the 'perfect day'. *The Sociological Review,* 65(1): 3–20.

Carver, R. (1997) *Fires.* London: Vintage Books.

Chase, E., Warwick, I., Knight, A. and Aggleton, P. (2009) *Supporting Young Parents: Pregnancy and Parenthood Among Young People from Care.* London: Jessica Kingsley.

Children's Rights Director for England (2014) *Children on the State of Social Care in England.* Children's Care Monitor 2013/14. London: Ofsted.

Clark, A. and Moss, P. (2011) *Listening to Young Children: The Mosaic Approach.* 2nd edn. London: National Children's Bureau.

Costa, R.P. (2013) Family rituals: Mapping the postmodern family through time, space and emotion: 'We are what we celebrate'. *Journal of Comparative Family Studies,* 44(3): 269–289.

Cooper, M. (2017) *Family Values: Between Neoliberalism and the New Social Conservatism*. Princeton: Zone Books.

Courtney, M.E., Dworsky, A., Brown, A., Cary, C., Love, K. and Vorhies, V. (2011) *Midwest Evaluation of the Adult Functioning of Former Foster Youth: Outcomes at age 26*. Chicago, IL: Chapin Hall Center for Children at the University of Chicago.

Cox, P., McPherson, S., Mason, C., Ryan, M. and Baxter, V. (2020) Reducing recurrent care proceedings: Building a local evidence base in England. *Societies*, 10(4): 88.

Crew, T. (2020) *Higher Education and Working-Class Academics: Precarity and Diversity in Academia*. Basingstoke: Palgrave Macmillan.

Critchley, A. (2022) Giving up the ghost: Findings on fathers and social work from a study of pre-birth child protection. *Qualitative Social Work*, 21(3): 580–601.

Crossley, S. (2018) *Troublemakers: The Construction of 'Troubled Families' as a Social Problem*. Bristol: Policy Press

Cunningham, H. (2006) *The Invention of Childhood*. London: BBC Books.

Cuzzocrea, V. (2018) A possibility to square the circle? Youth uncertainty and the imagination of late adulthood. *Sociological Research Online*, 23(3): 671–686.

Davies, K. (2015) Siblings, stories and the self: The sociological significance of young people's sibling relationships. *Sociology*, 49: 679–695.

DeNora, T. (2000) *Music in Everyday Life*. Cambridge: Cambridge University Press.

Department for Education (DfE) (2015) The Children Act 1989 Guidance and Regulations: Volume 2 – Care Planning, Placement and Case Review. June. London: DfE.

DfE (2018) Applying Corporate Parenting Principles to Looked-After Children and Care Leavers: Statutory Guidance for Local Authorities. https://assets.publishing.service.gov.uk/government/uploads/system/uploads/attachment_data/file/683698/Applying_corporate_parenting_principles_to_looked-after_children_and_care_leavers.pdf [Accessed 10 September 2021].

DfE (2019) Children Looked After by Local Authorities in England: Guide to the SSDA903 Collection, 1 April 2018 to 31 March 2019 – Version 1.3. https://assets.publishing.service.gov.uk/government/uploads/system/uploads/attachment_data/file/795375/CLA_SSDA903_2018-19_Guide_Version_1.3_.pdf [Accessed 10 September 2021].

DfE (2020) Children's Social Care Innovation Programme: Insights and Evaluation. https://www.gov.uk/guidance/childrens-social-care-innovation-programme-insights-and-evaluation#about-the-programme [Accessed 23 July 2021].

Dermott, E. and Seymour, J. (2011) *Displaying Families: A New Concept for the Sociology of Family Life*. Basingstoke: Palgrave Macmillan.

Dermott, E. and Pomati, M. (2016) 'Good' parenting practices: How important are poverty, education and time pressure? *Sociology*, 50: 125–142.

De Waal, K. (2016) *My Name is Leon*. London: Penguin.

Dolbin-MacNab, M.L. and Few-Demo, A.L. (2018) Grandfamilies in the United States: An intersectional analysis. In V. Timonen (ed) *Grandparenting Practices Around the World*. Bristol: Bristol University Press, pp 189–208.

Drew, C. (2016) Wholesome homosexuality: Normative childhoods in same-sex family advertisements. *Global Studies of Childhood*, 6: 324–335.

Edwards, R. (2020) Challenging landscapes of sociological thinking on everyday family lives in the UK: Taking the yellow brick road, *Gender, Place & Culture*, 27: 704–716.

Edwards, R., McCarthy, J.R. and Gillies, V. (2012) The politics of concepts: Family and its (putative) replacements. *The British Journal of Sociology*, 63: 730–746.

Edwards, R. and Weller, S. (2014) Sibling relationships and the construction of young people's gendered identities over time and in different spaces. *Families, Relationships and Societies*, 3: 185–199.

Ellingsen, E., Shemmings, D. and Størksen, I. (2011) The concept of 'family' among Norwegian adolescents in long-term foster care. *Child and Adolescent Social Work Journal*, 28: 301–318.

Elliott, M. (2020) Child welfare inequalities in a time of rising numbers of children entering out-of-home care. *British Journal of Social Work*, 50: 581–597.

Emmel, N. and Hughes, K. (2014) Vulnerability, intergenerational exchange and the conscience of generations. In J. Holland and R. Edwards (eds) *Understanding Families Over Time: Research and Policy*. Basingstoke: Palgrave Macmillan.

Farmer, E. (2014) Improving reunification practice: Pathways home, progress and outcomes for children returning from care to their parents. *The British Journal of Social Work*, 44(2): 348–366.

Farmer, E. (2018) *Reunification from Out-of-Home Care: A Research Overview of Good Practice in Returning Children Home from Care*. University of Bristol. https://research-information.bris.ac.uk/ws/portalfiles/portal/174570240/web_Reunif_LitRev_12_.pdf [Accessed 24 July 2022].

Farmer, E. and Wijedasa, D. (2012) The reunification of looked after children with their parents: What contributes to return stability? *British Journal of Social Work*, 43: 1611–1629.

Farrugia, D. (2021) Youth, work and global capitalism: New directions. *Journal of Youth Studies*, 24(3): 372–387.

Featherstone, B., White, S. and Morris, K. (2014) *Re-imagining Child Protection: Towards Humane Social Work with Families*. Bristol: Policy Press.

Featherstone, B., Gupta, A., Morris, K. and Warner, J. (2018a) Let's stop feeding the risk monster: Towards a social model of 'child protection'. *Families, Relationships and Societies,* 7: 7–22.

Featherstone, B., Gupta, A., Morris, K. and White, S. (2018b) *Protecting Children: A Social Model*. Bristol: Policy Press.

Fernandes, S. (2017) *Curated Stories: The Uses and Misuses of Storytelling*. New York: Oxford University Press.

Finch, J. (2007) Displaying families. *Sociology,* 41: 65–81.

Finch, J. and Mason, J. (1993) *Negotiating Family Responsibilities*. London: Tavistock/Routledge.

Fine, M. (1994) Working the hyphens: Reinventing self and other in qualitative research. In N.K. Denzin and Y.S. Lincoln (eds) *Handbook of Qualitative Research*. London: Sage, pp 70–82.

Fine, M. (2016) Participatory designs for critical literacies from under the covers. *Literacy Research: Theory, Method, and Practice,* 65: 47–68.

Foucault, M. (1983) On the genealogy of ethics: An overview of work in progress. In P. Rabinow (ed) *The Foucault Reader*. London: Penguin, pp 340–372.

Fowler, P.J., Marcal, K.E., Zhang, J., Day, O. and Landsverk, J. (2017) Homelessness and aging out of foster care: A national comparison of child welfare-involved adolescents. *Children and Youth Services Review,* 77: 27–33.

Fraser, N. (2001) Recognition without ethics? *Theory, Culture and Society,* 18: 21–42.

Fraser, N., Honneth, A. and Golb, J. (2003) *Redistribution or Recognition? A Political-Philosophical Exchange*. London: Verso.

Furlong, A. (2015) Unemployment, insecurity and poor work: Young adults in the new economy. In J. Wyn and H. Cahill (eds) *Handbook of Children and Youth Studies*. Singapore: Springer, pp 531–542.

Furlong, A. and Cartmel, F. (2003) Explaining transitions through individualised rationality. In L. Roulleau-Berger (ed) *Youth and Work in the Post-Industrial City of North America and Europe*. Leiden: Brill, pp 136–153.

Furstenberg, F.F. (2020) Kinship reconsidered: Research on a neglected topic. *Journal of Marriage and Family,* 82: 364–382.

Furstenberg, F.F., Harris, L.E., Pesando, L.M. and Reed, M.N. (2020) Kinship practices among alternative family forms in western industrialized societies. *Journal of Marriage and Family,* 82: 1403–1430.

Gabb, J. (2011a) Family lives and relational living: Taking account of otherness. *Sociological Research Online,* 16(4): 141–150.

Gabb, J. (2011b) Troubling displays: The affect of gender, sexuality and social class. In E. Dermott and J. Seymour (eds) *Displaying Families: A New Concept for the Sociology of Family Life*. Basingstoke: Palgrave Macmillan, pp 38–59.

Galloway, A., Boland, B. and Williams, G. (2018) Mental health problems, benefits and tackling discrimination. *British Journal of Psychiatry Bulletin*, 42: 200–205.

Gilbert, N. (2012) A comparative study of child welfare systems: Abstract orientations and concrete results. *Children and Youth Services Review*, 34: 532–536.

Gillies, V., Edwards, R. and Horsley, N. (2017) *Challenging the Politics of Early Intervention: Who's 'Saving' Children and Why*. Bristol: Policy Press.

Gillis, J.R. (1996) *A World of Their Own Making: Myth, Ritual and the Quest for Family Values*. Cambridge, MA: Harvard University Press.

Glynn, N. and Mayock, P. (2021) Housing after care: Understanding security and stability in the transition out of care through the lenses of liminality, recognition and precarity. *Journal of Youth Studies*, 1–18.

Gobo, G. (2004) Sampling, representativeness and generalizability. In C. Seale, G. Gobo and J.F. Gubrium (eds) *Qualitative Research Practice*. London: Sage, pp 405–426.

Gowen, S.M., Hart, C.S., Sehmar, P. and Wigfield, A. (2021) 'It takes a lot of brain space': Understanding young carers' lives in England and the implications for policy and practice to reduce inappropriate and excessive care work. *Children & Society*, 36: 118–136.

Grietens, H. (2018) *Studying Historical Abuse of Children in Foster Care: Reflections on a Researcher's Journey*. EUSARF XV International Conference: Plenary Presentation: (Re)Victimization of Children in Care, 2–5 October.

Grunwald, K. and Thiersch, H. (2009) The concept of the 'lifeworld orientation' for social work and social care. *Journal of Social Work Practice*, 23(2): 131–146.

Gubrium, J.F. and Holstein, J.A. (1998) Narrative practice and the coherence of personal stories. *The Sociological Quarterly*, 39(1): 163–187

Gulløv, E. and Winther, I.W. (2021) Sibling relationships: Being connected and related. In A-M. Castrén, V. Česnuitytė, I. Crespi, J-A. Gauthier, R. Gouveia, C. Martin, et al (eds) *The Palgrave Handbook of Family Sociology in Europe*. Basingstoke: Palgrave Macmillan, pp 301–319.

Gunaratnam, Y. (2003) *Researching Race and Ethnicity*. London: Sage.

Gundersen, T. (2021) Embedded in relations: Interactions as a source of agency and life opportunities for care experienced young adults. *Children & Society*, 35(3): 680–693.

Gupta, A. and Blumhardt, H. (2016) Giving poverty a voice: Families' experiences of social work practice in a risk-averse child protection system. *Families, Relationships and Societies*, 5: 163–172.

Hadley, A., Ingham, R. and Chandra-Mouli, V. (2016) Implementing the United Kingdom's ten-year teenage pregnancy strategy for England (1999–2010): How was this done and what did it achieve? *Reproductive Health*, 13: 139.

Häggman-Laitila, A., Salokekkilä, P. and Karki, S. (2018) Transition to adult life of young people leaving foster care: A qualitative systematic review. *Children and Youth Services Review*, 95: 134–143.

Hall, S.M. (2019) *Everyday Life in Austerity: Family, Friends and Intimate Relations.* Basingstoke: Palgrave Macmillan

Hamilton, P. (2022) *Black Mothers and Attachment Parenting: A Black Feminist Analysis of Intensive Mothering in Britain and Canada.* Bristol: Bristol University Press.

Hanrahan, F., Boddy, J. and Owen, C. (2020) 'Actually there is a brain in there': Uncovering complexity in pathways through education for young adults who have been in care. *Children & Society*, 34(1): 46–61.

Hantrais, L., Brannen, J. and Bennett, F. (2020) Family change, intergenerational relations and policy implications. *Contemporary Social Science*, 15: 275–290.

Harris, T., Hodge, L. and Phillips, D. (2019) *English Local Government Funding: Trends and Challenges in 2019 and Beyond.* London: Institute for Fiscal Studies.

Havlicek, J. (2021) Systematic review of birth parent–foster youth relationships before and after aging out of foster care. *Children and Youth Services Review*, 120: 105643.

Heaphy, B. (2011) Critical relational displays. In E. Dermott and J. Seymour (eds) *Displaying Families: A New Concept for the Sociology of Family Life.* Basingstoke: Palgrave Macmillan, pp 19–37.

Heaphy, B. (2018) Troubling traditional and conventional families? Formalised same-sex couples and 'the ordinary'. *Sociological Research Online*, 23: 160–176.

Herlofson, K. and Hagestad, G.O. (2011) Challenges in moving from macro to micro: Population and family structures in ageing societies. *Demographic Research*, 25: 337–370

Hetherington, R. and Nurse, T. (2006) Promoting change from 'child protection' to 'child and family welfare': The problems of the English system. In N. Freymond and G. Cameron (eds) *Towards Positive Systems of Child and Family Welfare: International Comparisons of Child Protection, Family Service and Community Caring Systems.* Toronto, ON: University of Toronto Press, pp 53–83.

Hey, V. (2013) Privilege, agency and affect in the Academy: Who do you think you are? In C. Maxwell and P. Aggleton (eds) *Privilege, Agency and Affect: Understanding the Production and Effects of Action.* London: Palgrave Macmillan, pp 106–125.

Hill, K., Hirsch, D. and Davis, A. (2021) The role of social support networks in helping low income families through uncertain times. *Social Policy and Society*, 20: 17–32.

HM Government (1989) Children Act. https://www.legislation.gov.uk/ukpga/1989/41/contents [Accessed 6 May 2023].

HM Government (2014) Care Act. https://www.legislation.gov.uk/ukpga/2014/23/contents/enacted [Accessed 6 May 2023].

Holland, J. and Thomson, R. (2009) Gaining perspective on choice and fate. *European Societies*, 11: 451–469.

Holmes, L., Connolly, C., Mortimer, E. and Hevesi, R. (2018) Residential group care as a last resort: Challenging the rhetoric. *Residential Treatment for Children & Youth*, 35: 209–224.

Holmes, L., Neagu, M., Sanders-Ellis, D. and Harrison, N. (2020) *Lifelong Links: Evaluation Report.* DfE Research Report RR 1037. London: Department for Education.

Honneth, A. (2012) *The I in We.* Cambridge: Polity Press.

Hunt, J. (2020) *Two Decades of UK Research on Kinship Care: An Overview.* London: Family Rights Group.

Iyer, P., Boddy, J., Hammelsbeck, R. and Lynch-Huggins, S. (2020) *Contact Following Placement in Care, Adoption, or Special Guardianship: Implications for Children and Young People's Well-Being – Evidence Review.* London: Nuffield Family Justice Observatory.

Jackson, A.Y. and Mazzei, L. (2012) *Thinking with Theory in Qualitative Research: Viewing Data Across Multiple Perspectives.* Abingdon: Taylor & Francis.

Jackson, S. and Cameron, C. (2012) Leaving care: Looking ahead and aiming higher. *Children and Youth Services Review*, 34(6): 1107–1114.

Jamieson, L. (1998) *Intimacy: Personal Relationships in Modern Societies.* Cambridge: Polity Press.

Jay, M.A. and McGrath-Lone, L. (2019) Educational outcomes of children in contact with social care in England: A systematic review. *Systematic Reviews,* 8: 155.

Jensen, T. (2010) Warmth and wealth: Re-imagining social class in taxonomies of good parenting. *Studies in the Maternal,* 2(1): 1–13.

Jensen, T. and Tyler, I. (2015) Benefits broods: The cultural and political crafting of anti-welfare commonsense. *Critical Social Policy,* 35: 470–491.

Join-Lambert, H., Boddy, J. and Thomson, R., (2020) The experience of power relationships for young people in care: Developing an ethical, shortitudinal and cross-national approach to researching everyday life. *Forum: Qualitative Social Research,* 21: 1.

Joseph, S., Sempik, J., Leu, A. and Becker, S. (2019) Young carers research, practice and policy: An overview and critical perspective on possible future directions. *Adolescent Research Review,* 5: 77–89.

Kääriälä, A., Berlin, M., Lausten, M., Hiilamo, H. and Ristikari, T. (2018) Early school leaving by children in out-of-home care: A comparative study of three Nordic countries. *Children and Youth Services Review*, 93: 186–195.

Kiraly, M. and Humphreys, C. (2016) 'It's about the whole family': Family contact for children in kinship care. *Child & Family Social Work*, 21: 228– 239.

Krause, A.E., North, A.C. and Hewitt, L.Y. (2015) Music-listening in everyday life: Devices and choice. *Psychology of Music,* 43: 155–170.

Koven, M. (2012) Speaker roles in personal narratives. In J.A. Holstein and J.F. Gubrium (eds) *Varieties of Narrative Analysis*. London: Sage, pp 151–180.

Leccardi, C. (2005) Facing uncertainty: Temporality and biographies in the new century. *Young,* 13(2): 123–146.

Lorde, A. (1984) *When I Dare To Be Powerful: Women So Empowered Are Dangerous.* London: Penguin.

Lorey, I. (2012/2015) *State of Insecurity: Government of the Precarious*, trans. A. Derieg. London: Verso.

Luttrell, W. (2020) *Children Framing Childhoods: Working Class Kids' Visions of Care.* Bristol: Policy Press.

Lynch, C. (2017) *Cooperation or Coercion? Children Coming into the Care System under Voluntary Arrangements: Findings and Recommendations of the Your Family, Your Voice Knowledge Inquiry.* London: Family Rights Group/Your Family, Your Voice.

Maillochon, F. and Castrén, A.M. (2011) Making family at a wedding: Bilateral kinship and equity. In R. Jallinoja and E.D. Widmer (eds) *Families and Kinship in Contemporary Europe: Rules and Practices of Relatedness.* Basingstoke: Palgrave Macmillan, pp 31–44.

Majamaa, K. (2011) Dismissed intergenerational support? New social risks and the economic welfare of young adults. *Journal of Youth Studies* 14 (6): 729–743.

Mannay, D. and Staples, E. (2019) Sandboxes, stickers and superheroes: Employing creative techniques to explore the aspirations and experiences of children and young people who are looked after. In D. Mannay, A. Rees and L. Roberts (eds) *Children and Young People 'Looked After?' Education, Intervention and the Everyday Culture in Care in Wales.* Cardiff: University of Wales Press, pp 169–182.

Mason, J. (2018) *Affinities: Potent Connections in Personal Life.* Cambridge: Polity Press.

May, T. (2016) Statement from the new prime minister Theresa May. https://www.gov.uk/government/speeches/statement-from-the-new-prime-minister-theresa-may [Accessed 25 July 2022].

MacAlister, J. (2022) *The Independent Review of Children's Social Care.* Final Report. https://childrenssocialcare.independent-review.uk/final-report/ [Accessed 3 August 2022].

McCartan, C., Bunting, L., Bywaters, P., Davidson, G., Elliott, M. and Hooper, J. (2018) A four-nation comparison of kinship care in the UK: The relationship between formal kinship care and deprivation. *Social Policy and Society*, 17(4): 619–635.

McCarthy, J.R. (2012) The powerful relational language of 'family': Togetherness, belonging and personhood. *The Sociological Review*, 60: 68–90.

McCarthy, J., Hooper, C.A. and Gillies, V. (2013) *Family Troubles?: Exploring Changes and Challenges in the Family Lives of Children and Young People*. Bristol: Policy Press.

McCarthy, J., Gillies, V., Hooper, C.A. (2019) 'Family troubles' and 'troubling families': Opening up fertile ground. *Journal of Family Issues*, 40: 2207–2224.

McDowell, L. (2020) Looking for work: Youth, masculine disadvantage and precarious employment in post-millennium England. *Journal of Youth Studies*, 23(8): 974–988.

Monk, D. and McVarish, J. (2018) *Siblings, Contact and the Law: An Overlooked Relationship*. London: Nuffield Foundation.

Morgan, D. (1996) *Family Connections: An Introduction to Family Studies*. Cambridge: Polity.

Morgan, D. (2011) *Rethinking Family Practices*. Basingstoke: Palgrave Macmillan.

Morgan, D. (2019) Family troubles, troubling families, and family practices. *Journal of Family Issues*, 40: 2225–2238.

Morgan, D. (2020) Family practices in time and space. *Gender, Place & Culture*, 27: 733–743.

Morriss, L. (2018) Haunted futures: The stigma of being a mother living apart from her child(ren) as a result of state-ordered court removal. *Sociological Review*, 66: 816–831.

Muxel, A. (1993) Family memory: A review of French work. In D. Bertaux and P. Thompson (eds) *Between Generations: Family Models, Myths and Memories*. Oxford: Oxford University Press, pp 191–197.

Neale, B., Henwood, K. and Holland, J. (2012) Researching lives through time: An introduction to the Timescapes approach. *Qualitative Research*, 12: 4–15.

Neale, B. and Clayton, C.L. (2014) Young parenthood and cross-generational relationships: The perspective of young fathers. In J. Holland and R. Edwards (eds) *Understanding Families Over Time: Research and Policy*. Basingstoke: Palgrave Macmillan, pp 69–87.

Neil, E., Beek, M. and Ward, E. (2015) *Contact After Adoption: A Longitudinal Study of Post-Adoption Contact Arrangements*. London: CoramBAAF.

Nico, M. (2016) 'Romantic turning points and patterns of leaving home: Contributions from qualitative research in a southern European country. *European Societies*, 18(4): 389–409

Nilsen, A. (2021) Independence and relationality in notions of adulthood across generations, gender and social class. *The Sociological Review*, 69(1): 123–138.

Nilsen, A. and Brannen, J. (2014) An intergenerational approach to transitions to adulthood: The importance of history and biography. *Sociological Research (Online)*, 19(2): 9.

O'Higgins, A., Sebba, J. and Gardner, F. (2017) What are the factors associated with educational achievement for children in kinship or foster care: A systematic review. *Children and Youth Services Review*, DOI: 10.1016/j.childyouth.2017.06.004.

Østergaard, J. and Thomson, R. (2020) Thinking through cases: Articulating variable and narrative logics on a longitudinal analysis of drug use and school drop out. *International Journal of Social Research Methodology*, 23(4): 423–436

Our Care, Our Say (2021) *'Is this the time people are actually going to listen?'* Report 2021. Care Experienced Conference. https://ourcareoursay.files.wordpress.com/2021/01/ocos-report-2021-finished-3.pdf [Accessed 3 August 2022].

Palmer, A., Norris, M. and Kelleher, J. (2022) Accelerated adulthood, extended adolescence and the care cliff: Supporting care leavers' transition from care to independent living. *Child & Family Social Work*, 27(4): 748–759

Paulsen, V. and Berg, B. (2016) Social support and interdependency in transition to adulthood from child welfare services. *Children and Youth Services Review*, 68: 125–131.

Pause (2017) *Pause Framework*, 1st edn. London: Pause.

Philip, G., Youansamouth, L., Bedston, S., Broadhurst, K., Hu, Y., Clifton, J. and Brandon, M. (2020) 'I had no hope, I had no help at all': Insights from a first study of fathers and recurrent care proceedings. *Societies*, 10: 89.

Phoenix, A. (1987) Theories of gender and black families. In G.W.A.M. Arnot (ed) *Gender Under Scrutiny: New Inquiries in Education*. London: Hutchinson.

Phoenix, A. (1991) *Young Mothers?* Cambridge: Polity Press, pp 50–63.

Phoenix, A. and Woollett, A. (1991) Motherhood: Social construction, politics and psychology. In A. Phoenix, A. Woollett and E. Lloyd (eds) *Motherhood: Meanings, Practices and Ideologies*. London: Sage, pp 13–27.

Phoenix, A., Woollett, A. and Lloyd, E. (1991) *Motherhood: Meanings, Practices and Ideologies*. London: Sage.

Phoenix, A., Squire, C., Brannen, J. and Andrews, M. (2021) Family lives, everyday practices and narrative research. In A. Phoenix, J. Brannen and C. Squire (eds) *Researching Family Narratives*. London: Sage, pp 1–14.

Punch, S. (2008) Negotiating the birth order: Children's experiences. In M. Klett-Davies (ed) *Putting Sibling Relationships on the Map: A Multi-disciplinary Perspective*. London: Family and Parenting Institute, pp 30–49.

Ravn, S. (2019) Telling life stories using creative methods in qualitative interviews. In A. Barnwell and K. Douglas (eds) *Research Methodologies for Auto/Biography Studies*. London: Routledge, pp 103–108.

Rebbe, R., Nurius, P.S., Ahrens, K.R. and Courtney, M.E. (2017) Adverse childhood experiences among youth aging out of foster care: A latent class analysis. *Children and Youth Services Review*, 74: 108–116.

Rees, P. and Munro, A. (2019) Promoting the education of children in care: Reflections of children and carers who have experienced 'success'. In D. Mannay, A. Rees and L. Roberts (eds) *Children and Young People 'Looked After'? Education, Intervention and the Everyday Culture in Care in Wales*. Cardiff: University of Wales Press, pp 56–68.

Rehill, J. and Oppenheim, C. (2021) *Protecting Young Children at Risk of Abuse and Neglect: The Changing Face of Early Childhood in Britain*. London: The Nuffield Foundation.

Reimer, D. and Schäfer, D. (2015) The use of biographical narratives to explain favourable and unfavourable outcomes for children in foster care. *Adoption & Fostering*, 39: 5–20.

Riessman, C.K. (2000) Stigma and everyday resistance practices: Childless women in South India. *Gender and Society*, 14: 111–135.

Roberts, L. (2021) *The Children of Looked After Children: Outcomes, Experiences and Ensuring Meaningful Support to Young Parents in and Leaving Care*. Bristol: Policy Press.

Roberts, L., Maxwell, N., Messenger, R. and Palmer, C. (2018) *Evaluation of Reflect in Gwent*. Final Report. Cardiff: CASCADE.

Roets, G., Roose, R. and Bouverne-De Bie, M. (2013) Researching child poverty: Towards a lifeworld orientation. *Childhood*, 20: 535–549.

Rogers, J. (2016) 'Different' and 'devalued': Managing the stigma of foster-care with the benefit of peer support. *The British Journal of Social Work*, 47: 1078–1093.

Roseneil, S. and Ketokivi, K. (2016) Relational persons and relational processes: Developing the notion of relationality for the sociology of personal life. *Sociology*, 50: 143–159.

Roseneil, S., Crowhurst, I., Santos, A.C. and Stoilova, M. (2016) Reproduction and citizenship/reproducing citizens: Editorial introduction. In S. Roseneil, I. Crowhurst, A.C. Santos and M. Stoilova (eds) *Reproducing Citizens: Family, State and Civil Society*. London: Routledge, pp 1–11.

Sánchez-Sandoval, Y., Jiménez-Luque, N., Melero, S., Luque, V. and Verdugo, L. (2020) Support needs and post-adoption resources for adopted adults: A systematic review. *British Journal of Social Work*, 50: 1775–1795.

Sanderson, E. (2020) Youth transitions to employment: Longitudinal evidence from marginalised young people in England. *Journal of Youth Studies*, 23: 1310–1329.

Schofield, G. and Beek, M. (2009) Growing up in foster care: providing a secure base through adolescence. *Child & Family Social Work*, 14: 255–266.

Schofield, G., Moldestad, B., Höjer, I., Ward, E., Skilbred, D., Young, J. and Havik, T. (2011) Managing loss and a threatened identity: Experiences of parents of children growing up in foster care, the perspectives of their social workers and implications for practice. *British Journal of Social Work*, 41: 74–92.

Schofield, G., Beek, M. and Ward, E. (2012) Part of the family: Planning for permanence in long-term family foster care. *Children and Youth Services Review*, 34: 244–253.

Schutz, A. (1932/1967) *The Phenomenology of the Social World*, trans. G. Walsh and F. Lehnert. Evanston, IL: Northwestern University Press.

Scott, S. (2009) *Making Sense of Everyday Life*. Cambridge: Polity Press.

Sebba, J., Berridge, D., Luke, N., Fletcher, J., Bell, K., Strand, S., et al (2015) *The Educational Progress of Looked After Children in England: Linking Care and Educational Data*. Commissioned report. London: Nuffield Foundation.

Shildrick, T., MacDonald, R., Webster, C. and Garthwaite, K. (2012) *Poverty and Insecurity: Life in Low-pay, No-pay Britain*. Bristol: Policy Press.

Sissay, L. (2011) *Foster Kid is Poetry Champ – A Superhero*. https://blog.lemnsissay.com/2011/12/09/foster-kid-is-poetry-champ-a-superhero/ [Accessed 17 September 2022].

Sissay, L. (2016) *Gold from the Stone*. Edinburgh: Canongate.

Sissay, L. (2019) *My Name is Why*. Edinburgh: Canongate.

Sjöberg, M. and Bertilsdotter-Rosqvist, H. (2017) Who is the mother? Exploring the meaning of grandparental support in young Swedish mothers' narratives. *Feminism & Psychology*, 27(3): 318–335.

Skattebol, J. (2011) 'When the money's low': Economic participation among disadvantaged young Australians. *Children and Youth Services Review*, 33(4): 528–533.

Skivenes, M. and Thoburn, J. (2016) Pathways to permanence in England and Norway: A critical analysis of documents and data. *Children and Youth Services Review*, 67: 152–160.

Skivington, K., Matthews, L., Simpson, S.A., Craig, P., Baird, J., Blazeby, J.M., et al. (2021) Framework for the development and evaluation of complex interventions: gap analysis, workshop and consultation-informed update. *Health Technology Assessment*, 25: 57.

Smart, C. (2011) Relationality and socio-cultural theories of family life. In R. Jallinoja and E.D. Widmer (eds) *Families and Kinship in Contemporary Europe. Rules and Practices of Relatedness*. Basingstoke: Palgrave Macmillan, pp 13–28.

Smetana, J.G. (2017) Current research on parenting styles, dimensions, and beliefs. *Current Opinion in Psychology*, 15: 19–25.

Squire, C. (2013) From experience-centred to socioculturally-oriented approaches to narrative. In M. Andrews, C. Squire and M. Tamboukou (eds) *Doing Narrative Research*. London: Sage, pp 47–71.

Staunes, D. and Kofoed, J. (2015) Hesitancy as ethics. *Reconceptualizing Educational Research Methodology*, 6(1): 24–39.

Steedman, C. (1986) *Landscape for a Good Woman*. London: Virago.

Steedman, C. (2000) Enforced narratives. Stories of another self. In T. Coslett, C. Lury and P. Summerfield (eds) *Feminism & Autobiography: Texts, Theories, Methods*. London: Routledge, pp 25–39.

Stein, M. (2006) Research review: Young people leaving care. *Child & Family Social Work,* 11: 273–279.

Stein, M. (2012) *Young People Leaving Care: Supporting Pathways to Adulthood*. London: Jessica Kingsley.

Stein, M. and Munro, E. (eds) (2008) *Young People's Transitions from Care to Adulthood: International Research and Practice*. London: Jessica Kingsley.

Stein, M. and Dumaret, A.C. (2011) The mental health of young people aging out of care and entering adulthood: Exploring the evidence from England and France. *Children and Youth Services Review*, 33(12): 2504–2511.

Stein, M. and Ward, H. (2021) Editorial: Transitions from care to adulthood – Persistent issues across time and place. *Child & Family Social Work*, 26: 215–221.

Stewart, K., Reeves, A. and Patrick, R. (2021) A Time of Need: Exploring the Changing Poverty Risk Facing Larger Families in the UK. *CASE/ 224*. London: Centre for Analysis of Social Exclusion, LSE.

Strandbu, Å., Stefansen, K., Smette, I. and Sandvik, M.R. (2019) Young people's experiences of parental involvement in youth sport. *Sport, Education and Society*, 24(1): 66–77.

Strawson, G. (2004) Against narrativity. *Ratio (new series)* XVII, 428–452.

Tarrant, A. (2021) *Fathering and Poverty: Uncovering Men's Participation in Low-Income Family Life*. Bristol: Policy Press.

Thoburn, J. and Courtney, M. (2011) A guide through the knowledge base on children in out-of-home care. *Journal of Children's Services*, 6(4): 210–227.

Thomson, R. (2009) *Unfolding Lives: Youth, Gender and Change*. Bristol: Policy Press.

Thomson, R. (2020) Too much too young? Revisiting young motherhood. *Studies in the Maternal*, 13(1): 1–9.

Thomson, R. and Holland, J. (2002) Imagined adulthood: Resources, plans and contradictions. *Gender and Education*, 14: 337–350.

Thomson, R. and Østergaard, J. (2021) Open-ended transitions to adulthood: Metaphorical thinking for times of stasis. *The Sociological Review*, 69: 434–450.

Thomson, R., Bell, R., Holland, J., Henderson, S., McGrellis, S. and Sharpe, S. (2002) Critical moments: Choice, chance and opportunity in young people's narratives of transition. *Sociology*, 36(2): 335–354.

Thomson, R., Kehily, M.J., Hadfield, L. and Sharpe, S. (2011) *Making Modern Mothers*. Bristol: Policy Press.

Toft, M. and Friedman, S. (2021) Family wealth and the class ceiling: The propulsive power of the bank of Mum and Dad. *Sociology*, 55: 90–109.

Trujillo, J. (2018) Intersubjectivity and the sociology of Alfred Schutz. *Bulletin d'analyse phénoménologique*. XIV(7): 1–30.

Tyler, I. (2013) *Revolting Subjects: Social Abjection and Resistance in Neoliberal Britain*. London: Zed Books.

Tyler, I. (2020) *Stigma: The Machinery of Inequality*. London: Zed Books.

Tyler, I. and Slater, T. (2018) Rethinking the sociology of stigma. *The Sociological Review Monographs*, 66(4): 721–743.

Vinnerljung, B. and Sallnas, M. (2008) Into adulthood: A follow-up study of 718 young people who were placed in out-of-home care during their teens. *Child & Family Social Work*, 13: 144–155.

Vygotsky, L. (1978) *Mind in Society: The Development of Higher Psychological Processes*. Cambridge, MA: Harvard University Press.

Wade, J. (2008) The ties that bind: Support from birth families and substitute families for young people leaving care. *British Journal of Social Work*, 38: 39–54.

Walsh, J., White, S., Morris, K. and Doherty, P. (2019) How do you solve a problem like Maria? Family complexity and institutional complications in UK social work. *European Journal of Social Work*, 22: 1050–1061.

Webb, C.J.R. and Bywaters, P. (2018) Austerity, rationing and inequity: Trends in children's and young peoples' services expenditure in England between 2010 and 2015. *Local Government Studies*, 44: 391–415

Webb, C.J.R., Bywaters, P., Elliott, M. and Scourfield, J. (2021) Income inequality and child welfare interventions in England and Wales. *Journal of Epidemiology and Community Health*, 75: 251.

Welch, V. (2018) Talking back to 'family', 'family troubles', and 'the looked-after child'. *Sociological Research Online*, 23: 197–218.

Wellings, K., Palmer, M.J., Geary, R.S., Gibson, L.J., Copas, A., Datta, J., et al (2016) Changes in conceptions in women younger than 18 years and the circumstances of young mothers in England in 2000–12: An observational study. *Lancet*, 388(10044): 586–95.

Wetherell, M. (2015) *Affect and Emotion: A New Social Science Understanding*. London: Sage.

White, S. and Wastell, D. (2017) The rise and rise of prevention science in UK family welfare: Surveillance gets under the skin. *Families, Relationships and Societies*, 6: 427–445.

Williams, A., Wood, S., Warner, N., Cummings, A., Hodges, H., El-Banna, A., et al (2020) *Unlocking the Facts: Young People Referred to Secure Children's Homes*. Cardiff: Cascade.

Willow, C. (2021) High Court gives go-ahead for discrimination claim to protect teenagers in care. Article 39: https://article39.org.uk/2021/08/17/high-court-gives-go-ahead-for-discrimination-claim-to-protect-teenagers-in-care/ [Accessed 12 August 2022].

Wilson, S. (2013) *Young People Creating Belonging: Spaces, Sounds and Sights*. ESRC End of Award Report, RES-061-25-0501. Swindon: ESRC.

Wilson, S. (2016) Visual activism and social justice: Using visual methods to make young people's complex lives visible across 'public' and 'private' spaces. *Current Sociology*, 64: 140–156.

Wilson, S. (2018) Haunting and the knowing and showing of qualitative research. *The Sociological Review*, 66(6): 1209–1225.

Wilson, S., Cunningham-Burley, S., Bancroft, A. and Backett-Milburn, K. (2012) The consequences of love: Young people and family practices in difficult circumstances. *The Sociological Review*, 60: 110–128.

Wissö, T., Johansson, H. and Höjer, I. (2019) What is a family? Constructions of family and parenting after a custody transfer from birth parents to foster parents. *Child and Family Social Work*, 24: 9–16.

Woodman, D. (2022) Generational change and intergenerational relationships in the context of the asset economy. *Distinktion: Journal of Social Theory*, 23(1): 55–69.

Woodthorpe, K. (2017) Family and funerals: Taking a relational perspective. *Death Studies*, 41: 592–601.

Worth, N. (2011) Evaluating life maps as a versatile method for lifecourse geographies. *Area*, 43: 405–412.

Wrobel, G.M. and Grotevant, H.D. (2019) Minding the (information) gap: What do emerging adult adoptees want to know about their birth parents? *Adoption Quarterly*, 22(1): 29–52.

Yuval-Davis, N. (2010) Theorizing identity: Beyond the 'us' and 'them' dichotomy. *Patterns of Prejudice*, 44(3): 261–280.

Index

References to endnotes show both the page number and the note number (231n3).

A

abjection 43, 153
absence of caring connections 78–79, 92
absent fathers 131–132, 157
abuse 25, 29, 53, 60, 104, 110–111
  see also domestic violence
Acosta, K.L. 71
addiction 132
Adichie, C.N. 1, 2, 16, 18, 153
adoption
  contact with birth family 107, 140
  family-at-a-distance 121
  looked-after children 19
  parental responsibility 13
  permanence of 19–20
  see also kinship care arrangements; removal of children from parental care
advertising and idealized families 9–10
  see also 'cornflakes packet family'
affective memories 47, 48–49, 50
  see also music; photography
affinities 54–55, 70, 75, 80
Against All Odds? study
  about the study 3–4, 18, 22, 31, 33–36
  becoming a parent 125
  bringing studies together 39–42, 152–166
  caring responsibilities 96
  complex family connections 51–53, 105
  corporate parenting 79
  defining the (extra)ordinary 56–57
  endpoints 158
  funding 28
  imagined futures 144, 146, 147
  ineffable kinship 80
  informal celebrations 60–61
  methods 31
  motherhood 121
  music 46–47, 49, 60, 64–65, 96, 98, 100, 109, 156
  not-family 86
  parenthood 134

photography 48–49, 81, 84–85, 108, 137–138, 156
residential units 89
scaffolding via family support 115–116
sibling relationships 98, 99, 102–103
significance of the mundane 46
tattoos 82
'unremarkable' practices 46–50
weddings and funerals 61–63, 64, 66–67
who counts as 'family' 80, 81, 84–85, 86, 89, 92
age of leaving home 22
alcohol *see* drugs and alcohol
Allen, S.H. 153
Andrews, M. 45–46, 54
anger 51, 52, 64, 114, 127–128
Article 39 22
artwork, children's 138, 157
attachment 132
austerity 2, 8–11, 14, 28, 96–97, 112–118, 160

B

Bach-Mortensen, A.J. 92
Backe-Hansen, E. 33, 161
Bakketeig, E. 4, 8, 11, 18, 28, 57, 146, 158, 161
Bassel, L. 123, 124, 127
Baumrind, D. 10
Become 161
bedroom tax 25
Bedston, S. 131, 133
Beek, M. 86
Bekaert, S. 24
belonging 84, 87, 89, 92–93, 156
'benefit brood' 72–73
Benjamin, W. 158
bereavement/loss 51, 52, 67, 97, 129, 139
Bernardi, L. 64
Berrington, A. 22
Bertilsdotter-Rosqvist, H. 24–25, 122, 135, 165

Beyond Contact study 105
Biehal, N. 84, 89, 155
binaries
  'good'/'bad' binaries 53
  'other'/'ordinary' binary 43
  'troubled'/'ordinary' binary 2, 9, 43, 72, 153, 159–160
biological/birth families
  complex family connections 110, 112–113
  contact with 20, 21, 92, 94, 105–107, 117, 140, 165
  dynamic connections with 105–107
  ineffable kinship 80–82
  parenting responsibilities/skills 110–111
  re-establishing contact with birth families 106–107
  'who counts' as family 74
birthdays 60–61, 75, 76, 139–140, 143, 155
black stereotypes 126–127
  see also racism
Blumhardt, H. 9, 14
Boddy, J. 4, 13, 14, 22, 28, 33, 34, 37, 41, 45, 55, 69, 79, 105, 115, 133, 137, 142, 143, 145, 149, 156, 160, 161
Bouamama, S. 124
boundaries of 'family' 70–94
boundary moves 83–86, 94
Bradly, J. 24
Brannen, J. 97, 148
bricolage 63, 66, 68
Broadhurst, K. 25, 124, 126, 128, 137, 142, 151
Burns, K. 13, 97
Butler, J. 14, 27, 29, 41, 68, 95, 96, 166

C

CAFCASS 25
Care Act 2014 101
'Care Cliff' 161
Care Experienced Conference 119, 165
Care Planning, Placement and Case Review (England) (Amendment) Regulations 2021 22
care plans 20
Carer's Allowance 113, 114
caring responsibilities 96, 98–101, 113–114, 164
Carter, J. 63, 66, 68, 150
Cartmel, F. 161, 164
Carver, R. 31, 32, 156
Castrén, A.M. 61
celebrations and rituals 59–68, 75, 76
  see also birthdays; Christmas; weddings and funerals
challenging behaviour 91–92
Child & Family Social Work 21
child protection systems 13, 14, 134
child-centred family service orientation 13
  see also humane social work

Children Act 1989 2, 8, 13, 14, 16, 19, 80, 164
children's homes *see* residential units
Children's Rights Director for England (CRDE) 98
Children's Social Care Innovation Programme 28, 36
chosen family 92–94, 163
Christmas 75, 85–86, 101
  see also rituals and celebrations
co-construction 32
'collateral' kin 76
colonialism 2
'common sense' 107, 120, 122, 124
community parenting 161–162
complex family connections 68–69, 70–94, 105–109, 153, 166
complex trauma 25, 37
connectedness 78–79, 95–119, 156
'contact', thinking beyond 69
contrast with other families 58–59
Cooper, M. 10–11
'cornflakes packet family' 5, 6, 9, 71, 72, 153
corporate grandparenting 24, 120, 121–122, 125, 165
corporate parenting
  connectedness 118, 121–122
  defining 'family' 79–80, 94
  definition of 165
  ordinary family experiences 67
  role of state 19, 23, 24, 164
  shift to 'community parenting' 161–162
Costa, R.P. 75
Courtney, M. 21
critical moments 104
critically engaged ethical approaches 33
Crossley, S. 73
cultural identity 109
Cunningham, H. 14

D

data analysis methods 41–42
De Waal, Kit 95, 98–99
deficit-focused approaches 131, 152
  see also 'single story'
Denmark 22, 33–34, 105
DeNora, T. 35–36, 46
Dermott, E. 6, 10
dignity 86
discharge grants 79
disenfranchised grief 142
display *see* family display
distance *see* family-at-a-distance
dividing practices 9, 15, 27
"do-able" life 146
'doing' family 6–7, 43, 71, 155
'doing well' 34
Dolbin-MacNab, M.L. 122
domestic violence 25, 117, 130

INDEX

dominant culture, and research 26, 27
'double thinking' 12, 76, 77, 155
Drew, C. 72
drugs and alcohol 79, 104, 131–132
Duncan, S. 63, 66, 68, 150

E

early parenthood 23–25
   see also young parents
educational disruption 23, 97, 123
Edwards, R. 5, 12, 98, 104, 156
emblematic representation 34
Emejulu, A. 123, 124
emergency arrangements 84
enduring kinship 78–80
essentialization 4, 31, 32, 76, 124
ethic of care 55
'ethical Narrativity thesis' 31
ethico-political choices 29–30
ethics 26–31, 33, 37, 155
ethnicity 11, 27, 109, 126
European Convention on Human Rights 13
Eurostat 22
Evaluation of Pause study
  about the study 3–4, 25, 31, 36–39
  absence of caring connections with family 78–79
  austerity 112–113
  becoming a parent 124–126
  bringing studies together 39–42, 152–166
  complex family connections 53–55, 110
  corporate parenting 79
  everyday/ordinary family practices 112
  family structures 73–74, 76–77
  family-at-a-distance 137
  focus on reducing repeated child removal 28, 128
  funding 28
  imagined futures 145, 147
  kinship care arrangements 157–158
  methods 31
  motherhood 121
  parenthood 133–134
  Pause 36–37
  practice of motherhood when children are in care 142–144
  professional support 143–144
  removal of children from parental care 139
  residential units 88–89
  scaffolding via family support 116–117
  siblings 99, 103
  tattoos 82
  'unremarkable' practices 50–51
  weddings and funerals 64, 67
everyday/ordinary family practices 43–69, 103, 113, 137–138, 154–157, 164
extended kin 60–61, 72, 76, 133, 157
extraordinary/ordinary practices 55–59, 76, 77, 78

F

'families we live by' 5
'family', conceptualizations of 4–12
'family', who counts as 70–94
family court proceedings 25
family display 7, 76, 78, 120, 136, 137–142, 154–155
family dynamics, managing 62–63, 75, 105–109, 153
family nucleus 72
family practices 71, 95, 121, 136–144, 154–155, 156
  see also everyday/ordinary family practices; rituals and celebrations
family resemblance 141, 157
Family Rights Group 55, 163
family structures 70–94, 97–98
family-at-a-distance 121, 136–144, 156
family-minded social work 55, 159–165
Farmer, E. 20
fatherhood 121, 130–133, 135, 156, 157
fear 52, 147
Featherstone, B. 4, 5–6, 9, 12, 14, 16, 55, 56, 159
feminism 122
Fernandes, S. 3, 27, 31
Few-Demo, A.L. 122
financial support 79, 113, 115, 164, 166
Finch, J. 6, 7, 8, 76, 78, 96, 136, 156, 158
Fine, M. 28–29, 30
forced moves 126
foster placements
  abuse 29, 103
  chosen family 163
  contact with birth family 141
  ethnicity 109
  everyday/ordinary family practices 56, 59
  ineffable connections 80–81
  learning from care experiences 21
  lifeworld orientation 59
  mother-and-baby foster placements 124–125
  scaffolding 134–135
  sense of family 155–156
  siblings 64, 104
  support at university 88, 116
  support for new parents 134–136
  'who counts' as family 82–85, 86–87, 89, 92
Foucault, M. 9, 15, 27, 29–30
Fraser, N. 7, 12, 129, 130, 137
Friedman, S. 8
friendships 62–67, 79, 132, 135–136, 161
fun times 47
  see also rituals and celebrations
funding 27–28
funerals 61–68, 164
Furlong, A. 161, 164
'furry children' 92, 93
  see also pets

Furstenberg, F.F. 72, 76
future imaginaries *see* imagined futures

G

Gabb, J. 93, 139, 153
Galloway, A. 113
gender normativity 72, 124, 131
geographical proximity 76, 77, 116, 163
gifts 60, 85–86
Gilbert, N. 13
Gillis, J.R. 5, 107, 136
global financial crisis 2008 97
global parenting responsibilities 101, 109–112
Gobo, G. 39, 41
'good enough' families 10
'good'/'bad' binaries 53
Gowen, S.M. 101, 104, 109, 162
grandparents 24–25, 60–61, 117, 122, 135, 157, 165
Grietens, H. 29
Grunwald, K. 44, 58, 86, 155, 163
Gubrium, J.F. 32
Gulløv, E. 158
Gunaratnam, Y. 27
Gupta, A. 9, 14

H

Hagestad, G.O. 72
Hall, S.M. 97
Hamilton, P. 126
Hanrahan, F. 34
Hantrais, L. 71–72
Harris, T. 160
'haunted motherhood' 137
Heaphy, B. 5, 12, 14, 71, 76, 136, 137, 153, 154, 155, 166
heritage 108
Herlofson, K. 72
Hetherington, R. 13
Hey, V. 27
Hill, K. 122
Holland, J. 35, 112
Holmes, L. 55, 71, 163
Holstein, J.A. 32
home, sense of 89, 102, 103, 155
homelessness 77, 129
Honneth, A. 135, 136, 139
horizontal lineage 76
household surveys 72
housing insecurity 79, 125–126, 128–129, 133, 149
humane social work 55, 159

I

idealised families 9–10
identity
  adoption 82
  connecting past and present 48
  cultural/heritage identities 109
  motherhood 111–112, 121, 137, 139, 140
    as narrative 68
    through memory 51
imaginary as resource for meaning making 81
imagined families 5
imagined futures 112, 121, 144–150, 157, 158
inconsistencies in accounts 32
independence, myth of 21, 119, 161
Independent Review of Children's Social Care 68, 119, 160, 161
individualization of responsibility 122
ineffable connections 80–86
informal celebrations 60–61
informal support 122, 125, 134
inhibition repertoires 125
interdependency
  austerity 112–118, 119
  connectedness 71, 95, 96–97
  and the meaning of 'family' 5
  precarity 8
  siblings 102
  supporting relational interdependency 161–165
  vulnerability 29
intergenerational relationships
  breaking the circle 148
  complex family connections 50, 156–157, 164
  corporate grandparents 24, 120, 121
  family support through 23–24, 75, 89, 122, 161, 164, 165
  and interdependence 119
  small stories 48
intergenerational resemblance 53–54, 55, 141, 157
intersectionality 26, 41, 123–124, 126, 128, 142
intersubjectivity 44, 48, 55
intervention thresholds 13
interview methods 38–39
intimate practices 6–7
intra-generational connections 158
  see also siblings
'I-Witness' 29
Iyer, P. 20, 69, 97, 104, 144, 165

J

Jackson, A.Y. 41, 42
Jamieson, L. 2–3, 4–5, 153, 156
Jensen, T. 11, 73
job insecurity 148
Johnson, B. 169n1
juxtaposition 4, 41, 77, 155

K

Ketokivi, K. 6, 92, 156
kin group membership 61

INDEX

kinship, defining 70–94
kinship care arrangements
  connectedness 99, 100, 110, 125
  contact with birth family 143
  grandparents 122, 157
  imagined futures 146, 150
  shifting boundaries of 'family' 92
kinship responsibilities 96
Kofoed, J. 33
Koven, M. 58

L

learning disabilities 129
leaving care placements 20, 79–80
Leccardi, C. 148
letterbox contact 139–140, 141, 143, 144
lifecourse events 59, 155, 162, 164
  see also rituals and celebrations
Lifelong Links 55, 163
lifeworld orientations 44, 48, 57–59, 86, 155–156, 163
limits of family support 115–118
"little fear" 52
longitudinal research 3–4, 33, 34, 37, 41, 112, 158
looked-after children 19
Lorde, A. 30, 42, 127
Lorey, I. 97, 160
loss/bereavement 51, 52, 67, 97, 129, 139
love 68, 135, 155, 158, 162, 164
Luttrell, W. 35

M

MacAlister, J. 68, 119, 160, 161–162, 165
Maillochon, F. 61
marriage 93
Mason, C. 25, 124, 126, 128, 137, 142, 151
Mason, J. 7, 8, 53, 54, 55, 70, 71, 75, 80, 94, 96
May, T. 9
Mazzei, L. 41, 42
McCarthy, J.R. 2, 5, 11, 12, 50, 94, 153, 165
McVarish, J. 98, 101–102, 158, 162
memory books 67–68
Mendez, S.N. 153
mental health 49, 86, 92, 97, 110, 114, 117
misrecognition 7, 12, 127, 128–130, 131, 137, 155
Monk, D. 97–98, 101–102, 158, 162
Morgan, D. 5, 6, 7, 15, 43, 44–45, 47, 59, 61, 71, 76, 136, 153, 155, 156, 157, 158, 164
Morriss, L. 25, 82, 112, 120, 124, 137, 144–145, 151
mother and baby placements 89, 124, 126–127, 129–130
motherhood 120–151, 157
multigenerational households 72
multimethod studies 37
multiple disadvantage 11, 25

multiple placement experiences 77, 88–89, 116–117, 134
mundane, significance of the 46–51
music 34–36, 46–48, 49, 60, 64–65, 96, 98, 100, 109, 156
Muxel, A. 51

N

name changes 78
narrative analytic lens 7, 41, 158
narratives
  applying narrative logic to single cases 41
  austerity story 9
  developing alternative 37
  'enforced narratives' 26, 34
  narrative coherence 31, 32
  narrative imagination 54
  narrative perspective on care experienced family lives 31–32
  political uses of storytelling 27
  'terrible tale' 14, 18, 30
  'vulnerability' 14, 19
Neale, B. 34
neighbours 126
Neil, E. 82, 107
neoliberalism 3, 11, 14, 97, 161
networks of support 95, 119, 162, 163, 164, 166
New Labour 23
Nilsen, A. 97, 119, 148, 161
'nkali' 1, 2, 18, 153, 165
non-traditional families 71, 72, 76, 92–94, 139, 153, 155
'normative absence and pathologized presence' 11–12, 155
normative narratives of 'family' 4–5, 9–10, 31, 148, 155, 166
Norway 9–10, 22, 28, 33–34, 119
not-family 71, 86–92, 94, 103, 156
not-home 103
nuclear family 72, 76
Nuffield Family Justice Observatory (FJO) 165
Nurse, T. 13, 14

O

Office for National Statistics 22
old neighbourhoods, returning to 89
open research methods 28, 38–39
Oppo, A. 64
ordinary family experiences 43–69, 76, 77, 78, 110
Østergaard, J. 4, 41, 96
'other' 8–11, 27, 28–29, 43
  see also 'troubled' families
Our Care, Our Say (2021) 119, 165
'outcomes' 158

P

parental responsibility 13
parenthood 120–151, 156, 157

parenting responsibilities 109–112
parenting 'styles' 10
Paris 124
participant recruitment 34, 37–38
pathologization 12
permanence, sense of 19–20, 84–86, 92
pets 92, 93, 116, 118, 149, 164
Philip, G. 131, 133, 151, 156, 157
Phoenix, A. 7, 11, 12, 30, 32, 120, 124, 134, 136, 137, 151, 155
photography 34–35, 48–49, 84–85, 107, 137–138, 156
PIP (Personal Independence Payments) 113, 114
placement breakdowns 86, 92, 109, 155
placement changes 20, 97, 124
  see also multiple placement experiences
politics 26–31
Pomati, M. 10
Poor Laws 21, 96
post-adoption contact 107
post-structuralism 27
poverty 56, 72–73, 96, 115, 122, 123
'poverty porn' 72–73
power 26–27, 28–29, 33, 42, 98, 123, 130, 142
pre-care experiences and later issues 97
precarity 15, 16, 96, 97, 160
  see also austerity; housing insecurity; poverty
pregnancy 124–125
prison 132–133
private domain, family as 14
privilege 26–27, 42, 123, 161
problem-focused work 2, 11, 12, 18, 27, 32, 159
professional support 118–119, 125, 133–136, 142–144, 151, 158, 160, 163–165
pseudonyms, use of 33, 40

Q

qualitative longitudinal research (QLR) 37
queer theory 71, 92, 153
quotation/reported dialogue 58

R

race 27
  see also ethnicity
racism 87–88, 126, 141
reality television 72
reciprocal help/support from family 96–97
recognition 60, 135, 137, 139, 155
  see also misrecognition
reconstituted families 72
re-establishing contact with birth families 106–107
regular, sense of the 59
rejection 93
relational continuity 55
relationality 6, 44, 50, 51–55, 159–160, 161–165
  see also complex family connections; interdependency

relationships with family breaking down 78, 103–104
removal of children from parental care 25, 121, 126, 128–130, 133, 137–145, 155, 157
repeat entries to care system 20
  see also multiple placement experiences
repetition of history, avoiding 147–148
'replacement' family 83, 84, 86
research funding 27–28
research methods 30–31, 34
researcher positionality 26–27, 28–31, 33
'resemblance stories' 53–54, 55
residential units 86–87, 88–90, 91–92, 124, 155
respect 86
return of children from care placements 21, 137
Riessman, C.K. 32, 38
rights, reciprocal 135–136
risk, focus on 124, 125, 131, 155
  see also problem-focused work; vulnerability
risk of disadvantage 18
risk of teenage pregnancy 23
rituals and celebrations 59–68, 75, 76
  see also birthdays; Christmas; weddings and funerals
Roberts, L. 24, 25, 89, 123, 151, 157
Roets, G. 155
role models 135
romantic relationships 115–116, 117, 132, 145, 148, 149
Roseneil, S. 6, 92, 153, 156

S

Sainsbury's advert 9, 72
same-sex families 12, 72, 76, 155
sampling 34, 37–38
scaffolding 24, 71, 115, 118, 134, 140, 161
Schofield, G. 25, 86
Schutz, A. 44, 48, 155
Scott, S. 55, 56
secure placements 91–92
self-esteem 136
semi-independent living 126, 161
sexuality 150
Seymour, J. 6
siblings
  on becoming a parent 125
  connectedness 96, 97–105, 109, 117–118, 119
  family structures 73–74
  implications for theory and practice 157, 162
  ordinary family experiences 64, 65
  'who counts' as family 75–76, 82–83, 158
'silent discourse' 119, 161
singing 47
'single story' 1, 2, 4, 32, 43, 45, 59, 68, 71, 144, 153–158, 166

Sissay, L. vii, 166
Sjöberg, M. 24–25, 122, 135, 165
Slater, T. 27
small stories 48, 51, 103, 111–112, 132
Smart, C. 6, 12, 81, 156
social justice 155
social negotiation 63
social representativeness 41
social workers, relationships with 77–78, 101, 125, 126–127, 133, 142, 145, 160
see also professional support
solidarity 136
Special Guardianship Orders (SGOs) 20, 76, 77, 78, 100, 101, 115, 116, 142
sporting events 60
Squire, C. 32
staff of residential placements 89–90, 102–103
state responsibilities 8, 19, 22
see also corporate grandparenting; corporate parenting
Staunes, D. 33
Steedman, C. 2, 7, 14, 18, 26, 30, 34, 43, 166
Stein, M. 21
step-parents 52, 105, 106, 108
stigma
  abjection 43, 153
  absent fathers 157
  care experience 11, 12
  family constructions 73
  inequality 9
  intersectionality 142
  low-income families 10
  'nkali' 153
  not-family 88
  'other' 27
  parenthood 121, 123, 124–128
  removal of children from parental care 128, 130
  researching objects of 30
  resistance to 155
  teenage pregnancy 24
  'troubled'/'ordinary' binary 153
  young parents 164
stories vs storytelling 32
see also narratives
Strandbu, Å 60, 61
Strawson, G. 31
structural inequalities 32
support networks 95, 119, 162, 163, 164, 166
supported living 102–103, 161
surveillance 130
Sweden 84, 122
symbolic families 5

T

taken-for-grantedness 11, 45, 56–58, 59, 110, 119, 153, 155
Tarrant, A. 122, 131, 157

tattoos 82, 137, 156
teenage pregnancy 123
see also young parents
Teenage Pregnancy Strategy (TPS) 23, 24
therapy 114, 119
Thiersch, H. 44, 58, 86, 155, 163
Thoburn, J. 21
Thomson, R. 4, 34, 35, 41, 42, 96, 104, 112, 119, 120, 121, 122, 124
Toft, M. 8
tradition 63–64, 66, 68, 76, 150
transcription conventions 42
transitions 8, 21–22, 89, 97, 115, 124–128, 156, 161
trauma 97, 126, 129, 155, 164
'troubled' families
  defining 73
  not necessarily large or complex 76
  thinking beyond 11–12
  'troubled'/'ordinary' binary 2, 9, 43, 72, 153, 159–160
Trujillo, J. 44
Tyler, I. 2, 27, 30, 43, 73, 130, 153

U

UK Medical Research Council (MRC)/National Institute for Health Research guidance 37
UN (United Nations), definition of family 71–72
UN Convention of the Rights of the Child 13
unconventional families 71, 76, 92–94, 139, 153, 155
Universal Credit 23, 123
university, starting 88, 115–116
'unremarkable' practices 46–51
US 10–11, 122

V

violence 103
see also abuse; domestic violence
vulnerability 27–28, 29, 30, 155
Vygotsky, L. 115, 140

W

Wade, J. 21, 68–69
Walsh, J. 159
Ward, H. 21
Wastell, D. 152, 159
weddings and funerals 61–68, 150, 155
Welch, V. 155, 159
welfare contexts
  austerity 2, 8–11, 14, 28, 96–97, 112–118, 160
  care experience 13
  fear of welfare dependency 21
  mental health difficulties and benefits 113
  policing the poor 11

'protective carapace' 96
typology of welfare systems 13
US 11
young parents 123
Weller, S. 98, 104
Wetherell, M. 32
Wheeler, B. 37, 55, 79, 137, 145
White, S. 152, 159
'who counts' as family 70–94, 97–98, 156, 158
Williams, A. 92
Willow, C. 22–23
Wilson, S. 35, 46, 80, 83, 94
Winther, I.W. 158
Wissö, T. 84
Woodthorpe, K. 66
Woollett, A. 136, 137
working class 26, 124

Y

young adults, focus on 7–8, 21–23, 97
young carers 97–105
young parents 23–25, 122, 123, 134
Yuval-Davis, N. 68

www.ingramcontent.com/pod-product-compliance
Lightning Source LLC
Chambersburg PA
CBHW051544020426
42333CB00016B/2082